International Entrepreneurship

This edited collection presents the latest research on the international aspects of entrepreneurship.

The volume is divided into two sections. Part One looks at conceptual issues in entrepreneurship, including discussion on trust and the entrepreneur, the importance of technology management and the facets of new business growth. In Part Two the discussion centres around a wide range of international case studies, including the role of networking in Japan, foreign direct investment in research and development as entrepreneurship, and the brewing industry in the UK.

Multidisciplinary in scope, this volume demonstrates that there is no single way to conduct research. The contributions illustrate the evolution of focus from the study of individual entrepreneurs, firms and countries to the embedding of such players in the wider context of organizational, regional and global environments and the interactions between them. Providing an excellent base for further study in the area, this volume will be a vital resource for researchers and students in entrepreneurship and international business.

Sue Birley is Director of Research and Professor of Management in the field of entrepreneurship at the Management School, Imperial College of Science and Technology, University of London.

Ian C. MacMillan is Executive Director of the Sol C. Snider Entrepreneurial Center and George W. Taylor Professor of Entrepreneurial Studies at the Wharton School, University of Pennsylvania.

International Entrepreneurship

Edited by Sue Birley
and Ian C. MacMillan

London and New York

First published 1995
by Routledge
11 New Fetter Lane, London EC4P 4EE

Simultaneously published in the USA and Canada
by Routledge
29 West 35th Street, New York, NY 10001

© 1995 Sue Birley and Ian C. MacMillan

Typeset in Times Ten by Florencetype Ltd, Stoodleigh, Devon
Printed and bound in Great Britain by Biddles Ltd,
Guildford and King's Lynn

British Library Cataloguing in Publication Data
A catalogue record for this book is available from the British Library

Library of Congress Cataloguing in Publication Data
International entrepreneurship / edited by Sue Birley and Ian
   MacMillan.
       p. cm.
   Includes bibliographical references and index.
   ISBN 0–415–11219–2
   1. International business enterprises – Management.
   2. International business enterprises – Managment – Case studies.
   I. Birley, Sue. II. MacMillan, Ian C., 1940– .
   HD62.4.I563   1995
   658'. 049–dc20   95–6160
                                                              CIP

ISBN 0–415–11219–2

Contents

vi *Contents*

Figures, tables and exhibits

FIGURES

TABLES

EXHIBITS

Notes on contributors

Howard E. Aldrich is Kenan Professor of Sociology and Adjunct Professor of Business at the University of North Carolina, Chapel Hill, North Carolina, USA. He is the author of *Organizations and Environments* (Prentice-Hall, 1979) and co-author of *Ethnic Entrepreneurs: Immigrant Businesses in Industrial Societies* (Sage, 1990).

Alexander Ardishvili is a research fellow at the Carlson Center for Entrepreneurial Studies. He received his doctorate from the Moscow State University, and MBA from the Carlson School of the University of Minnesota, USA. Dr. Ardishvili was previously visiting professor at the Carlson School of Management, researcher at the Russian Academy of Sciences at Moscow, and held a teaching position at the Management Development Institute in Tbilisi, Republic of Georgia.

Sue Birley is Professor of Management in Entrepreneurship at the Management School, Imperial College, London. She has taught at Cranfield School of Management, the London Business School, and City University, all in the UK, and at the University of Notre Dame, USA.

William D. Bygrave, MA, DPhil (Oxford), MBA (Northeastern University), DBA (Boston University) is the Frederic C. Hamilton Professor for Free Enterprise and Director of the Center for Entrepreneurial Studies at Babson College, and Visiting Professor at INSEAD, the European Institute of Business Administration, in France.

Richard N. Cardozo holds the Curtis L. Carlson Chair in Entrepreneurial Studies and is Professor of Marketing in the Carlson

School of Management at the University of Minnesota, USA. He received his PhD from the University of Minnesota, and MBA from Harvard Business School, and AB from Carleton College. He currently serves as Director of the Case Development Center at the Carlson School of Management.

Alain Fayolle is Professor of Small and Medium-Sized Business Policy at Lyon Graduate School of Business, France. He is Deputy Director of Groupe ESC Lyon's Innovation and Entrepreneurship Centre, and Professor and Researcher in Entrepreneurship and Business Policy at Saint Etienne Graduate School of Business, France.

Dennis Hanlon is a lecturer at the Faculty of Business Administration, Memorial University of Newfoundland, Canada, and a doctoral candidate at the University of Stirling, Scotland.

Brian Harmon is an independent consultant, and serves as a core member of the research staff at the Carlson Center for Entrepreneurial Studies, University of Minnesota, USA.

Mitsuko Hirata is a doctoral candidate at the Graduate School of Business Administration at Keio University. She received a BA at Tsuda University and MBA at the Graduate School of Business Administration at Keio University, both in Japan.

Walter Kümmerle is a doctoral student at Harvard University's Graduate School of Business Administration in the USA. He holds a degree in commerce from Ecole Superieure de Commerce de Lyon, France and a masters-level degree in industrial economics from the Koblenz School of Corporate Management in Germany.

Kalevi Kyläheiko is Senior Lecturer in economics at the Lappeenranta University of Technology in Lappeenranta, Finland. His research interests lie in the field of industrial engineering where he studies inventory models and issues of technological change.

Benôit F. Leleux is Assistant Professor of Finance at Babson College, USA. He holds the equivalent of an MSc in Agricultural Engineering and an MA in Education from the Université Catholique de Louvain in Belgium, and an MBA from the Virginia Polytechnic Institute and State University in the USA.

Yves-Frédéric Livian is a researcher at IRE at Groupe ESC Lyon, Lyon Graduate School of Business, France. He works in the areas of organization theory and human resources management.

Murray B. Low is Assistant Professor in the Management of Organizations Division of the Graduate School of Business at Columbia University. He received his doctorate from the University of Pennsylvania in 1991.

Ian C. MacMillan is the Executive Director of the Sol C. Snider Entrepreneurial Center and George W. Taylor Professor of Entrepreneurship Studies at the Wharton School of the University of Pennsylvania, USA. His previous posts were Director of the Center for Entrepreneurial Studies at New York University, Associate Professor at Columbia University, and Visiting Professor at Northwestern University. He received a BSc from the University of Witwatersrand, South Africa, and an MBA and DBA from the University of South Africa.

Colin Mason is Senior Lecturer in Economic Geography at the University of Southampton, UK. He is currently engaged in a major study of the informal venture capital market in the UK.

Rita Gunther McGrath received her doctorate from the Wharton School, University of Pennsylvania, USA, and is Assistant Professor in the Management of Organizations Divisions at Columbia Business School.

Kevin McNally graduated from the University of Southampton, UK in 1992 with first class honours. He is currently a doctoral candidate in the Department of Geography, University of Southampton.

Asko Miettinen is Professor of Management at the Lappeenranta University of Technology in Lappeenranta, Finland. He researches small business management and entrepreneurship.

David Molian is Teaching Fellow in Marketing and Business Policy and a doctoral candidate at the Management School, Imperial College, London. After graduating from Oxford University and the Cranfield School of Management, he worked in advertising and marketing consultancy.

Daniel F. Muzyka is IAF Professor of Entrepreneurship and Director of Entrepreneurship Programs at INSEAD. Dr. Muzyka received his BA from Williams College, USA, MBA from the Wharton School, and DBA from the Harvard Business School.

Akihiro Okumura is a professor at Keio University's Graduate School of Business Administration in Japan. He received his MBA from Northwestern University, USA, and DBA from Keio University. He is also an active consultant to leading Japanese companies.

Rémy Paliard is Professor of Finance and Head of the Finance and Management Accounting Department at Groupe ESC Lyon, Lyon Graduate School of Business, France. His experience includes the post of treasurer of a family-owned firm. Professor Paliard serves on the board of the European Capital Markets Institute.

Pat Ray Reese received her PhD in Sociology from the University of North Carolina, Chapel Hill, North Carolina, USA in 1992. She is currently Pharmaeconomic Manager, International Research Department, in Glaxo Research and Development Ltd, England.

Michael G. Scott is Scottish Amicable Professor of Entrepreneurial Studies, and Director of the Scottish Enterprise Foundation, University of Stirling, Scotland.

Stephen Spinelli graduated with a BA in Economics from Western Maryland College and with an MBA from Babson College, USA. He is currently working on his doctorate at the Management School, Imperial College, London. He also teaches New Venture Creation as a part of Babson College's entrepreneurship faculty.

V. Srivatsan is Visiting Professor in the Management of Organizations Division of the Graduate School of Business at Columbia University, USA. He received his doctorate from Columbia University. Dr. Srivatsan teaches and conducts research in the areas of international business and leadership.

S. Venkataraman is Paul Yeakel Term Assistant Professor of Management at the Wharton School of the University of Pennsylvania, USA. He received his PhD in strategic management from the Carlson School of Management, University of Minnesota. He is a research associate of the Sol C. Snider Entrepreneurial Center at the Wharton School.

Foreword

It was a pleasure and an honour for us here at the Lyon Graduate School of Business to host the Third Annual Global Conference on Entrepreneurship Research. Lyon has for centuries proven to be an entrepreneurial city, notably in the silk, finance and pharmaceutical industries, and we try within Groupe ESC Lyon's Centre des Entrepreneurs to maintain and reinforce this spirit among our students and local entrepreneurs.

Our six-month programme for entrepreneurs already has 250 participants and has generated 150 new ventures, of which 100 are still alive (as of October 1993). We also offer a variety of entrepreneurship courses in the MBA curriculum. We hope, through such programmes, to contribute both to the economic development of our area and to an increased knowledge of entrepreneurship and new venture creation.

Each new conference opens up new ideas, new developments, new theoretical models and a host of new questions. The Third Annual Global Conference on Entrepreneurship Research held in Lyon in March 1993 was no exception. We are very pleased with our sponsorship of this forum and proud of the result.

Rémy Paliard
Guest Editor

Preface

As you will discover in the following volume of research, the Third Annual Global Conference on Entrepreneurship Research included a wide selection of themes, methodological approaches, fields and organization types. In this, it reflects our aims to provide young scholars with a global perspective on a variety of possible approaches in entrepreneurship research.

Another objective of this conference is to give these young scholars an opportunity to present their ongoing research to positive, supportive, helpful senior researchers, and to benefit from their critiques in improving the papers for publication. The feedback on papers has been constructive and most of the papers have been rewritten in accordance with suggestions.

A serious issue arose when the large increase in number of papers submitted to the conference made it impossible to include all of them in the proceedings. A panel therefore selected the papers to be published. We apologize to those authors who were excluded.

We decided, in the interests of space and cost considerations, against publishing the critiques.

This book is divided into two sections. Part I, titled 'Theoretical explorations in entrepreneurship', contains research on conceptual issues in entrepreneurship. Part II – 'Empirical findings in entrepreneurship' – deals with a variety of empirical studies. They have been further organized into four subgroups according to similarity of subject matter.

The topics presented at the conference suggest some interesting evolutions in entrepreneurship research. There would appear to be a movement:

1 From studying entrepreneurs themselves to studying the entrepreneurs and their organizations as a whole,

2 From the analysis of new ventures individually to the global analysis of factors which affect entrepreneurship in a region, be it local or national,

3 From national analysis to cross border analysis,

4 From empirical, descriptive work to theory development along rigorous, analytical lines.

We hope to continue participating in entrepreneurship research that remains multidisciplinary in spirit, multi-method in measurement and fascinating in its results.

Rémy Paliard
Sue Birley
Ian C. MacMillan

Acknowledgements

We are indebted to the Conseil Général du Rhône for financing a large part of the conference costs.

We are grateful to Groupe ESC Lyon's Centre des Entrepreneurs, The Management School at Imperial College, and the Sol C. Snider Entrepreneurial Center of the Wharton School of the University of Pennsylvania for their help in organizing the conference and supporting this publication. Special thanks to Mark Howland for patiently solving problems in the production of graphics.

Part I

Theoretical explorations in entrepreneurship

1 Understanding new business growth

Richard N. Cardozo, Brian Harmon
and Alexander Ardishvili

INTRODUCTION

Despite the acknowledged importance of business growth in entrepreneurial thought, we understand growth only imperfectly, largely
because we have not identified the processes involved, or developed
a coherent theory of business growth. As a first step in addressing this
deficiency, we sought to 'map' growth by describing the processes
involved and the sequence(s) in which those processes take place.
The resulting preliminary map holds promise as an analytic and diag-
nostic device, as well as a basis for future research.

The topic of business growth captures the attention of entrepreneurs,
investors, policymakers, analysts, and scholars. Many entrepreneurs
hope to grow their businesses into public companies. Investors try to
assess the growth potential of individual new businesses and their
likelihood of yielding double- and triple-digit returns. Policymakers
want to support new businesses that will increase employment.
Analysts seek to identify members of businesses with high growth
potential. As scholars, we search for answers to all these questions –
how to grow a business, how much profit and employment will a
particular business generate – and we want to know why the answers
to these questions come out as they do. Indeed, we wish to be able to
generalize about growth across businesses and time periods.

At the present time, our ability to address these questions is
limited. Most entrepreneurs do not grow their businesses. Investors'
success rates vary widely, testifying to the uncertainty of 'guessing
correctly'; venture capital yields have fallen dramatically (Keeley and
Turki 1992). No policymaker has reported success in crafting criteria
to direct aid toward growth and away from no-growth new firms.
Analysts, like investors, differ widely in their success; each appears to

use a different set of heuristics. As for us scholars, we really do not know *how* growth occurs, much less *why*.

PRESENT KNOWLEDGE OF GROWTH

Strange as it may appear, our literature contains no accepted standard definition of growth. Most studies do not bother to define it at all. Penrose (1959) argues that the lack of definition, or imprecise and confusing definitions, leads to chaos in research on growth.

Two years ago, two colleagues and I at the Carlson Center addressed this problem. We concluded that we could define growth as a change in size or magnitude from one period to another of any or all of the following measures: resource base of the firm, physical output, sales revenue, market share, or profits. We also showed how these five measures were related to one another (Bailey, Montero, Cardozo 1991). This work provided a necessary foundation block, but did not help us understand why some businesses grow, while others did not; nor did it help us to distinguish high growth firms from low growth firms.

In an attempt to address the lack of a useful formulation of growth, we developed for purposes of our own discussion within the Center, the following conceptual definition:

> For a specified level or unit of analysis, organization growth is an increase in size, measured by structural or functional characteristics of the unit. Negative growth, or shrinkage, involves a decrease in size.
>
> Measures of change in size may include *input* (acquiring resources such as employees, capital, etc.; purchases of goods and services for use and/or resale), *throughput* (combination/integration of resources, management routines and development of relationships, all of which together enable the firm to develop its special capabilities or competencies), *resource base* (capabilities or competencies, employees, real estate, physical and financial assets) and *output* (transactions, units produced, units shipped/sold, dollar sales, profits (in dollars and as percentages of sales, assets, investment) and market share).
>
> Because these several measures of growth may move in different directions during a specified time period (e.g., reductions in employment and physical output, increases in sales and profits) it is oversimple to speak of a firm as a whole growing or not growing; we should specify the particular measure(s) under consideration. Level of analysis is also critical: a firm may, through

training, increase competence of *individual employees*. Unless mechanisms are activated to harness this increased competence, however, competence of the *subunit* or firm may not increase or grow.

Organization growth involves increases in quantity for specified levels of quality; increases in quality alone do not necessarily involve growth.

Organization growth is a subset of organization change. Organizations may change what they do and how they look without increasing (or decreasing) in size. But growth involves a change in size measured in structural or functional terms. Growth and change may occur independently or together. For example, an organization may add a product line to its existing portfolio. If sales of the new line simply replace sales of existing lines, and no change in total sales occurs, we would say that change has occurred, but not growth. If sales of existing lines remained the same and sales of the new line increased total sales, both growth and change have occurred.

In a seminal article that built on previous work in organization growth, Churchill and Lewis (1983) identified multiple stages in the growth of a business, and linked passage through those stages to (1) the interests and abilities of the entrepreneurs, and (2) the resource base of the firm. Other articles in this 'stage' tradition offer no additional help in addressing the questions of interest.

A parallel approach to the study of business growth involves attempts to identify factors or antecedent variables that correlate with some measure of growth. A group in the Carlson Center recently identified and reviewed what we call 'factor studies' (Cardozo *et al.* 1993). To our surprise, we found fewer than thirty papers, a small number given the importance and widespread interest in the phenomenon. Because there was little overlap among factors studied and measures used, this small set of studies provided few clues to our questions of interest. A larger set of coordinated studies might inform us to some extent about the questions and provide some clues, but could not explain the process, because they were not intended to do so. Our own experience with 'factor' studies (e.g., Cardozo, *et al.* 1990) made us very clearly aware of the need for a conceptual framework to address these questions.

While exploring questions of how growth occurs, we also asked how many businesses demonstrated significant growth. Studies of longitudinal panels of small businesses (e.g., Reynolds and Miller 1986, Cardozo, Harmon *et al.* 1991) showed that distributions of

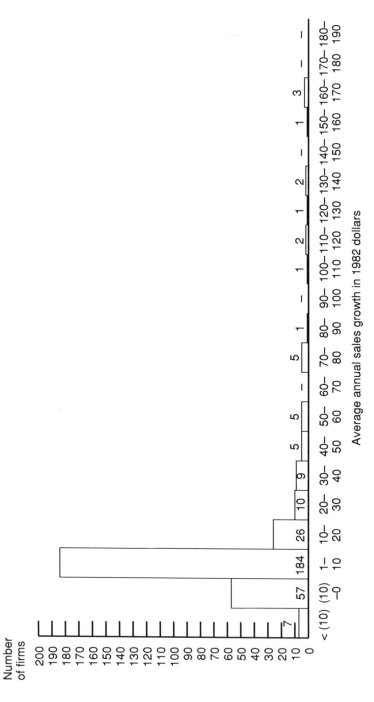

Exhibit 1.1 Age adjusted average annual sales growth in 1982 dollars (n=326) (in thousands)
Source: Cardozo *et al.* 1991

growth were highly skewed to the right, with low mode and median values (see Exhibit 1.1).

This observation prompted us to turn the question around – if so few businesses grow, perhaps we should be asking, 'Why don't new businesses grow?' We pursued that latter question and identified several additional questions and roadblocks to growth (Cardozo and Ardishvili 1992). Like the 'factor' studies, this analysis yielded some insights, but could not by itself enable us to describe the process of growth.

REACHING OUTSIDE THE DISCIPLINE

Frustrated by what we could not find in our literature, we looked to other disciplines to understand how they thought about growth. We discovered that physical science concepts allied to growth dealt primarily with changes of state or combinations. Notions of overcoming inertia and changes in rate of growth, which can be modelled mathematically, have proved useful in the study of diffusion of innovations, and may have application here.

Apart from mathematical models, we found no concepts from other social sciences with which we were not already familiar from business and economics literature. One such concept, which has not been generally employed to date in the study of growth, is that of organizational learning. What an organization learns – or what individuals in an organization learn – should enrich the resource base of an organization and, hence, its growth potential (Bailey *et al.* 1991).

Our richest yield of concepts came from conversations with colleagues in the biological and health sciences. Botanists described processes by which plant tendrils seek foundations for growth; marine biologists attributed similar behaviour to coral, clams and other organisms that attach themselves to a substrate or object.

Physicians and biologists noted that growth involves increases in size of individual cells and multiplication of cells to increase their number. These increases in size and number of cells may in some instances be accompanied by differentiation of cells to perform specialized functions; this differentiation may also take place independently of increases in cell size and number.

All these phenomena are triggered by biochemical signals that follow certain pathways. Cell changes may occur in a predictable sequence, and will be arrested by still other biochemical signals. The timing, pace, and extent of growth in an individual organism are specific to each species. These processes depend upon genetic programming interacting with the environment of the individual organism. More fecund environments typically favour growth to a greater extent than less rich ones.

If the level of analysis is raised to that of the species (or some subset of it) or a whole population of individual organisms, then the environment, or the interaction of organisms and environment, takes on greater importance. Concepts from population ecology have been introduced into our literature, which suggests that population age, density, growth rate, together with characteristics of the environment, influence growth and size of individual organizations (e.g., Hannan and Carroll 1992).

Biologists also told us that growth has a 'mirror' process, namely, decay. The latter may not exactly mimic the former in reverse. Decay and growth may occur at the same time as complementary processes; for example, more complex animals lose cells and grow new ones to replace them continuously.

Colleagues in health sciences suggested that we distinguish 'normal' from 'pathological' patterns of growth. They also reminded us that normal growth differs among individual organisms, as do pathological growth and decay. They admitted that distributions of normal activity and pathological activity might well overlap to some extent.

A PRELIMINARY MODEL OF THE ORGANIZATIONAL GROWTH PROCESS

As a starting point for mapping growth of new businesses, we focused on growth of individual businesses, rather than populations, and on normal growth only. If we can build an adequate map of normal individual growth, we can next venture into growth of populations and into pathology. We took whatever concepts appeared useful, without regard to their origin, and with no attempt to use all the constructs from any one discipline.

We consider the conceptual frameworks developed in other disciplines as metaphors or analogies, which are to be adapted to our use rather than simply being overlaid on the phenomena of interest to us. We distinguish positive growth from negative growth, choosing the latter term in preference to 'decay'.

Our 'map' of positive growth appears in Figure 1.1. The words in the figure name the processes we have identified in normal growth. The arrows in that figure describe the direction or flow of growth from one process to the next. The numbers in that figure represent our current beliefs about the sequence in which the various processes named occur in normal growth.

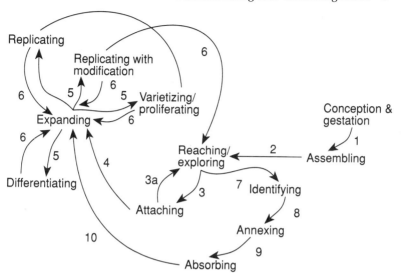

Figure 1.1 Positive growth processes and pathways

The process of normal growth begins with *conception and gestation* of the business concept or vision. The next step involves *assembling* resources to turn the vision into reality. These resources include financial, physical, human and intellectual resources, and relationships with stakeholders.

As resources are being assembled, the fledgling organization is *reaching/exploring* for appropriate niches in order to *attach* itself or find positions to lodge in those niches, which may be defined in terms of products/services and markets (or segments). *Reaching/exploring and attaching* may involve an iterative process of trial-and-error or deliberate experimentation.

Once the new business has made some attachment, it *expands*. We measure expansion from the first sale of a specific product or service to a customer. Additional sales of the same products to that customer represents expansion. Sales to similar customers that require no changes in product or marketing programmes are considered *replications*. As customers and products of services depart from the original, the process becomes *replicating with modification*. Addition of new customer segments, models, products, and lines constitute *varietizing/proliferating*.

These processes (*replicating, varietizing,* etc.) describe not only product–market growth but also internal growth. Adding a second telemarketing representative, for example, is replicating. Adding a second manufacturers' representative typically involves a modified replication, as there are differences in presentation and customer. Additional locations – stores or factories – may be replicates or replicates with modifications. These replicates and proliferates often must reach out and attach themselves in their own environments before expanding. Once put in place, these replicates expand themselves, thus continuing the process of growth.

Along with these expanding–replicating processes, a process of *differentiating* occurs. By differentiation we mean specialization within the firm, rather than in the marketplace. Churchill and Lewis (1983) recognized that, as functions expanded in a growing organization, they became specialized. The marketing function, for example, might grow from a single individual performing all the marketing functions for the business to several salesmen, a sales manager, a marketing operations manager, all with support staff and all reporting to a vice-president of marketing.

As the new business grows, it may come to a point at which internal growth (the kind described above) may be supplemented with growth through acquisition. The reaching out/exploring activity leads

Table 1.1 Golden Valley Microwave Foods

Process	Example of process
Conception/gestation	Identifying opportunity for vended line of microwave foods
Assembling	Agreement with six vending operators to fund startup
Reaching/exploring	Trying and discarding different versions of individual entrees, entrees themselves, line of entrees; adding popcorn
Attaching	Using extant popcorn sales and distribution system
Expanding	Increasing production volume
Differentiating–Marketing	Brokers and CEO => brokers and regional manager
Operations	Specialization within lab, production functions
Finance	Bookkeeper and CEO => CFO, controller and staff
Replicating	Multiple regional managers
Replicating with Modifications	Caramel, cheese flavours (line extensions)
Varietizing/Proliferating	Pancakes
Identifying	Opportunity in french fries
Annexing	Lamb-Weston potatoes
Absorbing	Integrated operations

to *identification* of prospective acquisition targets, some of which are *annexed* to the growing firm, which then *absorbs* them.

These processes are illustrated in the case of two companies, Golden Valley Microwave Foods, a manufacturer of microwave food packets, and Best Buy Company, an electronics superstore company, in Tables 1.1 and 1.2 respectively.

The positive growth process begins when the entrepreneur or entrepreneurial team is driven to produce and sell more than the first unit to a single customer. The rate and extent of growth depends on entrepreneurial drive; amount, type, and deployment of available resources; the breadth, stability, and durability of attachment; and the profit-maximization curve (see Exhibit 1.2). Entrepreneurial drive will propel growth either to local optima (where revenue minus cost equals maximum profit) or beyond them in pursuit of the next optimum. Opportunity, represented by the level of total revenues that might be obtained, differs among situations.

Figure 1.2 displays our conception of the processes and pathways of negative growth. By and large these mirror the positive growth activity in Figure 1.1 and described above. The process begins at the left and centre of the Figure, rather than the right.

Table 1.2 Best Buy Company

Process	Example of process
Conception/gestation	Vision of large-scale, low-overhead retail store for home electronics, to displace neighbourhood and industrial specialty shops selling hi-fi components
Assembling	Supplier extended credit (on promise of market expansion); banks; real estate acquisition; hiring staff
Reading/Exploring	Experimenting with merchandise mix, staffing levels, location
Attaching	Settled on 'concept one' store
Expanding	Sales growth in 'comparable stores'
Differentiating	Specialization within merchandising, MIS, store management functions
Replicating	Geographic roll out of stores
Replicating with modification	—
Varietizing/Proliferating	Addition of major appliances to merchandise mix
Identifying	Similar stores in markets targeted for expansion
Annexing	Acquisition of small regional chains
Absorbing	Reconfiguration acquired store

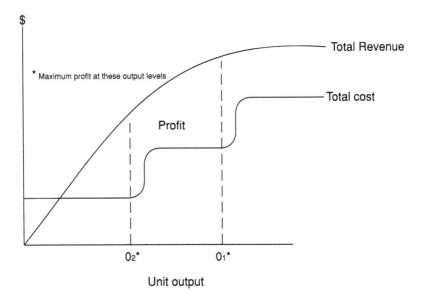

Exhibit 1.2 Profit-maximization curve

Negative growth begins with a *withdrawal* or *turning inward*, which leads to *narrowing, compressing,* and *sloughing off* of products and markets. At the same time, functions may be *combining* internally. All these processes lead to a *shrinking* of the business or subunit. That shrinking in turn leads to *detachment, separation,* and *rejection,* further withdrawal, *disassembly* and *release* of resources, and finally *disappearance* of the organism.

UTILITY OF THE MODEL

We evaluate the usefulness of this, or any other, model of growth with respect to (1) its descriptive accuracy, and (2) its ability to generate research propositions of interest. Ultimately, the model is useful or not to the extent that it helps us address the questions listed at the beginning of this paper. Perhaps because this model arose from our observations of growing firms, we believe it to be descriptively accurate, albeit possibly incomplete.

To test the fecundity of this model, we listed some of the research questions or propositions that it prompted:

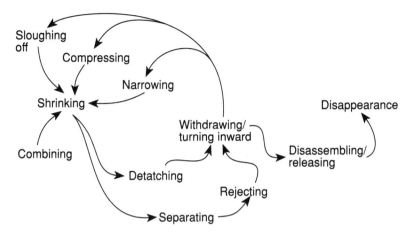

Figure 1.2 Negative growth processes and pathways

1 The more efficiently each process works, the faster the growth.
2 The more frequently each process occurs, the greater the growth, and
3 the more stable the process, the more consistent the growth.
4 Expanding will occur more frequently than any other process, once a threshold of growth and size are reached.
5 Replicating propels growth faster than expansion.
6 Replicating drives growth at a faster rate than varietizing/proliferating; for any rate of growth, replicating will lead to higher profits than varietizing/proliferating.
7 The relationship between varietizing/proliferating and growth is curvilinear; at low levels, the firm does not experiment, does not learn and therefore does not grow its resource base. At high levels, the firm lacks time to absorb the lessons, and thus fails to enrich its resource base, the engine for further growth. (Adapted from Singh and Chang 1993).
8 Growth that follows the sequence indicated will be more stable and durable than that not following the sequence.
9 The growth sequence differs in elapsed time required across firms, industries, and environmental circumstances.
10 Variations in motivation/drive/objective at the beginning of the sequence (up through replicating) will be related to variations in growth.
11 Once replication begins, inertia drives growth.

12 Specialization leads to expansion, as specialized units create activity for themselves.
13 Except for exploring and expanding, which are continuous functions, all others are discrete or step functions.

We consider this list illustrative, not exhaustive, but believe that it demonstrates the usefulness of the model in generating research questions, answers to which should help us to address the basic questions with which we began.

QUESTIONS FOR THE FUTURE

If this preliminary model appears to hold promise, then we face a wide range of development issues, among them the following.

Negative growth may occur simultaneously with positive growth on similar dimensions, for example, a firm may add employment in one department, while cutting payroll in another department. Negative growth may be reversible, for example, laid off employees may be rehired. Nevertheless, the model portrays the growth process as organic, not mechanical, so not all processes may be reversible (for example, relationships). The kind of growth envisioned by conception and birth, for example, is not the mirror image of decline and death.

Organizations may experience negative growth gradually or abruptly. When an organization fails or disappears, its resources may retain their value and simply be recycled into other organizations (Cardozo *et al.* 1991). [This notion implies that any organization may be simply a temporary institutional home for specified resources (employees, assets, capabilities).] If positive and negative growth occur simultaneously on multiple dimensions, management of growth may require continuous effort, much like the continuous small movement involved in steering an automobile on stretches of roadway.

1 Have we identified all the major processes? What subordinate processes need to be added?
2 Are there thresholds and limits to growth in any process? Optimum levels under certain circumstances.
3 Is the sequence descriptively accurate? To what extent do variations in this sequence occur? With what impact on growth?
4 Do positive and negative growth processes occur continuously in organizations?
5 Which pathways require what amount and type of resources, and produce what outcomes? Does the resource/outcome balance

differ under specifiable circumstances? Thus, are there more and less profitable paths to growth? Do those vary systematically throughout the life of an organization?

6 What factors external to the organization affect individual processes, sequences and outcomes?

The emergence of these questions appears to be further evidence of the richness of the model.

CONCLUSION

We began by asking how entrepreneurs could grow their businesses, how investors could estimate growth potential, and how analysts and scholars could identify high-growth businesses in populations. We argued that a first step in addressing these questions was to understand how and why new businesses grew. Since existing literature did not provide this information, we outlined a preliminary model to map growth. This model appears to offer promise as a sufficiently rich descriptive vehicle that it will provide a basis for us to address the key questions of interest.

REFERENCES

Bailey, J., M. Montero, and R.N. Cardozo (1991) 'A Framework for Analyzing Business Growth', in *Research at the Marketing/ Entrepreneurship Interface*, Hills, J.E. *et al.* (eds), Chicago: University of Illinois at Chicago.

Cardozo, R.N. and A. Ardishvili (1992) 'Identifying Roadblocks to New Business Growth', in *Research at the Marketing/Entrepreneurship Interface*, Hills, J.E. *et al.* (eds), Chicago: University of Illinois at Chicago.

Cardozo, R.N., J.M. Bailey, P.D. Reynolds, and B. Miller (1991) 'Entrepreneurial Recycling of Economic Resources', in *Frontiers of Entrepreneurship Research 1991*, Churchill, N.C. *et al.* (eds), Babson College, Babson Park, MA.

Cardozo, R.N., R. Dobbins, T. Kibler, W. Peterson, and J. Baltzell (1993) 'Factors Affecting New Business Growth', Working Paper, Carlson Center for Entrepreneurial Studies, University of Minnesota.

Cardozo, R.N., B. Harmon, P.D. Reynolds, and B. Miller (1991) 'Initial Financial Partnering and New Firm Growth', Proceedings of the 36th ICSB Annual World Conference, Vienna.

Cardozo, R.N., K. McLaughlin, B. Harmon, P.D. Reynolds, and B. Miller (1990) 'Product Market Strategies and New Business Growth', in Apple, L.E. and T.P. Hustad (eds), *Product Development: Prospering in a Rapidly Changing World*, Product Development and Management Association, University of Indiana at Indianapolis.

Churchill, N.C. and V.L. Lewis (1983) 'The Five Stages of Small Business Growth', *Harvard Business Review*, May–June, No. 3, 30–51.

Hannan, M.T. and G.R. Carroll (1992) *Dynamics of Organizational Populations*, Oxford: Oxford University Press.

Keeley, R.H. and L.A. Turki (1992) 'New Ventures: How Risky Are They?', in *Frontiers of Entrepreneurship Research 1992*, Center for Entrepreneurial Studies, Babson College.

MacMillan, I., R. McGrath, and S. Venkataraman (1993), 'Global Dimensions of New Competencies: Creating a Review and Research Agenda', paper presented at the third Global Entrepreneurship Conference, Groupe ESC Lyon, Lyon, France.

Penrose, E.T. (1959) *Theory of the Growth of the Firm*, Oxford: Blackwell.

Reynolds, P.D. and B. Miller (1986) *1984 Minnesota New Firms Study*, Center for Urban and Regional Affairs, University of Minnesota.

Singh, H. and S.J. Chang (1993) 'Corporate Reconfiguration: A Resource Perspective', working paper, the Wharton School, University of Pennsylvania.

2 Strategy formulation in the entrepreneurial small firm

Dennis Hanlon and Michael. G. Scott

INTRODUCTION

While much has been written on the nature of business strategy, little of it has focused on the entrepreneurial small firm, and there is still imperfect understanding of the strategy process. Specifically, there is tension between normative statements and the findings of empirical research. The latter increasingly stress the apparently iterative way in which strategy emerges (or *post facto* can be said to have emerged), and the need to take account of the complex interactions between managers, other stakeholders and their environments. Within all this there remains to be explained the role of 'vision', which may drive the social-construction-of-reality process. This paper attempts to assess the importance of each of these elements and to contribute a preliminary model by which they can be better understood.

Consider the following scenario: A federal government, faced with a burgeoning deficit and desperately in need of greater revenues, announces that a new tax on goods and services will be introduced within a year. Small businesses across the country, faced with a likely drop in consumer confidence and the unpleasant prospect of collecting, accounting for and remitting the tax, protest loudly and bitterly. Ten months later, an informal survey by a small group of business students at one university indicates that the vast majority of small businesses have taken no preparatory action whatsoever. Of those who have decided how they will price their stock, the same survey indicates most have chosen the method least attractive to consumers. Meanwhile, a small bakery displays large, colourful posters which outline purchase strategies minimizing the amount of tax to be paid by the consumer and passes out brochures to its customers which explain the workings of the new tax using everyday language.

The behaviour of this bakery is certainly different from most of these other businesses. Did it occur by chance, or is this distinctive behaviour explainable? This paper seeks to develop and describe a model capable of explaining this and similar behaviours by drawing on and synthesizing recent concepts from the fields of strategic management and visionary leadership.

THE PROBLEM OF STRATEGY IN A SMALL FIRM CONTEXT

How would we describe the nature of the bakery's behaviour? Few would label the firm's behaviour strategic. Indeed, many would maintain that strategic management is a concept which should be reserved for large corporations with large planning departments. Small businesses, it is usually argued, are too busy dealing with operational problems and events on a day-to-day basis to devote time to strategic management. Some authors have gone so far as to suggest that strategy may even be detrimental to small firm performance.

It is quite natural that these critics place so much emphasis on the planning process, since the discipline of strategic management has its historical roots in the normative (planning) model of strategy. Yet this view of strategy has been subjected to strong criticism (McMillan 1980). One widely recognized dimension of the concept of strategy is the distinction between content and process (see, for example, Berg and Pitts 1979; Bourgeois 1980; Ginsberg 1988; Hofer 1975; Huff and Reger 1987; Jauch 1983; Miller 1989; Montgomery 1988; Pettigrew 1987). Huff and Reger (1987) described process research as focusing on the actions that lead to and support strategy. Traditionally, the distinction between 'leading to' and 'supporting' strategy has been an important one; these two aspects of the strategy process are commonly characterized as strategy formulation (how decisions are generated) and strategy implementation (how decisions are translated into action), respectively (Huff and Reger 1987). Many authors have come to use the term 'strategic management' to describe the strategy process.

Several streams of research have examined the phenomenon of strategy within the context of small business. This literature can be roughly organized into four categories:

1 Prescriptive and theoretical literature which seeks to identify the differences between the planning requirements of large and small firms (e.g. Birley 1982; Curtis 1983; Nagel 1981; Van Hoorn 1979).
2 Empirical studies which seek to establish the extent and usefulness

of planning behaviour in small firms (e.g. McKiernan 1986; Unni 1981).

3 Empirical studies aimed at identifying factors which influence the performance of small firms. These are often labelled 'success/failure factors' (e.g. Gibb and Scott 1985).

4 Empirical studies which attempt to identify and describe the types of product/market and competitive strategies adopted by small firms (e.g. Bamberger 1989).

Bearing in mind that these research categories are quite informal, several useful observations can be made concerning the nature and scope of research on small business strategy. First, it can easily be seen that studies of small business strategy have examined both strategy process and strategy content; the first two categories focus primarily on process-related issues whereas the latter two categories are concerned with content (the focus of this paper is on process). Second, it is apparent that, to date, the research on process has tended to emphasize the formulation of strategy; the issue of strategy implementation is sadly under-researched. A third observation is that the process-related research has focused almost exclusively on the planning model (this may help to explain how the implementation process has come to be separated, and consequently ignored), despite the fact that several alternate models of strategy formation exist. As will be shown shortly, these more recent models appear to hold greater promise in their ability to explain how strategies actually develop in firms, and especially in small firms.

A BRIEF OVERVIEW OF MODELS OF STRATEGY FORMATION

Most of the literature on the strategic process concerns the normative model – the planning model which seeks to describe how firms should go about formulating their strategies. Interestingly, however, those who have chosen to examine how firms actually make strategy are virtually unanimous in their rejection of the applicability of the rational, planning model. For example, Mintzberg *et al.* (1976: 258) write, 'Our study (of 25 strategic decision processes) reveals very little use of such an analytic approach, a surprising finding given the importance of the decision processes studied. Of the 83 instances of evaluation choice activity, in only 18 could evaluation be distinguished from choice.' Similarly, in a study of 78 strategic decisions, each in a separate organization, Nutt (1984: 446) concluded that 'nothing remotely resembling the normative methods described in the literature was carried out'.

It is unfortunate that the terminology used to describe the strategic management process remains rooted in the linear model of strategy, for the work of Mintzberg *et al.* (cited above) clearly demonstrates that the distinctions between these stages are often blurred. Many textbooks on strategic management still implicitly or explicitly describe a sequential model (Johnson *et al.* 1989: 11), but Johnson *et al.* strongly reject this notion: 'in practice, the stages do not take this linear form. . . . A linear representation of the process gives the impression that one stage is totally distinct from or precedes or follows another when, in fact, they are part of the same process.'

Such findings have cast much doubt on the value of the traditional view of strategy, for it appears that these models are incapable of explaining strategic behaviour in large firms as well as small. For this reason, Huff and Reger (1987: 227) have criticized the field of strategic management for its 'continuing practice of prescribing before describing'. Moreover, barring a few exceptions (see, for example, Gibb and Scott 1985) research on how strategies are actually formed in entrepreneurial small firms is virtually nonexistent. We therefore conclude that while some small businesses do make formal plans, this model is not sufficient to account for the behaviour of most small firms; furthermore, the applicability of rigid planning models to the entrepreneurial context is especially questionable.

Beyond the rational planning model

Of those taking exception to the traditional view of strategy, Mintzberg has been one of the most articulate and influential. (See especially his 1990 review of 1,495 publications related to strategic management, categorized into ten schools of thought.) He writes:

> All these definitions treat strategy as (a) explicit, (b) developed consciously and purposefully, and (c) made in advance of the specific decisions to which it applies. In common terminology, a strategy is a 'plan'. . . . this definition is incomplete for the organization and nonoperational for the researcher.
>
> (1978: 935)

Making a subtle but powerful distinction between strategy formulation and strategy formation, Mintzberg argued that strategies could form gradually and sometimes unintentionally over time. He thus distinguished between 'intended strategies' and 'realized strategies'. This thinking led him to define strategy as 'a pattern in a stream of decisions'. Mintzberg described three further types of strategies:

(1) deliberate strategies, which are intended strategies that get realized, (2) unrealized strategies, which represent intended strategies that do not get realized, and (3) emergent strategies, which are realized strategies that were never intended.

Mintzberg subsequently (1985) identified eight strategies lying along the continuum between deliberate and emergent strategies: planned, entrepreneurial, ideological, umbrella, process, unconnected, consensus and imposed. He argued that for a strategy to be purely deliberate, three conditions must be satisfied: (1) the existence of precise intentions, articulated in concrete detail, (2) the intentions must be shared or completely accepted by all actors within the organization, and (3) the environment must be perfectly predictable, totally benign, or capable of being fully controlled by the organization. In referring to the perfect planned strategy, Mintzberg noted (1985: 259): 'here (and only here) does the classic distinction between "formulation" and "implementation" hold up.' While it would be highly unlikely to find situations where the three conditions are fully met, equally rare, however, would be the purely emergent strategy. Thus, Mintzberg saw most strategies as tending to fall somewhere between these extremes, sharing characteristics of both.[1]

In a cogent and influential analysis of the various approaches to strategic management, Chaffee (1985) argued that the lack of consensus on a definition of strategy stems in part from differing mental models. She identified three distinct models implicit in the strategy literature. The *linear* model views strategy as methodical, deliberate and sequential, with a heavy emphasis on planning. Thus, organizations set goals and formulate and implement plans to achieve their objectives. Decision-making is viewed as rational, and the environment tends to be considered a nuisance. According to Chaffee, Chandler's definition of strategy typifies this model. Some authors have labelled this approach to strategy the 'normative' or 'prescriptive' approach, since the overriding concern tends to be how organizations should make strategy as opposed to how organizations actually make strategy.

Chaffee used Hofer and Schendel's definition to exemplify the second model, which she termed the *adaptive* model. Hofer and Schendel (1978: 4, 11) defined strategy as 'the basic characteristics of the match an organization achieves with its environment', and more elaborately, as 'the match between an organization's resources and skills and the environmental opportunities and risks it faces and the purposes it wishes to accomplish'. By focusing on the match between the environment and the organization, Hofer and Schendel adopt an adaptive perspective. One important implication of this definition (and model) warrants mention here. As the authors note,

> all organizations can be said to have a strategy. Thus, while the match between an organization's resources and its environment may or may not be explicitly developed and while it may or may not be a good match, the characteristics of this match can be described for all organizations.

(1978: 4)

According to the adaptive model, small firms as well as large firms can be said to possess strategies, whether or not there exists a formal plan.

At the core of the debate between the linear model and the adaptive model lies the issue of choice or free will. Andrews' definition of strategy, representing the linear model, has more or less become the dominant influence in the strategy literature (Noel 1989) and provides for proactive, purposeful choices made by the CEO of the organization. Child (1972) was one of the earliest proponents of the free-will perspective; Hambrick and Mason (1984) have also been influential advocates of choice or voluntarism. At the other extreme is a rather deterministic view of organizational development, represented by the adaptive model. Pfeffer and Salancik (1978) have argued that organizations are dependent on their external environments for the availability of critical resources. Hannan and Freeman (1977) adopt an evolutionary biological perspective, suggesting that organizational development represents a process of natural selection of species, with executives having a minimal impact.

At the risk of over-simplification, the linear model is voluntaristic but mechanistic, whereas the adaptive model is deterministic but organic.

Chaffee's third, or *interpretive*, model is of a more recent nature, and has not been as fully developed as the other two. Accordingly, Chaffee provides us with her own definition: 'Strategy in the interpretive model might be defined as orienting metaphors or frames of reference that allow the organization and its environment to be understood by organizational stakeholders' (1985: 93). The model bases itself on a social contract, assumes that reality is socially constructed (Berger and Luckmann 1966), and emphasizes symbolic action and communication or language. In a similar vein, Pennings (1985) referred to a 'rationalized strategy', where strategy is viewed as a social construction or rationalization used to give meaning to prior activities. (There are implications here for the operationalization of relevant methodologies. The researcher can deal with the linear model *ex ante*; by definition, emergent strategies and the adaptive and interpretive models can only be understood through longitudinal process studies and *post facto*.)

SOME BROADER PERSPECTIVES

Recent empirical and theoretical developments, particularly those during the past ten to fifteen years, have provided some novel and highly useful concepts which can now be used to explain strategy formation in the entrepreneurial small firm. These concepts have been drawn from the literatures of both strategy and leadership, and rest upon the assumptions in Chaffee's interpretive model of strategy. According to an interpretive view, human actors enact their environments (Weick 1979). Enactment consists of meaning-making; this meaning is created through action and the process of attention. To the extent that organizations enact or create their environment versus passively perceiving the environment, they are engaging in active, intrusive behaviour (Daft and Weick 1984). Indeed, according to Daft and Weick, in certain situations it is possible for the interpretation to shape the environment more than the environment shapes the interpretation. (The extent to which small firms can in fact shape their environments remains empirically open to study at present.)

What factors account for differences between organizational beliefs about the environment? Daft and Weick suggest that two factors are involved: the characteristics of the environment itself and the previous experience of the individual(s). An individual creates meaning from an environmental stimuli based on attention to what has already occurred (past experience); at the same time, the individual's understanding of what is happening now is simultaneously affecting his perceptions of the past (Johnson 1987).

The foregoing relates to central concerns of the social sciences over the last century. To what extent is man shaped by his society (a Durkheimian view) and to what extent is society a product of man's actions (a Weberian view)? 'Society in man' versus 'man in society', determinism versus the social construction of a reality which in turn reacts as a constraint (Berger and Luckmann 1966). As a first step, let us turn to the work of Mary Douglas on social and cultural environments.

Grid–Group environments

Mary Douglas (1978) has developed a two-dimensional framework based on the sociological theories of Weber and Durkheim concerning social control; this framework consists of different social environments which assist in explaining how an individual will choose to interpret a situation. For our purposes, the framework makes two important contributions. First, it assists in explaining why and when we might expect different modes of strategy formation in firms. Second, the framework provides a specific context for entrepreneurial behaviour.

The first dimension of the framework, that of *group*, consists of the claims the corporate or social group makes on its members, the boundaries it draws around them, and the rights it confers on them. This dimension thus measures the degree to which an individual is embedded in a larger group. *Grid*, the second dimension, represents the degree of rule-based social control exerted on an individual. Consequently, a high-grid context is a highly regulated context; low-grid suggests a powerful emphasis on the unique value of the individual.

When the grid and group dimensions are taken together they suggest a four-category typology of social environments (see Figure 2.1), each of which is associated with a unique cosmology (Douglas 1978; Thompson *et al.* 1990). High group and low grid represents an egalitarian social environment. All people are classified into insiders and outsiders, with the latter considered hostile. Emphasis is placed

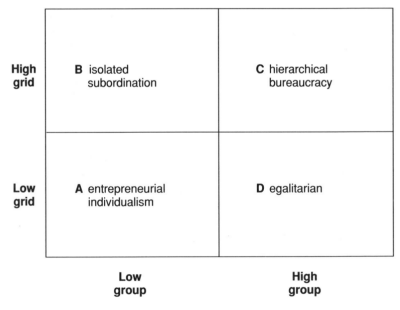

Figure 2.1 Typology of social environments
Source: Caulkins 1988, after Douglas 1978

on the group boundary (us versus them) since the world outside is intrinsically evil and characterized by predatory wolves. Small is considered beautiful and insiders are considered equals. High group and high grid results in the belief system of the hierarchist. Here boundaries not only define the outside, but also the internal roles of specialization. Many rules exist and tradition is emphasized. Inequality and authority are justifiable in this environment. The fatalist is a person located in a low group and high grid environment. These individuals feel controlled from without, and thus tend to behave in a passive manner. They are controlled by the nature of their social roles, but do not enjoy the support of group membership.

The fourth and final quadrant is that of low group and low grid; Caulkins has termed this the environment of entrepreneurial individualism. In this environment all boundaries are provisional and subject to negotiation. Although this person is not under the control of another, it is possible for this person to exert control over others. This is a highly competitive environment where individuals are responsible only for themselves. In this quadrant individuals will be biased toward interpreting their experiences as an unfolding series of opportunities (Caulkins 1988).

Preferences can often be explained by their consequences for social relations. According to Thompson *et al.* (1990), grid/group theory (or 'cultural theory') limits the number of possible biases by embedding them in social relations. What decision theorists have labelled 'heuristics' these authors term 'cultural biases' – the shared meanings, convictions and expectations that shape our way of life and constantly shape our preferences. The theory therefore predicts responses to the important themes of social theory: blame, envy, risk, etc. Consider the subject of blame, which the authors suggest is the greatest drama of all. According to the theory the individualist will blame failure on bad luck or personal failing; such persons will not, however, place any blame on the system, whereas a fatalist would be strongly inclined to blame fate. There is some empirical evidence in the literature to support this. Bowman (1976), for example, found that less successful food-processing companies tended to complain more about the weather and government price controls than did their more successful counterparts.

As stated earlier, the framework has implications for differing modes of strategy formation. Firms located in the high-group/high-grid quadrant will likely adopt a very systematic and rule-based approach to strategy formation, with specialists assigned to the task. The approach of these firms is best described by the rational planning model. Although this quadrant will tend to be characterized by large firms, smaller and medium-sized firms may also be present if role specialization or rigid lines of authority are important. High-group/low-grid firms will emphasize the process of strategy formation more so than the actual outcome. For these organizations, it is considered more important that everyone be consulted and a consensus reached than it is for the correct decision to be made. This quadrant will likely contain a greater proportion of partnerships and team-based high-technology ventures. Low-group/high-grid firms are less consistent in their choice of strategy. It is difficult to assign one particular process to this group of firms, and it is probable that the process of strategy formation will be least discernible in a portion of these. These firms seem to typify Miles and Snow's (1978) 'reactor' firm and may range in size from 'mom and pop' operations to large multinational organizations. Despite their outward differences, they will likely share a common attitude toward the usefulness of strategy, viewing it as relatively inconsequential in the long run.

Environments are therefore not homogenous. This should alert us to the possibility of multiple strategies, even within one firm, at the level of individual and collectivities. (What are the strategies of the CEO and the Union boss?)

Although we expect firms to operate in each of these environments, it is the low-group/low-grid quadrant that is the subject of particular interest, for this is where we would expect to find the entrepreneurial small firm. Clearly, large firms may also be present in this quadrant as well (consider the Walt Disney or Polaroid organizations), but they will tend to be the exception rather than the rule because it is more difficult to maintain the appropriate entrepreneurial social environment in a large organization. This quadrant is least constrained by rule-based and group social control and it is therefore here that we can expect boldness and imagination to flourish. The nature of strategy formation in this quadrant is the subject of the next section.

TOWARD A MODEL OF STRATEGY FORMATION

We now have to assemble a number of key elements: an interactive stance, the social construction of reality, heterogeneous environments, and the role of 'charismatic' vision.

Charismatic vision and the entrepreneur

The German sociologist Max Weber is particularly insightful into the key social processes of power and authority and their role in organizations. His implied question 'how is it possible for some individuals to have power over others, to get things done?' is clearly central to any discussion of strategy formulation. Weber identified three types of legitimate power, or authority – *traditional*, *legal rational* and *charisma*. The first two are represented by feudal systems and 'bureaucracy', the latter used by Weber in a technical sense, and seen as the most efficient form of organization, likely to drive out other forms.

It is, however, *charisma* which is of special interest to us here. Charisma is of course that special power of an individual which of itself gives rise to leadership; charisma is often seen as pure 'vision', and typically refers to religious leaders. Charisma is seen by Weber and others as crucial to the institution-building process, the way in which (revolutionary) ideas are put into social reality (Dow 1978). There is an axiom, 'All great things achieved must first be imagined.' The link between charisma and entrepreneurship has been explored by Scott (1976, 1980) at the micro level. Certain individuals react to situations in such a way as to break the circle of routine behaviour and set off a completely new train of events. Such creative responses – innovatory, inner-directed – are essentially concerned with the role of individual ideas in the historical process: the way in which human creativity, acting in a social context, alters that process.

However, it is one thing theoretically to pose the existence of charisma as the source of ideas around which new social reality can crystallize, and quite another to demonstrate the process concretely. Weber refers to the 'routinization' of charisma, by which the charismatic 'band' would (after the demise of the leader) revert to one or the other forms of organization. Empirically it is necessary to identify charismatic vision and explore the actual process by which (through social construction of reality) that vision is modified and implemented.

The enactment of the entrepreneur's personal vision

Sooklal (1991) developed a grounded theory which explains how a personal vision can be enacted into a social reality. The theory makes an important distinction between vision and dream, with vision considered a private and personal construct based on a single or multiple values, and leadership dream a social construct. Sooklal reproduces a passage from Levinson *et al.* (1978) describing the dream as follows:

> In its primordial form, the Dream is a vague sense of self-in-adult world. It has the quality of vision, an imagined possibility that generates excitement and vitality. At the start it is poorly articulated

and only tenuously connected to reality ... A young man's Dream becomes increasingly rational and reality based as he works to build it into his life. He gains admission to appropriate institutions, he develops the needed skills and qualities of character, makes concrete plans and strives to reach his goal.

Sooklal argues that a personal vision will gain clarity and social support through the leadership process; as it does so, it gradually evolves into the social construct known as the leadership dream (see Figure 2.2). In order to construct a dream sufficiently powerful to change the firm, the leader (entrepreneur) requires a support system. This system consists of four components: value-based insiders, value-based outsiders, convenience-based insiders and convenience-based outsiders. A value is defined as a core preference or preference set. Value-based support thus refers to contributions to a 'cause' or principle, without the expectation of reciprocal benefit. Convenience-based support comprises support or assistance which is based upon transactional exchange.

One framework which can be used to help identify individuals and groups which constitute these support groups is the stakeholder

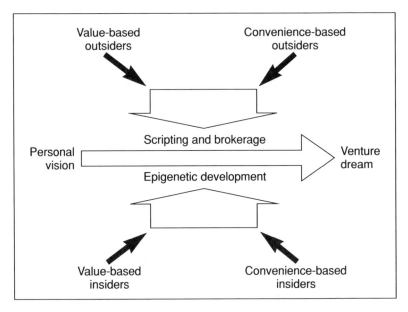

Figure 2.2 Vision enactment process
Source: after Sooklal 1991

approach provided by Freeman (1984). A stakeholder is defined as any individual or group who can affect, or is affected by, the achievement of an organization's objectives (1984: 25). The concept is applicable to both insiders and outsiders, although Freeman's view of inside stakeholders as internal groups which are troublesome (1984: 216) seems unnecessarily restrictive. Freeman suggested that proactive firms may have a high degree of stakeholder management capability.

Sooklal proposed that the leader acts as a *broker* who assembles a leadership dream by providing critical interest support groups with a stake in defining corporate intention, and hence, the reality which is ultimately enacted. This leadership dream consists of a set of social intentions which are modified and clarified through brokerage activities. A leadership dream must be scripted in order to be implemented. A script is a knowledge schema held in memory that describes expectations about the behaviours, and possibly the sequence of behaviours, appropriate for a particular context (Goia and Poole 1984). Scripts thus enable understanding of a situation and provide a guide to behaviour. They can be acquired through experience directly and indirectly. If scripts are acquired through direct experience, then repetition, reward and reinforcement are necessary in order for people to learn the new behaviours required by the script.

Scripts can also be acquired indirectly; in this case they are transferred or communicated through a variety of media, such as conversations, speeches, and reading materials. An emphasis on repetition is highly consistent with the practitioner literature. Campbell (1989), for instance, provides the following examples: 'He continually reminds everyone of Carrier's goals and the need to perform . . . exudes enthusiasm when he talks about what the team has done – consistently reminding everyone that the National's first responsibility is to its customers . . . He has found no danger of over-communicating his beliefs.' Westley and Mintzberg (1989) also confirm the importance of repetition and the interactive nature of the visionary leadership process. Starbuck (1985) pointed out that repetition can increase the strength of retrospective rationalizations.

The definition of the entrepreneur's intentions, through the medium of the venture dream, will be moderated by the need to appeal to different stakeholders with differing expectations. Sooklal suggests that the purpose of the brokerage process between the leader (entrepreneur) and the support system is to define intention and to assist in translating it into reality. Brokerage will involve negotiations, consultation, compromise, and clarification, during which participants will be given the opportunity to buy into the dream. The process is very much a bi-directional one: 'Thus, not only was the leader trying to produce change within his support network; he was also being acted upon by it' (Sooklal 1991: 849).

Sooklal's theory also incorporated Erikson's (1963) theory of epigenetic change as a means of resolving the endless debate between voluntarism and determinism, since neither of these two extremes supports a mode of leadership that is engaging, inspirational and healthy at once. According to Erikson, for healthy development to occur, an individual's needs must unfold in a predictable sequence: hope, willpower, purpose, competence, fidelity, love, care, and wisdom. By incorporating epigenetic change theory, the timing and pace of organizational change, although moderated by choice and the environment, are regulated in accordance with the needs of the leader.

The model: further considerations and elaborations

The nature of this model suggests that strategy processes do not occur in a neat sequential order. For example, Sooklal (1991) proposed that implementation occurred concurrently with the evolution of the dream. Smircich and Stubbard (1985) argued that enactment involves thinking and acting. Weick (1990) suggested that a map (or a plan) could not be understood merely by passive observation; instead, to be useful, a map must be intimately intertwined with action. Gibb and Scott (1985) make related points concerning the incremental and interactive nature of the way owner-managers of small firms develop personal commitment to emerging strategies.

Weick (1987) also suggests that the presence of strong beliefs can serve to bring events into existence:

> The lesson of self-fulfilling prophecies for students of strategy is that strong beliefs that single out and intensify consistent action can bring events into existence. Whether people are called fanatics, true believers, or the currently popular phrase 'idea champions', they all embody what looks like strategy in their persistent behaviour. Their persistence carries the strategy; the persistence is the strategy. True believers impose their view on the world and fulfil their own prophecies.
>
> (1987: 227)

The proposed model provides a very dynamic view of the strategy process, where strategy can be viewed as a continual process of 'becoming', corresponding to the transformation of vision to dream. The model has not provided for the total attainment of the vision, whereby the dream becomes fully realized. As Quinn (1984: 38) observed, 'external forces and internal potentials intersected to suggest better – but never perfect – alignments. The process was dynamic with neither a real beginning nor end.'

Several authors have suggested that the attainment of the dream can actually be detrimental to the firm. Quinn (1984) argues that continuing dynamics and eroding consensus must immediately follow initial implementation lest old recipes and crusades become institutionalized. Johnson *et al.* (1989) describe how culture and ideology can serve as constraints which are dysfunctional and serve to reduce the number and scope of possibilities available to the firm. Adopting a prescriptive approach, Hurst, Rush and White (1989) proposed a creative model of management which specifically provided for the ongoing recreation of the business and of the logic by which it is managed. Such an approach, they argued, is particularly necessary in an unstable environment.

Some biologists would term this cultural hardening, or 'freezing' as it is often called, overspecialization. But the phenomenon is not unique to business or biology. Sahlins (1964) observed:

> In fact a culture's downfall is the most probable outcome of its successes. The accomplished, well-adapted culture is biased. Its design has been refined in a special direction, its environment narrowly specified, how it shall operate definitively stated. The more adapted a culture, the less therefore it is adaptable. Its specialization subtracts from its potential, from the capacity of alternate response, from tolerance of change in the world. It becomes vulnerable in proportion to its accomplishments. . . . In other words advanced and dominant cultures create their own eclipse.
>
> (1964: 138, 144)

It may well be that this is a particularly vulnerable period for a firm or a species. Birch (1987), in his landmark study, encountered what seems to be a very similar phenomenon:

> It appears to be a tortuous route, indeed. The entrepreneurial firm is in a constant state of flux. Just when management thinks it has figured out how to grow forever, something unexpected comes along and the firm falls flat on its face. Typically management learns from these setbacks, however, and the firm comes back

stronger than before. This process appears to continue throughout the life of the firm – a constant pulsation, growing and contracting, taking false paths, retreating, and trying again, up and down, down and up. The ups are progressively higher, however, and the downs do not seem more than a detour when viewed in retrospect.

(1987: 38)

The strategy process, as depicted by the model, is quite unlike traditional notions of strategy formulation. However, several perspectives on strategy are sympathetic toward this model of strategy formation – perspectives which share in their process orientation. It was Mintzberg (1987), for instance, who reminded us that strategy normally consists of stability rather than change. Quinn's (1984) notion of incremental strategies has greatly contributed to our understanding of strategy change as an incremental, evolutionary process. Johnson (1987) and Mintzberg (1990) have both made outstanding efforts to reexamine and reinterpret Quinn's espoused normative model, taking into account perspectives which provide for concepts such as vision, learning, culture, recipe, etc.

The two-way interactive shaping of the vision central to the model also has support in the literature. Westley and Mintzberg (1989) note that although the original idea may come from the leader, it is the process of co-creation, the sharing of the vision, that generates the necessary excitement. They likened the need for an active audience to a need for assistance, which is analogous to Sooklal's concept of a support system. Filion (1990) found that the key factor associated with the development of a vision and subsequent visionary achievements was the entrepreneur's internal relations system.

However, Bryson (1988) argues that the existence of numerous stakeholders with conflicting agendas will make it more difficult to develop a detailed vision. For this reason, he places the vision development step at the end of the formulation process, where, he suggests, it is more likely to guide implementation rather than formulation. It appears to us that this point is also empirically open at present.

CONCLUSION

Mintzberg (1990) has described the entrepreneurial school as viewing strategy formation as a visionary process. He does criticize the school, however, for its inability to elaborate on the strategy formation process, which he likens to a black box. At the same time, Mintzberg's view of this school does not coincide precisely with the proposed model since Mintzberg attributes strategy formation to a single leader. Recently there has been some work which attempts to address the dearth of theory and empirical research in this area (Noel 1989; Westley and Mintzberg 1989; Filion 1990).

The model outlined in this paper specifically addresses Mintzberg's complaint by incorporating leadership mechanisms which explain the transformation from vision to dream. Moreover, this model differs from Mintzberg's conception of entrepreneurial strategy (1991) since Mintzberg consistently emphasized the solitary character of the vision, which he described as 'locked in a single brain' (p. 609).

A number of advantages can be associated with this proposed model. First, most models of strategy have treated culture solely as a constraint or obstacle to strategic change. Although the popular press is replete with examples of how culture can also be viewed as an important (although not necessarily distinct or separable) component of strategy, there has been very little theory available to support this view. This model provides a much larger role for culture. It suggests that while culture can be a constraint at certain times (i.e. when dramatic change is required), culture must always be considered an important dimension of strategy, even during periods of stability. Moreover, culture can also be seen to influence our 'sense-making processes'; it therefore has a profound impact on not only how we see the world, but also what we see.

A second advantage of the model is its capacity to account for the simultaneity of formulation and implementation processes, consistent with the body of literature on strategy process. Those studies which have studied the strategy process as it actually occurs rather than how it should occur are virtually unanimous in their rejection of the view of formulation and implementation as separate, distinct stages. Mintzberg (1991: 609) also suggests how vision is inextricably linked to implementation: 'a clear, imaginative, integrated strategic vision depends on an involvement with detail, an intimate knowledge of specifics. And by closely controlling implementation "personally", the leader is able to reformulate enroute, to adapt the evolving vision through his or her own process of learning.'

While the model does not resolve the choice versus determinism debate, it is perhaps more realistic in its recognition that strategy formation probably shares characteristics of both views. Moreover, although the ability to proactively manage the environment is usually considered a strategic activity of the highest level, this ability is usually only ascribed to large firms. This model, however, suggests that small firms are capable of managing their environments through the enactment process. It thus provides for the possibility of proactive behaviour, and in particular, proactive behaviour without planning.

IMPLICATIONS

The model suggests several possible directions for future research, two of which are presented here. First, Sooklal's theory is based on a single case involving a relatively large organization; more studies are clearly needed to record and describe the enactment process in small firms and start-ups. With enactment and process as the focus, longitudinal methodologies sufficiently sensitive to capture context and ambiguity are desirable. Ethnographic research and participant observation are therefore particularly suitable for this type of endeavour.

To date, the literature on venture support systems has tended to emphasize support provided by convenience-based outsiders such as accountants, consultants, venture capital firms and government agencies, while the potential for value-based support and the contribution of insider support has been largely neglected. This paper argues that we should begin to examine support systems in their totality; we need a greater understanding of the composition of these systems and the types of support they provide (which is probably much more varied than the literature suggests). Given the fragmentary nature of our current understanding, these questions are perhaps best initially addressed through in-depth interviews.

For the practitioner, the model holds promise for at least three reasons. First, despite the fact that the entrepreneur alone is responsible for providing the imagination and initial vision that forms the seed of the venture dream, it is apparent that the venture dream is not the result of a solo effort. Rather, a reluctance to let others buy into and actively participate in shaping the dream is likely to inhibit the healthy development of the dream and the venture itself. Second, entrepreneurs can be trained to plan, develop and assess their support systems strategically. A more effective support system should result in a stronger dream and ultimately, better performance. Finally, it should be noted that value-based support does not come with a price tag attached – it is instead perfectly free.

NOTE

1 It was also at this time that Mintzberg redefined strategy as a pattern in a stream of actions rather than decisions, arguing that decisions must represent intentions.

REFERENCES

Andrews, K. (1971) *The Concept of Corporate Strategy*, Homewood, Ill.: Dow-Jones-Irwin.

Bamberger, I. (1989) 'Developing Competitive Advantage in Small and Medium-size Firms', *Long Range Planning*, 22 (5), 80–88.

Berg, N. and Pitts, R.A. (1979) 'Strategic Management: the Multi-business Corporation', in D.E. Schendel and C.W. Hofer (eds), *Strategic Management: A New View of Business Policy and Planning*, Boston: Little, Brown and Company, 339–348.

Berger, P. and Luckmann, T. (1966) *The Social Construction of Reality: A Treatise in the Sociology of Knowledge*, New York: Doubleday.

Birch, D.L. (1987) *Job Creation in America*, New York: Free Press.

Birley, S. (1982) 'Corporate Strategy and the Small Firm', *Journal of General Management*, 8 (2), 82–86.

Bourgeois, L.J. III (1980) 'Strategy and Environment: A Conceptual Integration', *Academy of Management Review*, 5 (1), 25–39.

Bowman, E.H. (1976) 'Strategy and the Weather', *Sloan Management Review*, 17 (2), 49–62.

Bryson, J.M. (1988) *Strategic Planning for Public and Nonprofit Organizations*, San Francisco: Jossey-Bass Publishers.

Campbell, A. (1989) 'How to Translate a Corporate Vision into Reality', *the Globe and Mail*, 24 April, A7.

Caulkins, D. (1988) 'Networks and Narratives: An Anthropological Perspective for Small Business Research', Occasional Paper Series no. 01/88, Stirling, Scotland: Scottish Enterprise Foundation.

Chaffee, E.E. (1985) 'Three Models of Strategy', *Academy of Management Review*, 10 (1), 89–98.

Chandler, A. (1962) *Strategy and Structure: Chapters in the History of American Industrial Enterprise*, Cambridge, MA: M.I.T. Press.

Child, J. (1972) 'Organizational Structure, Environment and Performance: the role of strategic choice', *Sociology*, 6 (1), 1–22.

Curtis, D.A. (1983) *Strategic Planning for Smaller Businesses*, Lexington, MA: D.C. Heath.

Daft, R.L. and Weick, K.E. (1984) 'Toward a Model of Organizations as Interpretation Systems', *Academy of Management Review*, 9 (2), 284–295.

Douglas, M. (1978) 'Cultural Bias', Occasional Paper, 35, Royal Anthropological Institute, reprinted in Douglas, M. (1982) *In the Active Voice*, London: Routledge & Kegan Paul, 183–254.

Dow, T.E. (1978) 'An Analysis of Max Weber's Work on Charisma', *British Journal of Sociology*, 29 (1), 83–93.

Erikson, E.H. (1963) *Childhood and Society*, New York: W.W. Norton.

Filion, L.J. (1990) 'Vision and Relations: Elements for an Entrepreneurial Metamodel', *Frontiers of Entrepreneurship Research*, Wellesley, MA: Babson College, 57–71.

Freeman, E.R. (1984) *Strategic Management: A Stakeholder Approach*, Boston: Pitman.

Gibb, A. and Scott, M. (1985) 'Strategic Awareness, Personal Commitment and the Process of Planning in the Small Business', *Journal of Management Studies*, 22 (6), 597–631.

Ginsberg, A. (1988) 'Measuring and Modelling Changes in Strategy: Theoretical Foundations and Empirical Directions', *Strategic Management Journal*, 9 (6), 559–575.

Goia, D.A. and Poole, P.P. (1984) 'Scripts in Organizational Behaviour', *Academy of Management Review*, 9 (3), 449–459.

Hambrick, D.C. and Mason, P.A. (1984) 'Upper Echelons: The Organization as a Reflection of its Top Managers', *Academy of Management Review*, 9 (2), 193–206.

Hannan, M.T. and Freeman, J. (1977) 'The Population Ecology of Organizations', *American Journal of Sociology*, 82 (5), 929–964.

Hofer, C.W. (1975) 'Toward a Contingency Theory of Business Strategy', *Academy of Management Journal*, 18 (4), 784–810.

Hofer, C.W. and Schendel, D. (1978) *Strategy Formulation: Analytical Concepts*, St. Paul: West Publishing Company.

Huff, A.S. and Reger, R.K. (1987) 'A Review of Strategic Process Research', *Journal of Management*, 13 (2), 211–236.

Hurst, D.K., Rush, J.C. and White, R.E. (1989) 'Top Management Teams and Organizational Renewal', *Strategic Management Journal*, 10 (5), 87–105.

Jauch, L.R. (1983) 'An Inventory of Selected Academic Research on Strategic Management', *Advances in Strategic Management*, 2, 141–175.

Johnson, G. (1987) *Strategic Change and the Management Process*, Oxford: Basil Blackwell.

Johnson, G., Scholes, K., and Sexty, R.W. (1989) *Exploring Strategic Management*, Scarborough, Ont.: Prentice-Hall Canada.

Levinson, D.J. *et al.* (1978) *The Seasons of a Man's Life*, New York: Alfred A. Knopf.

McKiernan, P. (1986) 'Corporate Planning in Small Companies in UK Manufacturing Industry', Proceedings of the Ninth National Small Firms Policy and Research Conference, Gleneagles, UK.

McMillan, C.J. (1980) 'Qualitative Models of Organizational Decision-making', *Journal of General Management*, 5 (4), 22–39.

Miles, R.E. and Snow, C.C. (1978) *Organizational Strategy, Structure and Process*, New York: McGraw-Hill.

Miller, D. (1989) 'Matching Strategies and Strategy Making: Process, Content, and Performance', *Human Relations*, 42 (3), 241–260.

Mintzberg, H. (1973) 'Strategy-making in Three Modes', *California Management Review*, 16 (2), 44–53.

Mintzberg, H., Raisinghani, D., and Theoret, A. (1976) 'The Structure of "Unstructured" Decision Processes', *Administrative Science Quarterly*, 21 (2), 246–275.

Mintzberg, H. (1978) 'Patterns in Strategy Formation', *Management Science*, 24 (9), 934–948.

Mintzberg, H. (1987) 'Crafting Strategy', *Harvard Business Review*, 65 (4), 66–75.

Mintzberg, H. (1990) 'Strategy Formation: Schools of Thought', in J.W. Fredrickson (ed.), *Perspectives on Strategic Management*, New York: Harper & Row, 105–235.

Mintzberg, H. (1991) 'The Entrepreneurial Organization', in H. Mintzberg and J.B. Quinn, *The Strategy Process*, Englewood Cliffs: Prentice-Hall, 604–613.

Montgomery, C.A. (1988) Guest editor's Introduction to the special issue on Research in the Content of Strategy, *Strategic Management Journal*, 9 (5), 3–8.

Nagel, A. (1981) 'Strategy Formulation for the Smaller Firm – A Practical Approach', *Long Range Planning*, 14 (4), 115–120.

Noel, A. (1989) 'Strategic Cores and Magnificent Obsessions: Discovering Strategy Formation through Daily Activities of CEOs', *Strategic Management Journal*, 10 (5), 33–49.

Nutt, P.C. (1984) 'Types of Organizational Decision Processes', *Administrative Planning Quarterly*, 29 (3), 414–450.

Pennings, J.M. (1985) 'Introduction: On the Nature and Theory of Strategic Decisions', in J.M. Pennings (ed.), *Organizational Strategy and Change*, San Francisco: Jossey-Bass, 1–34.

Pettigrew, A. (1987) 'Introduction: Researching Strategic Change', in A. Pettigrew (ed.), *The Management of Strategic Change*, Oxford: Basil Blackwell, 1–13.

Pfeffer, J. and Salancik, G.R. (1978) *The External Control of Organizations: A Resource Dependence Perspective*, New York: Harper and Row.

Quinn, J.B. (1980) *Strategies for Change: Logical Incrementalism*, Homewood, Ill.: Richard D. Irwin.

Quinn, J.B. (1984) 'Managing Strategies Incrementally', in R.B. Lamb (ed.), *Competitive Strategic Management*, Englewood Cliffs: Prentice-Hall.

Sahlins, M.D. (1964) 'Culture and Environment: The Study of Cultural Ecology', in S. Tax (ed.), *Horizons of Anthropology*, Chicago: Aldine Publishing Company, 132–147.

Scott, M.G. (1976) 'Entrepreneurs and Entrepreneurship: A Study of Organizational Founding', unpublished Ph.D. thesis, University of Edinburgh.

Scott, M.G. (1980) 'Independence and the Flight from Large Scale: Some Sociological Factors in the Founding Process', in A. Gibb and T. Webb (eds), *Policy Issues in Small Business Research*, Farnborough: Saxon House.

Smircich, L. and Stubbard, C. (1985) 'Strategic Management in an Enacted World', *Academy of Management Review*, 10 (4), 724–736.

Sooklal, L. (1991) 'The Leader as a Broker of Dreams', *Human Relations*, 44 (8), 833–856.

Starbuck, W.H. (1985) 'Acting First and Thinking Later: Theory versus Reality in Strategic Change', in J. Pennings (ed.), *Organizational Strategy and Change*, San Francisco: Jossey-Bass, 336–372.

Thompson, M., Ellis, R. and Wildavsky, A. (1990) *Cultural Theory*, Boulder, CO: Westview Press.

Unni, V.K. (1981) 'The Role of Strategic Planning in Small Businesses', *Long Range Planning*, 14 (2), 54–58.

Van Hoorn, T.P. (1979) 'Strategic Planning in Small and Medium-sized Companies', *Long Range Planning*, 12 (2), 84–91.

Weick, K.E. (1979) *The Social Psychology of Organizing*, Reading, MA: Addison-Wesley.

Weick, K.E. (1987) 'Substitutes for Corporate Strategy', in D.J. Teece (ed.), *Competitive Challenge*, Cambridge, MA: Ballinger.

Weick, K.E. (1990) 'Introduction: Cartographic Myths in Organizations', in

A.S. Huff (ed.), *Mapping Strategic Thought*, Chichester: John Wiley and Sons.

Westley, F. and Mintzberg, H. (1989) 'Visionary Leadership and Strategic Management', *Strategic Management Journal*, 10 (5), 17–32.

3 Technology management and entrepreneurship
A critical view

Kalevi Kyläheiko and Asko Miettinen

INTRODUCTION

There have been two recent trends in the debate about strategic management. First, there is the attempt to delineate the backgrounds of new directions in the theories of the firm (Teece 1984; Rumelt 1984, 1987.) Second, there is a clear interest in technology as part of 'corporate strategy' (Pavitt 1990; Nelson 1991). Although the importance of technological development as a determinant of the competitive advantage of a firm is accepted, the dynamo of development, the entrepreneur creating 'new combinations', is to a large extent outside the analysis.

The first part of this essay provides a look at the economics-oriented theories of strategic management, and focuses on their ability to cope with technology. The second part focuses on entrepreneurship. Because 'the change generating actor' is missing in the neoclassical explanations, the concept of the entrepreneur is not found in them either. Evolutionary approaches seem to be suitable for analysing entrepreneurship.

POSING THE QUESTION

Traditionally, studies in strategic management research, economics, organization theory and business history have analysed the relationship between firm strategies and technological change in isolation. The last decade, however, has witnessed some convergence of theories. This development has cast new light on many empirical findings from a number of detailed case studies of the process of technological innovation from the 1960s onwards. In spite of the dialogue, the theoretical domain of technology management studies is still incoherent and some more classifications are needed.

Empirical case studies and detailed business history studies (Chandler 1990; Mowery and Rosenberg 1989) can be used as starting points when formulating the propositions on which theoretical technology management research is to be based:

Proposition 1:   Technological change cannot be analysed without the analysis of dynamic processes.

Proposition 2:   All innovation decisions are ultimately interwoven with problems of uncertainty.

Proposition 3:   Innovation activities depend on the internal organization and the production structure of a firm.

The main 'economics-based' strategic technology management frameworks to be analysed are as follows: (1) the neoclassical theory of the firm (production function approach (PF) and new industrial organization (NIO)), (2) Porter's competitive advantage framework (IO), (3) transaction cost economics (TCE), (4) resource-based theory (RBT), (5) evolutionary theories of the firm (ET). Figure 3.1 characterizes these potential approaches by taking into account the three main distinctions of the propositions; (i) static (stationary) versus dynamic, (ii) certainty versus uncertainty and, (iii) exchange-oriented versus production-oriented.

Our definition of uncertainty deserves some explanation. Knight introduced the distinction between certainty, risk, and uncertainty. Unfortunately this triad has been interpreted narrowly by mainstream economists. For instance, for Arrow (1974: 33) uncertainty means that the world is in one or another of a range of fully known states and we just do not know which state is the true one. This view is easily combined with the neoclassical 'profit maximization' assumption but it leaves the problems of radical uncertainty ('not knowing which states and outcomes are possible') outside the very definition.

In the context of technological change the idea of radical uncertainty is of vital importance and we prefer the distinction between parametric and structural uncertainty (Langlois 1984). The former, neoclassical one is based on a certain knowledge of the underlying choice structure. Structural uncertainty, in turn, is based on imperfect structural knowledge, which implies bounded rationality. This endogenized view of uncertainty helps to explain internal organization (structures, routines, habits) and deliberate strategies of a firm as behavioural responses to complex and uncertain environments.

By combining the two matrices of Figure 3.1 we see that our selection criteria discriminate between different approaches. Our comments on different approaches will be restricted to the selection

	CERTAINTY	RISK AND PARAMETRIC UNCERTAINTY	STRUCTURAL UNCERTAINTY
STATIC OR STATIONARY	PF	IO	TCE RBT
DYNAMIC		NIO	Dynamic RBT EE

			TC
EXCHANGE-ORIENTED			TC
PRODUCTION-ORIENTED	PF	IO NIO	RBT EE

Figure 3.1 Typology of different theories of the firm

criteria, and the main question asked will focus on how it is possible to create and sustain quasi-rents derived from innovations.

NEOCLASSICAL THEORY OF THE FIRM AND TECHNOLOGY

The neoclassical production function theory (PF) views the firm as a set of given, feasible, production plans from which a rational manager, with perfect or parametrically uncertain information, chooses that plan that maximizes expected net present value of future profit (Hart 1989: 1757). Resources, technology, institutions and preferences are given and the firm (= the owner = the entrepreneur) is treated as a black box. Technological change is exogenous ('manna from heaven'). All the differences between firms are determined by the external conditions they face and by the assets they possess. There is no scope for internal organization or discretionary firm-specific technology strategies.

The nature of adopted technological knowledge carries an engineering blueprint connotation and no distinction between the concepts of 'information' and 'technology' is made. From Arrow (1962) onward, investments in technology are treated similarly to any other public investments with externalities. This view is at odds with recent empirical innovation studies. According to Pavitt (1986: 178–179) most technology does not have the properties of information; it is specific, often tacit and uncodified.

More interesting is the new industrial organization theory (NIO). It utilizes game theory and focuses on innovation strategies in a dynamic and production-oriented framework. The analyses of the impact of R&D investment in innovations and different characterizations of R&D rivalries between firms (Reinganum 1989) are useful. They overcome static limitations and open up (at least a little bit) the black box. Even these models suffer from the lack of a theory of the firm and from the parametric uncertainty assumption. Accordingly, no special internal organization is needed and the explanation of the behaviour of different agents can be traced back to initial and equilibrium conditions and luck. The models concentrate also on a very small number of variables and fix many empirically essential variables. Given the same conditions, all the firms will do the same thing (Nelson 1991: 65–66). From the entrepreneurship point of view this is a fundamental drawback.

PORTER'S COMPETITIVE ADVANTAGE FRAMEWORK

Porter's analysis is based on the Bain–Mason industrial organization paradigm (IO). The message was that the supply and demand conditions in a particular industry determine the relevant market structure, which affects the conduct of the firm, which, in turn, determines the performance of firms. The goal was to increase social welfare by promoting effective industrial policy. Porter's (1980) idea was to combine this paradigm with the concept of strategy by turning the normative social welfare message upside down. The performance of a firm depends drastically upon its environment, which can be characterized by five forces: bargaining power of suppliers and buyers, threat of new entrants and substitute products or services and rivalry among current competitors.

Porter's competitive advantage is externally determined (due to its neoclassical heritage). Only the rivalry component depends on internal capabilities . This is not very important, however, because the firms within an industry are assumed to be almost identical in terms of their capabilities. The framework is static and cannot give any good explanation of the sustainability of monopoly rents. The role of technology and innovation is theoretically disconnected and *ad hoc* (Porter 1981: 616).

Porter (1983: 3) states that technology is unique as a strategic variable because of its considerable power to change the competitive rules of a game. By combining his strategic framework ('differentiation or low-cost strategies') with the product cycle curve, Porter generates some technology strategies as an element of an overall competitive strategy. Nevertheless, Porter's considerations are externally determined. Market structure dominates and the role of technology is subordinated. This is due to his trust in the IO-paradigm and its (often implicit) maximization and parametric uncertainty assumptions.

Porter (1985) focuses more on the understanding of the sources of sustained competitive advantage (the value chain concept) and enriches the analysis of internal factors. He (1990, 1991) extends this analysis into national level and makes some attempts to dynamize his formerly static framework. 'Competitive Advantage of Nations' (1991: 19) argues that the location ('a home base') is a key success factor, since it shapes the structure, the strategy, and the organizational and technological capabilities of a firm. Domestic rivalry pressures the firms to upgrade competitive advantages continuously by improving the quality and by innovating.

'New' Porter still holds the 'old' IO-Porter view of the importance of the five forces. What is new is the emphasis on dynamics and the innovation process. This contradicts the premises of Porter's old analysis which was based on the static but theoretically well-founded matching of external and internal factors. What is needed is a Schumpeterian view where competitive advantages are continuously in flux and it is no longer enough to capture monopoly rents by erecting mobility barriers. One cannot help thinking that the theoretical underpinnings of this endeavour have not been well articulated and 'the quasi-dynamization' has been articulated at the cost of theoretical coherence. Schumpeterian ideas ('history matters', disequilibria, and path-dependency) cannot be reconciled with the modified IO-framework. Porter's new contribution seems to be based inductively upon historical observations. Hence, it is rather a description than an explanation of the competitive advantages of nations.

TRANSACTION-COST ECONOMICS AND TECHNOLOGY

Since Coase's (1937) famous seminal paper, economists have utilized transaction costs in explaining the internal structure and boundaries of the firm. The (controversial) sources of transaction costs are summarized as a cost of using the price mechanism. According to Williamson all microeconomic activities are organized to minimize the sum of production and transaction costs (in his jargon 'to economize on costs of production and transactions'). The main factors that give rise to transaction costs are as follows (Williamson 1991: 79–80): (1) bounded rationality (behaviour is intentionally rational, but only limitedly so), (2) opportunism (self-interest seeking with guile), (3) information impactedness (asymmetric information), (4) frequency of transactions (small numbers of trading relationship possibilities reinforce the dependence), (5) uncertainty and complexity (the contracts are incomplete), (6) asset (site, physical, or human asset) specificity.

Conditions (1) to (3) are behavioural and (4) to (6) are attributes of transactions. Condition (6) refers to the ease with which an asset can be redeployed to alternative uses (the problem of irreversibility). This is an important aspect from the technology strategy viewpoint. The owners of specific assets are in a danger of losing their rents to their contractual partners. In order to avoid this they can either use less specific assets (and incur efficiency losses) or internalize the partner using vertical integration (and incur more bureaucratic costs). Here one is facing the Penrosian–Arrowian (1974) 'flexibility versus efficiency' dilemma in a disguise.

By combining the conditions (1–6) one can construct transaction difficulties which usually speak for more integration as a technology management strategy. For instance, if there are only a few transactions and the asset specificity is high, the best alternative is to internalize. Williamson concludes that vertically integrated large-scale organizations are typical where opportunistic potential is significant. Asset specificity, small numbers, and uncertainty increase this potential and vice versa.

The recent shift from highly integrated innovation and R&D systems towards more disintegrated network solutions (especially in the rapidly changing high-tech industries, see Antonelli 1992 for this) offers new challenges to TCE. One possible explanation can be found when comparing market transaction costs (TC) with internal bureaucratic costs (BC). In conditions where the relative level of TC is small with respect to the level of BC, market solutions are preferred and vice versa. When the entrepreneur is facing a situation where both the TC and BC components are high because of rapidly changing, uncertain and turbulent environments and very specialized research efforts, the best way to organize is to utilize 'hybrid' network solutions (joint ventures, strategic alliances, etc.: Hagedoorn 1993). On the other hand, the existence of remarkable economies of scale and scope increases the tendency towards more integrated solutions.

Williamson (1988) admits that his theory is profoundly static and hence unable to say much about technological change. The idea is to take 'snapshots' concerning asset specificity conditions (relating to technology) and to analyse each period separately. There is no room for endogenous technology in this exercise. Williamson clings to his opinion that the static TCE really can differentiate the efficient governance structure from the inefficient one. Here we have a quasi-functionalist explanation in action or perhaps even worse, a Panglossian statement. If one knows nothing else but some observed governance structures, one cannot make any efficiency judgements. More information is needed in order to specify the underlying causal mechanism. One is tempted to argue that Williamson's typically neo-classical minimization logic is at stake.

Referring back to Figure 3.1, one can find another problem in the TCE analysis of technological change. It is exchange-based and its basic unit of analysis is 'the transaction' (Williamson 1985: 41). Focusing on transactions and a static economizing on costs results in abstract deduction from given data just as in the neoclassical general equilibrium tradition. Hence TCE cannot explain the role of specific, path-dependent characteristics of a firm's assets, in particular cumulative learning processes. This is a major drawback when analysing technology strategies.

'PROFITING FROM TECHNOLOGICAL INNOVATIONS'

Teece has made fruitful attempts to apply TCE directly to the problems of innovation. His starting point (1984) was that technological innovations are asset-specific and need high quality control. Both increase transaction costs of arm's-length contracts and speak for the vertical integration solution. In his celebrated article, Teece (1986) goes deeper into the problems of innovation. He introduces two key concepts, complementary assets and appropriability regime. The former consists of those assets that are needed with the firm's core assets. A regime of appropriability (Teece 1986: 191) refers to the factors that govern the ability to capture the rents of innovations. The tighter the protection, the more preferred a market solution (or a hybrid form) and vice versa.

Teece offers powerful analytical results for integration versus contract design. The pure vertical integration solution is preferable when appropriability is weak, some critical specialized complementary assets are needed and some core capabilities are idiosyncratic. The market solution is preferred when protection is tight and there is no particular asset specificity. It is not surprising that neoclassical models typically produce market solutions; they are based on the very special assumptions of iron-clad patents and zero transaction costs. Teece shows that one can utilize the abstract idea of 'defining the boundaries of a firm' fruitfully when making strategic innovation decisions. Potential losers and winners of the innovation race can be outlined by analysing the sources of transaction costs. In comparison with Porter's competitive advantage approach, one now has more analytical tools for evaluation. For example, one can understand the symbiotic relationship between large and small firms much better. It depends on different complementary asset portfolios and different appropriability conditions. It is also easy to see why there are deliberate technology strategies.

The main problem of Teece's framework is once again its stasis. It cannot cope well with technological change. One can demonstrate this by introducing the time factor into the analysis (Langlois 1988: 651–652). In the (neoclassical) stationary state the uncertainty is low and hence TC as well. Hence the market solution is preferred. The question of appropriability is secondary. Also the learning by doing (and using) is easy and reduces TC. In the world of rapid change the radical innovations are the engines of growth. Turbulent times also make learning difficult. Uncertainty is high and so are the TC. Complementary assets become critical and asset specificity increases. Even tight appropriability could not countervail these strong integration tendencies. Consequently, the integrated solution is preferred.

More problematic is the moderate growth and incremental innovations scenario that could characterize a stable technological trajectory (Dosi 1988). Now one has to know the initial conditions because the direction towards contracting/internalizing depends upon the (tranquil or turbulent) conditions at the starting point. This indicates roughly the path-dependency problem of the dynamic processes; the observed internal organizations (and all the other institutions) depend drastically on their history. For this very reason one cannot make Williamsonian static efficiency comparisons. When the growth rate is unbalanced (as typical) the analysis becomes even more complicated.

THE RESOURCE-BASED THEORY AND TECHNOLOGY

The resource-based theory (RBT) developed rapidly during the 1980s. It balanced considerably the externally-oriented strategic matching discussion by focusing on the rents accruing to the owners of internal resources and skills (or taken together, capabilities) of the firm (see Wernerfelt 1984; Rumelt 1984; Barney 1991). The RBT has its roots both in strategic theory and in economics. Such strategy classics as Barnard, Selznick, Ansoff, and Chandler have emphasized the idea of strategy as a fit between the internal capabilities (the focus of analysis) and external opportunities. In economics the roots are in the works of Ricardo, Chamberlin, and Penrose (1959).

Chamberlin's monopolistic competition theory from 1933 demonstrated that firm-specific resources (technical know-how, management, patents, trade marks, etc.) can affect competitive advantages. Selznick introduced in 1957 the term 'distinctive competence' to illustrate those capabilities that an organization can do very well compared with its rivals. Chandler (1962) based these ideas upon extensive historical evidence. He introduced a useful triad: (technological and organizational) capabilities – strategy – structure. The idea was that all these elements are rather stable and closely interconnected. Because the structure is essentially based on those accumulated (and partly tacit) core capabilities which the firm does exceptionally well, it is very difficult to change the firm's structure profoundly. This inertia sets a limit to the choice of strategy, too.

Edith Penrose (1959: 24–26) regarded the firm both as an administrative organization and as a collection of productive (tangible) resources and human (intangible) resources. In the spirit of Schumpeter, she distinguished between managerial and entrepreneurial competencies (1959: 34–35). The former relates to running an existing business and the latter to discovering and realizing new opportunities for growth. She concluded also that uncertainty limits expansion and introduced the trade-off between efficiency and flexibility.

It was left to Wernerfelt (1984) and Rumelt (1984) to bring the many strands together. Wernerfelt developed a kind of dual Porter-inspired strategy theory. He stated that 'for the firm, resources and products are two sides of the same coin'. Indeed, in a static optimization and equilibrium context, the dual structures are identical. More interestingly, Wernerfelt's (1984: 174–179) strategy formulations are different from Porter's strategies. The reason is that the RBT framework can be dynamized. The knowledge base needed to build up core capabilities is the result of a cumulative process. Firms are heterogenous just because they have an irreversible history of their own. This is in accordance with recent empirical innovation studies (Pavitt 1991). Accordingly, one cannot anticipate a very easy imitation of these assets. The message of RBT literature can now be summarized as follows:

1 The firm's success is based on the chain: skills and resources → organizational and technological capabilities → core competence → competitive advantage.

2 Isolation mechanisms try to prevent the equalization of rents by increasing causal ambiguity. This presupposes (at least partly) tacit, complex and specific competencies based on the partly heterogenous and immobile resources.
3 It is a question of a historical and structurally uncertain process. One cannot analyse the position of a particular firm just by looking at its contemporary situation.
4 The RBT entrepreneurship theory distinguishes between managerial and entrepreneurial competencies. Rumelt (1987: 143) defines 'entrepreneurial rent' as the difference between a venture's *ex post* value and the *ex ante* anticipated cost. This rent brings together neatly the aspects of 'uncertainty' and 'discovering something new'.

The static RBT is vulnerable to the same criticism as TCE and Porter's approach. It cannot handle learning processes and identify relevant competencies. It reveals its worst in many popular articles, which argue in a functionalist, vicious circle. The celebrated essay of Prahalad and Hamel (1990) is close to tautological reasoning. However, the dynamic RBT seems to be a serious candidate for a relevant strategic technology management framework.

EVOLUTIONARY SYNTHESIS OF TECHNOLOGY MANAGEMENT

There has been a long evolutionary tradition in economics (see Hodgson 1993) but the recent revival is the most influential. It consists of many approaches both in economics and in organization research. All have in common an opposition to the neoclassical received view, and a commitment to the 'Blind Variation–Selection–Retention' (BVSR) cultural evolution paradigm created by Campbell (1969). Also we regard evolution as the historical transformation of a system through endogenously generated change and apply the BVSR framework. Metcalfe (1989: 58) relates it to technology analysis by stating that technological change is most capable of generating variety in the long run. Hence, in order to understand the dynamics of organizations one has to analyse the evolution of technology. There are three elements in Campbell's paradigm: blind variation (BV), selection (S), and retention (R). For each, an economic explanation is given. In the cultural evolution theory, the concept of 'blindness' does not mean random development but purposeful actions under circumstances of structural uncertainty.

In the context of strategic technology management, the principle of variation means that there are heterogenous firms with idiosyncratic resources, skills, and capabilities so that selection is possible. Also the 'Lamarckian' features, such as imitation and learning, are allowed. The variation works through the hierarchy of skills and routines, which both are capable of learning and imitating. Through variety, the firm generates new routines and capabilities (= innovations). The path-dependent, cumulative nature of a firm's development along a natural or technological trajectory is emphasized. It can be described as the incremental development of a particular technology within the techno-economic paradigm (Dosi 1988: 224–226) which has pervasive effects throughout the whole economy. A paradigm change means a radical transformation of the dominating engineering and managerial views and results in drastic new organizational and social changes (see Freeman 1991: 222–224).

Variation is a necessary but not a sufficient condition for economic progress. Two other principles, namely 'the principle of heredity' (retention) and 'the principle of selection', are also needed. The former means that there are mechanisms that guarantee necessary stability and continuity over time. Nelson and Winter (1982: 99–107) put stress on the continuity by analysing the role of routines as an organizational memory. New information will be conceptualized in the framework of old, established hierarchical routines. Routines are also the basis of replication and imitation processes. Because of their partly tacit nature these two processes cannot be carried out quickly, easily, and without costs as the NC theory often seems to think.

The mutations of routines ('innovations' interpreted as 'genes') are possible too. All innovations (technological, organizational, marketing, financial or managerial) are connected with the problems of structural uncertainty. First, innovating means discovering something new that cannot be wholly characterized *ex ante* (Schumpeter 1934: 65–66). Second, most innovations imply unanticipated changes in routine(s) that can result in new structures in the organization, which may introduce problems or even a crisis.

The task of the selection principle is to set limits to the scale and scope of variety by increasing the relative significance of the characteristics which are better fitted for the environmental pressure (Metcalfe 1989: 56). The direct unit of the selection is a new product or a new process and the selection criterion is the profitability (profit motive, not profit maximization!). There are also non-market selection environments consisting of political, regulatory, control, and generic technological knowledge created by science and technology development work.

The role of organization is of vital importance when appraising the interplay of variation and selection. Selection needs time to operate and pick up the fittest artefacts (products/processes). This, in turn, depends on organizational inertia. Hence, organizations have a double role: the source of 'new combinations' ('variety') and the stable hierarchial network of routines ('retention'). The result is path-dependent evolution based on routines and incremental innovations.

In order to explore the dynamics, some new concepts are needed. Innovations can be characterized as incremental (minor) when they occur continuously for existing products, processes, organizations, management styles, and distribution or financial systems. Innovations are radical (major) when they result in discontinuities in technological or organizational capabilities. Typically, quantitative changes transform into qualitative changes. The technological trajectory can now be analysed, too. When there are only incremental innovations, the learning process functions effectively and the economies of scale and scope strengthen the trajectory. There is evidence that after long periods of gradual change, technologies can be punctuated by technological discontinuities. The role of selection mechanisms is then drastic. The analysis of such a 'leaping' development has been called the 'punctuated equilibrium' approach (Gersick 1991).

In the light of empirical evidence, punctuated discontinuities of technologies are divided into two classes by Tushman and Anderson (1986). Discontinuity is competence-enhancing when it is based on the established trajectory and thus organized by existing firms thanks to their effective search mechanism. The discontinuity is competence-destroying when it is based on radically new routines. In this case the existing firms cannot (always) cope with the new discoveries because of their organizational rigidity and will therefore be the losers. Entrants with new routines and competencies will be the winners. High uncertainty and asset specificity results in inflexibility and large coordination problems that can prevent established corporations from reaching the advanced frontier of the new technological regime. In this case the turbulent period of different competing trajectories lasts until a new dominant design (or technological trajectory) has been established.

The studies (Chandler 1990; Freeman 1991; Pavitt 1986, 1991) show that dramatic punctuations are not typical and that large corporations can often cope even with new challenges using their firm boundaries as strategic variables. In such a situation, increasing fuzziness of the boundaries of firms occurs due to simultaneous increase of both transaction and bureaucratic costs. This leaves room for hybrid forms and results in the symbiotic life between strongly path-dependent large firms (with dominant designs) and more flexible small firms which generate variety through new routines.

IN SEARCH OF A THEORY OF ENTREPRENEURSHIP

This section deals with entrepreneurship approaches in the context of technological change. In the 1980s many valuable empirical analyses concerning entrepreneurship were published, but the problems of technology management did not receive much attention. The main problem with this empirically oriented field of inquiry is the lack of a substantial theoretical foundation. Our evaluation is based on the following two propositions:

Proposition 4:   The essence of entrepreneurship consists of creative acts of discovery. It is a question of an uncertain disequilibrium process.

Proposition 5:   The main sources of economic opportunities to be discovered depend upon technological change.

It is clear that the further from standard NC theory we are, the more room there is for entrepreneurs as new generating agents. The reason is to be found in the distinction between 'externally' versus 'internally' determined. In the former case the role of a manager is to calculate the necessary profit maximization exercises subject to the well-known constraints (given preferences, technology, initial resources). No deliberate strategies are possible. The assumptions of unbounded rationality, perfect information (or parametric uncertainty), smooth adjustment, and efficient prices do not leave room for genuine entrepreneurs. Then we have only externally 'programmed', rule-following calculators. Due to the black box assumption, no heterogenous firms or firm-specific routines exist and the static nature renders the history superfluous. Neither Porter nor TCE have any special theory starting from the change-generating agent. Entrepreneurs can, however, have useful ideas about economizing on production and transactionary costs, and it is possible to combine many ideas of TCE with ideas of evolutionary schools, as Jarillo (1988) does.

The dynamized RBT version can be used as a germ of a theory of entrepreneurship. Managerial competencies are needed for a well-established technological trajectory and entrepreneurial competencies are demanded especially when discontinuities are apparent. The distinction is not clear-cut, of course, but offers a useful point of departure for empirical studies covering the qualifications of an entrepreneur. A bridge between theory and crude facts can be found by using the concept of entrepreneurial rent. It is based on the difference between *ex post* value and *ex ante* 'costs'. Only under conditions of uncertainty can this rent be positive, functioning then as an incentive to entrepreneurs. This brings us to evolutionary thinking.

Evolutionary entrepreneurship ideas are based on the works of Schumpeter, Kirzner, and Hayek. Curiously enough, Schumpeter never wrote any suitable theory for technological change and his most cited ideas did not take more than six pages in the chapter on *Capitalism, Socialism and Democracy* (1943). However, in spite of crude empirical data, Schumpeter did represent a rich source of insights concerning the role of an entrepreneur. In the *Theorie der wirtschaftlichen Entwicklung* (1934) he introduced a distinction between managerial ('hedonistic–static') and entrepreneurial ('energetic–dynamic') subjects. The dynamo of capitalistic development was an entrepreneur who needed help from a hedonistic mass of managers. Schumpeter also utilized the concept of 'the circular flow' in order to describe equilibrium conditions where rationality and daily routines would work well and uncertainty would be negligible. Economic development would be smooth but slow. It is the task of an entrepreneur to create 'new combinations' and destroy this tranquil circle (Schumpeter 1934: 85) in order to reach the new 'far from equilibrium' state. If the intuition proves to be right and '*ex post* value' exceeds '*ex ante*' costs, the prize is a positive profit.

In the terminology of evolutionary theory, Schumpeter saw entrepreneurs as creating the necessary variation which selection mechanisms try, through competitive processes, to hammer down and restore the stationary circular flow. This interplay between variation and selection was the focal point of *Business Cycles* (1939), where Schumpeter analysed innovations as disturbing factors. He distinguished between innovations and inventions and thought that every new innovation was created by a new firm (or at least by new men). He was clearly equating innovations with radical innovations.

The six famous pages (1943) focused on the evolution of capitalism. The driving force was the businessman's hunt for pure profits. Schumpeter was growing more sceptical and predicted (1943: 134) that capitalist enterprise, by its very achievements, tends to make itself superfluous. This false prediction originated in his inability to see the fundamental role of incremental innovations and path-dependent learning processes. He could not see anything productive in routines and thought that stable development along the trajectory impossible due to diminishing returns. Schumpeter's main problem was a lack of a theory and the exaggerated role given to radical innovations.

Kirzner and Hayek see the capitalist markets as a discovery process that conspires 'to push back the fog of mutual ignorance' (Kirzner 1985: 11). The alertness of an entrepreneur to the errors of the past or the creation of something new are the sources of pure profits. Radical uncertainty results in the errors but it is a source of success, too. Another connected element is 'the disequilibrium situation' where the price signals are wrong, thus creating opportunities to achieve arbitrage or speculative profits. Kirzner (1985: 84–86) distinguishes between three different types of entrepreneurial activities: (a) arbitrage activity consists of discovering profitable price discrepancies, (b) speculative activity consists of intertemporal arbitrage, and (c) innovative activity consists of the creation of something new. It is suggested that managerial competencies are developed to solve arbitrage problems, and entrepreneurial competencies are acquired to create new combinations.

TOWARDS A SYNTHESIS

The typology of entrepreneurship can now be introduced. Figure 3.2 charts two important environmental variables, the change and the nature of technological and market knowledge (compare Clark 1987: 62–64), and enables us to list four different types of entrepreneurial characteristics needed in different situations.

	INCREMENTAL AND FAIRLY CERTAIN	RADICAL AND FAIRLY UNCERTAIN
INCREMENTAL AND FAIRLY CERTAIN	Routine manager	Schumpeterian entrepreneur ('Innovator')
RADICAL AND FAIRLY UNCERTAIN	Knightian entrepreneur ('Niche Discoverer')	Kirznerian entrepreneur ('Visionary')

Figure 3.2 Typology of entrepreneurship

The situation in the upper left-hand corner is close to Schumpeterian 'circular flow'. Managerial competencies for running daily routines are needed. The appropriate type of entrepreneur is called simply a routine manager. In the upper right-hand corner, we have Schumpeter's 'creative destruction' box dominated by great technological uncertainty and radical innovations. What is needed is a Schumpeterian entrepreneur, an innovator, who is able to generate new skills, habits, routines, and capabilities. In the lower left-hand corner, markets are changing rapidly but technological change is incremental (a well-established trajectory exists). An ability to grasp new market opportunities is badly needed. Because of market uncertainty, this type is called a 'Knightian' entrepreneur (or a niche discoverer). In the lower right-hand corner is the most demanding situation, where both technological and market knowledge are struc-

	ESTABLISHED FIRM	EMERGING FIRM
CONTINUOUS TECHNICAL TRAJECTORY • path-dependent learning processes dominate • target: "dynamic efficiency"	Competitive advantage due to dominant design • effective isolating mechanisms • scale and scope and learning • core competence due to specific routines and tacit knowledge *Manager*	No chances to challenge directly • integration or subcontracting • generic complementary assets and new products needed *Innovator and/or Niche Discoverer*
DISCONTINUOUS TECHNOLOGICAL TRAJECTORY • selection environment dominates • target: "flexibility"	Competitive disadvantage due to learning inertia and switching costs • new specific complementary assets needed • vertical integration or cooperation *Innovator and/or Niche Discoverer*	Competitive advantage due to flexibility and new capabilities • how to establish a new dominant design? *Visionary Entrepreneur*

Figure 3.3 Technological (dis)continuity and the type of entrepreneurship

turally uncertain and there are competing technological trajectories. In this situation great vision is needed. Also, the opportunities are manifold. Because this corner presupposes both arbitrage and innovative competencies, the type of entrepreneur is called 'Kirznerian'. The next step is to take into account the nature of technological trajectories. The focal point is to analyse the opportunities and threats of two different firm types, established and emerging, when facing either continuous or discontinuous trajectory.

Figure 3.3 clarifies the idea that the evolution of the capabilities of firms depends drastically upon the progress of technological development (cf. Hamilton 1989). The results are straightforward. In the upper left-hand quadrant an old, well-established firm has the competitive advantage because of dominant design. Causal ambiguity and other isolating mechanisms are strong and cumulative learning strengthens the position. Managerial entrepreneurship is needed.

In the upper right-hand box, a new emerging firm tries to come into the established trajectory. It can be realized only (*i*) by generating new complementary routines needed by established firms (the innovator) or (*ii*) by discovering a new niche based on specific competencies (the niche discoverer). In the lower left-hand box, the technological paradigm has been challenged by competence-destroying capabilities of competitors. The organizational inertia of an established firm decreases its capacity to create new combinations. The best strategy seems to be to integrate with new competitors (if possible). In the lower right-hand cell, there are even opportunities for a new entrant to establish a new dominant design. Only the visionary entrepreneur (or a team of different types of entrepreneurs) can handle such challenges.

As an exercise one could think of the idealized development process of an entrant with superior new capabilities. This firm starts from the upper right-hand box by networking with an emerging firm. Its next step is to challenge the established firms and develop a truly dominant design. If this succeeds there will be a shift into the upper left-hand box. Thereafter there is always a danger of dropping into the lower left-hand box.

CONCLUSIONS

The strategic technology management message of the evolutionary synthesis can be summarized as follows (cf. Pavitt 1986, 1991; Metcalfe 1989):

1 Innovative activities consist of firm-specific, partly tacit, and path-dependent routines. All the strategies have to be based on them

and rapid and radical changes are not possible. Imitation and technology transfers are not easy and cost-free.

2 Structural uncertainty is inherent.

3 In order to create enough internal variety, innovative activities have to be based on flexible collaboration and on generating different, even conflicting visions.

4 The planning procedure cannot be based on the simple problem-solving methods of neoclassical management literature where the uncertainties are parametric, the future price and cost structures are taken for granted and the internal organization is overlooked.

5 There are great differences between different industries. One cannot find any general recipe. The interplay between technological and organizational capabilities is of great importance.

6 The roles of internal variation (search mechanisms) and external selection pressures (exit/entry) change depending upon the nature of the technological trajectory.

7 The more turbulent the times are, the more coordination and involvement of senior management is needed.

8 Even under seemingly tranquil circumstances on the well-established trajectory, continuous learning and incremental innovations are needed.

9 The core competencies of a firm set limits to its structure which, in turn, condition the strategy. There are not many degrees of freedom when formulating technology strategies.

REFERENCES

Antonelli, C. (1992) 'Information Economics and Industrial Organization', *Human Systems Management*, 11, 53–60.

Arrow, K. (1962) 'Economic Welfare and the Allocation of Resources for Inventions', in R.R. Nelson (ed.), *The Rate and Direction of Inventive Activity: Economic and Social Factors*, Princeton: Princeton University Press, 353–358.

Arrow, K. (1974) *The Limits of Organization*, New York: Norton.

Barney, J.B. (1991) 'Firm Resources and Sustained Competitive Advantage', *Journal of Management* , 17, 99–120.

Campbell, D.T. (1969) 'Variation and Selective Retention in Sociocultural Evolution', *General Systems*, 69–85.

Chandler, A. (1962) *Strategy and Structure: Chapters in the History of the American Industrial Enterprise*, Cambridge, MA: the M.I.T. Press.

Chandler, A. (1990) *Scale and Scope: The Dynamics of Industrial Capitalism*, Cambridge, MA: Harvard University Press.

Chandler, A.D. (1992) 'What is a Firm?' *European Economic Review*, 36, 483–494.

Clark, K. (1987) 'Investment in New Technology and Competitive Advantage' in Teece, D. (ed.) *The Competitive Challenge: Strategies for Industrial Innovation and Renewal*, New York: Harper & Row, pp. 59–82.

Coase, R.H. (1937) 'The Nature of the Firm', *Economica*, 4, 386–406.

Dosi, G. (1988) 'Sources, Procedures, and Microeconomic Effects of Innovation', *Journal of Economic Literature*, 26, 1120–1171.

Freeman, C. (1991) 'Innovation, Changes of Techno-economic Paradigm and Biological Analogies in Economics', *Revue Économique*, 42, 211–231.

Gersick, C.J.G. (1991) 'Revolutionary Change Theories: A Multilevel Exploration of the Punctuated Equilibrium Paradigm', *Academy of Management Review*, 16, 10–36.

Hagedoorn, J. (1993) 'Understanding the Rationale of Strategic Technology Partnering', *Strategic Management Journal*, 14, 371–385

Hamilton, W.F. (1989) 'The Dynamics of Technology and Strategy', *European Journal of Operational Research*, 47, 141–152.

Hart, O. (1989) 'An Economist's Perspective on the Theory of the Firm', *Columbian Law Review*, 89, 1757–1774.

Hodgson, G.M. (1993) 'Theories of Economic Evolution: A Preliminary Taxonomy', *The Manchester School*, 61, 125–143.

Jarillo, J.C. (1988) 'On Strategic Networks', *Strategic Management Journal*, 9, 31–41.

Kirzner, I.M. (1985) *Discovery and the Capitalist Process*, Chicago: University of Chicago Press.

Langlois, R.N. (1984) 'Internal Organization in a Dynamic Context', in M. Jussawalla and H. Ebenfield (eds), *Communication and Information Economics: New Perspectives*, Amsterdam: Elsevier, 23–49.

Langlois, R.N. (1988) 'Economic Change and the Boundaries of the Firm', *Journal of Institutional and Theoretical Economics*, 144, 635–657.

Metcalfe, S. (1989) 'Evolution and Economic Change', in A. Silberstain (ed.), *Technology and Economic Progress*, London: Macmillan, 54–85.

Mowery, D.C. and Rosenberg, N. (1989) *Technology and the Pursuit of Economic Growth*, Cambridge: Cambridge University Press.

Nelson, R.R. (1991) 'Why do Firms Differ, and How Does it Matter?', *Strategic Management Journal*, 12, 61–74.

Nelson, R.R. and Winter, S. (1982) *An Evolutionary Theory of Economic Change*, Cambridge, UK: Harvard U.P.

Pavitt, K. (1986) 'Technology, Innovation, and Strategic Management', in J. McGee and H. Thomas (eds). *Strategic Management Research*, London: John Wiley & Sons, 171–190.

Pavitt, K. (1990) 'What We Know about the Strategic Management of Technology', *California Management Review*, 32, 17–26.

Pavitt, K. (1991) 'Key Characteristics of the Large Innovating Firm', *British Journal of Management*, 2, 41–50.

Penrose, E.T. (1959) *The Theory of the Growth of the Firm*, Oxford: Basil Blackwell (2nd edn 1980).

Porter, M.E. (1980) *Competitive Strategy: Techniques for Analyzing Industries and Competitors*, New York: Free Press.

Porter, M.E. (1981) 'The Contributions of Industrial Organization to Strategic Management', *Academy of Management Review*, 6, 609–620.

Porter, M.E. (1983) 'The Technological Dimension of Competitive Strategy', *Research on Technological Innovation, Management and Policy* (1), 1–33.

Porter, M.E. (1985) *Competitive Advantage*, New York: Free Press.

Porter, M.E. (1990) *The Competitive Advantage of Nations*, New York: Free Press.

Porter, M.E. (1991) 'Towards a Dynamic Theory of Strategy', *Strategic Management Journal*, 12, 95–117.

Prahalad, C.K. and Hamel, G. (1990) 'The Core Competence of the Corporation', *Harvard Business Review*, 68, 79–91.

Reinganum, J. (1989) 'The Timing of Innovation: Research, Development and Diffusion', in R. Schamalense and R. Willig (eds), *Handbook of Industrial Organization*, New York: North Holland, 849–908.

Rumelt, R.P. (1984) 'Towards a Strategic Theory of the Firm', in R.B. Lamb (ed.), *Competitive Strategic Management*, Englewood Cliffs, NJ: Prentice-Hall, 556–570.

Rumelt, R.P. (1987) 'Theory, Strategy, and Entrepreneurship', in D.J. Teece (ed.), *The Competitive Challenge: Strategies for Industrial Innovation and Renewal*, New York: Harper & Row, 137–158.

Schumpeter, J.A. (1934) *The Theory of Economic Development*, Cambridge MA: Harvard University Press (original edition 1912).

Schumpeter, J.A. (1939) *Business Cycles*, vol. I. New York: McGraw-Hill.

Schumpeter, J.A. (1943) *Capitalism, Socialism and Democracy*, New York: George Allen & Unwin, 1987.

Teece, D.J. (1984) 'Economic Analysis and Strategic Management', *California Management Review*, 26, 87–110.

Teece, D.J. (1986) 'Profiting from Technological Innovation: Implications for Integration, Collaboration, Licensing and Public Policy', *Research Policy*, 285–305.

Tushman, M.L. and Anderson, P. (1986) 'Technological Discontinuities and Organizational Environments', *Administrative Science Quarterly*, 439–465.

Wernerfelt, B. (1984) 'A Resource-based View of the Firm', *Strategic Management Journal*, 5, 171–180.

Williamson, O.E. (1985) *The Economic Institutions of Capitalism*, New York: Free Press.

Williamson, O.E. (1988) 'Technology and Transaction Cost Economics', *Journal of Economic Behavior and Organization*, 10, 355–363.

Williamson, O.E. (1991) 'Strategizing, Economizing, and Economic Organization', *Strategic Management Journal*, 12, 75–94.

Winter, S. (1988) 'On Coase, Competence, and the Corporation', *Journal of Law, Economics, and Organization*, 4, 163–180.

4 What does it mean to trust an entrepreneur?

Murray B. Low and V. Srivatsan

Abstract

A fundamental requirement for successful entrepreneurship is the ability to secure the support of critical stakeholders. This paper examines how entrepreneurs build stakeholder confidence. It argues that confidence has two dimensions: trust and competence. A process model is presented to illustrate how entrepreneurs demonstrate their trustworthiness and competence. The metaphor of drama is invoked and a fundamental paradox is revealed. In order to build confidence, entrepreneurs need to be skilled actors. However, as such, they are also capable of deception. Under such conditions, how is it possible to secure stakeholder support? The resolution of the paradox lies in making the distinction between the entrepreneur's character and the entrepreneur as a character, and the recognition by all parties that while entrepreneurship is inherently concerned with moral issues, the role of the entrepreneur is amoral and requires highly-developed impression management skills. Directions for future research are explored.

INTRODUCTION

A fundamental requirement for successful entrepreneurship is the ability to secure the support of critical stakeholders (MacMillan 1983). These stakeholders have diverse preferences, bear varied kinds of risk, and may be complete strangers to the entrepreneur. Given the uncertainty and risk associated with a start-up business, how is their cooperation obtained?

Forging cooperative stakeholder relations is important for all enterprise, but it is particularly salient in entrepreneurial contexts. This paper examines how entrepreneurs build stakeholder confidence. It argues that confidence has two dimensions: trust and competence. A process model is presented to illustrate how entrepreneurs demonstrate their trustworthiness and competence. The complexity of the confidence-building process is revealed by invoking the metaphor of drama and pointing to a fundamental paradox. We show that in order to build confidence, entrepreneurs need to be skilled actors. However, as skilled actors, they are also capable of deception. Under such conditions, how is it possible to secure stakeholder support? The resolution of the paradox lies in making the distinction between the entrepreneur's character and the entrepreneur as a character, and the recognition by all parties that while entrepreneurship is inherently concerned with moral issues, the role of the entrepreneur is amoral and requires highly-developed impression management skills. The paper begins with an exposition of the nature of trust.

TRUST – NATURE AND CHARACTERISTICS

The issue of trust has a long history in the social sciences. It has been examined from a number of theoretical perspectives and applied to a broad range of issues (see Gambetta 1988). The need for trust arises because of what has been called the problem of cooperation (Axelrod 1984). It exists in situations where two parties stand to gain through cooperative action; however, once the commitment to cooperate has been made, each party has an incentive to cheat. The classic illustration of the cooperation problem is the prisoner's dilemma game. In this game, non-cooperation is the dominant strategy since it results in the best payoff no matter what the other player chooses.[1]

The cooperation problem does not in itself dictate the need for trust. One way to overcome the problem of cooperation is for each player to make a credible commitment not to defect. Credible commitments not to defect can be made in many ways that do not involve trust. For example, in the case of the prisoner's dilemma, a prisoner might provide the other with self-incriminating information about a second crime that could be used against them should they defect. More commonly, transaction partners provide some sort of binding guarantee that can be invoked in the case of defection.[2]

We argue that it is uncertainty and bounded rationality in the context of the cooperation problem that dictates the need for trust. Uncertainty and bounded rationality make it impossible to specify all possible contingencies and corresponding payoffs *ex ante*. Furthermore, even after outcomes are known, it may not be possible to identify defectors, since outcomes may not be completely determined by the parties' actions.

For example, Joe and Harry want to open a garage. Joe is a first-rate mechanic and Harry is a financial whiz. By pooling their talents they have the requisite skills to run a successful garage. However, once the business is up and running, Joe can accept kickbacks from suppliers and Harry can skim cash, each doing well at the other's expense with little chance of detection. While the business might not be doing as well as expected, it is not clear why. In this circumstance, assuming strictly self-interested behaviour and a focus on the short term, cheating is the dominant strategy, because each will do better by cheating, regardless of whether the other is honest.

One possibility of addressing this problem is to monitor behaviours instead of outcomes. Harry could listen in on Joe's conversations with suppliers, and Joe could occasionally count the cash. However, it is impossible to eliminate all opportunities to cheat undetected. Furthermore, such monitoring is costly, distracting each from his own duties and reducing the returns from their cooperative division of labour. Excessive monitoring can also have the perverse effect of creating an atmosphere of distrust and making cheating more likely. Finally, since each lacks the expertise of the other, its not even clear what behaviours to monitor. Joe might be buying more expensive equipment than necessary because he likes playing with the latest gadgets. Harry observes the purchases but does not realize they are unnecessary. In the literature on principal–agent relations, these kinds of problems are classified as either hidden action (skimming cash) or hidden information (equipment not necessary) (Arrow 1974).

The need for trust arises when outcomes are only partly affected by actions and it is not practical or cost effective to monitor behaviours. Transaction partners need to trust one another not to cheat, even when cheating may go undetected. Without such trust, the potential for cooperative action is severely circumscribed. In the next section, trust is defined and an attempt is made to reconcile the concept with self-interested behaviour.

THE DYNAMICS OF TRUST

Trust might be defined as the expectation that transaction parties will not defect, even when it is in their self-interest to do so. The problem with this definition is that it violates a fundamental tenet of economic reasoning, namely self-interested behaviour. In doing so, it sidetracks the discussion into an investigation of factors that lead individuals to act against their self-interest. Without denying the possibility of altruism, the assumption that individuals systematically violate self-interest seems an inappropriate starting point for an exploration of stakeholder relations in entrepreneurial contexts.

One way to reconcile the assumption of self-interested behaviour with the observation that some individuals appear to be more altruistic than others is to argue that individuals have different utility functions. For example, assume that utility functions are comprised of two dimensions, instrumental payoffs and the satisfaction that comes from 'doing the right thing'. Individuals that place a high value on 'doing the right thing' will appear more altruistic and trustworthy than those who do not. In our fictitious garage start-up, Joe does not take kickbacks from suppliers because he values his self-image as an honest person more than the money he would receive from cheating.

Retaining the axiom of self-interested behaviour and invoking the concept of a utility function with non-instrumental payoffs in order to explain apparent acts of altruism highlights two critical factors that explicate the nature of trust. First, trust is never absolute. If individuals are self-interested, then there is always a chance they will defect. Second, trust is context specific. In order to determine trustworthiness, it is necessary to understand both the individual's utility function and the payoffs associated with the specific circumstance.

Following the above logic, trust is defined here as the belief that it is in the trusted party's self-perceived best interest not to defect. This belief is based upon the perceptions of the trusting party concerning (1) the character of the trusted individual, (2) the context in which the trust is extended, and (3) the interaction between character and context.

Determining trustworthiness involves complex calculations using multiple factors. For example, for Joe to trust Harry not to receive kickbacks from suppliers, he needs to estimate the value Harry places on the additional cash, net of the disutility associated with not 'doing the right thing'. He also needs to estimate Harry's perception of the chances of getting caught, the consequences of getting caught, and the disutility of these consequences. In order to impute Harry's valuation of a good reputation, Joe needs to know the relative value Harry places on short-term versus long-term payoffs. He also needs to estimate Harry's perception of the likelihood of future interactions (what is the chance they will want to open a second garage?).

Finally, Joe also needs to know about potential conflict among the various dimensions of Harry's utility function. For example, Harry might place a high priority on not cheating his partner, but an even higher priority on providing medical care for his children. If Harry perceives taking kickbacks as the only way to care for his children, then he is likely to do so, despite the high value he places on honesty.

The process of determining trustworthiness is not only complex, it is dynamic. As new information is gained through ongoing inter-actions about either the context or the individual, or as the context changes as a result of exogenous events, the assessment of trust-worthiness is revised. In the above example, Harry might be perfectly trustworthy until his kids get ill.

SIGNALLING AND DETECTING TRUSTWORTHINESS

Given the important role that trust plays in facilitating cooperative exchange, combined with complex and subtle calculations required to determine trustworthiness, it is rational for individuals to learn how to signal their trustworthiness (Frank 1983). Doing so will better enable them to secure the benefits of cooperation. It is also rational for individuals to learn how to detect trustworthiness, since this will reduce the danger of being cheated. A simple example of trust signalling is the willingness to share information. A simple example of trust detecting is looking for corroborative information. More complex and dynamic examples will be provided later.

In addition to trust signalling and detection, it is also rational for individuals to learn how to signal and detect willingness to retaliate should trust be violated, especially if the apparent costs of retaliation exceed the benefits. For example, Joe might indicate to Harry that he will quit the business and take legal action if he finds Harry skimming cash. While Joe stands to lose more by this course of action than he would gain (lose the entire business and incur significant legal costs in the hope of recovering a small amount of money), if the threat to retaliate is credible, it will deter Harry from skimming cash. The threat of retaliation does not affect the size of the payoff from cheat-ing, nor the likelihood of detection, but it does affect the costs asso-ciated with getting caught. By raising the perceived costs of defection, a person is able to induce trustworthiness in another.

A person's ability to signal trustworthiness (or willingness to retali-ate) may or may not correspond to their true nature. While trustwor-thy individuals on average may be better able to signal trustworthiness, the profession of acting and existence of confidence men demonstrate it is possible to fake it. It is also possible that individuals unskilled in the art of signalling trust (e.g. do not understand the importance of sharing information), may appear untrustworthy when they are not. Therefore, regardless of a person's true nature, it is important to learn how to appear trustworthy.

The realization that even a trustworthy person needs to learn how to signal trustworthiness greatly complicates the trust detection process. Since everyone engages in such performances, determining trustworthiness it not simply a matter of distinguishing between those who are acting at being trustworthy from those who are not. Everyone is acting. The observation that an individual is consciously manipulating trust is not an indication that the person is insincere. The challenge is to determine the extent to which the performance is authentic. While we regularly make judgements of this sort, we are often left with doubts.

In the *Presentation of Self in Everyday Life*, Goffman (1959: 71) develops the notion of social life as drama, and points out that:

> Some performances are carried off successfully with complete dishonesty, others with complete honesty; but for performances in general, neither of these extremes is essential, and neither, perhaps, is dramaturgically advisable.

Goffman's point is that successful performances appeal to a socially constructed reality (in our case, the nature of trustworthiness), and too much reliance on one's inward view of reality may rob the actor of the flexibility required to put on a good performance. The suggestion is that trustworthiness is not an innate individual characteristic, but rather a learned behaviour. To be considered trustworthy, an individual must conform to a set of socially constructed norms (Berger and Luckmann 1966). Goffman makes the further observation that while the subject matter of a performance is fundamentally moral in nature, the performance itself is amoral:

> In their capacity as performers, individuals will be concerned with maintaining the impression that they are living up to the many standards by which they and their products are judged. Because these standards are so numerous and so pervasive, the individuals who are performers dwell more than we might think in a moral world. But, *qua* performers, individuals are concerned not with the moral issue of realizing these standards, but the amoral issue of engineering a convincing impression that these standards are being realized. Our activity, then, is largely concerned with moral matters, but as performers we do not have a moral concern with them. As performers we are merchants of morality.
>
> (1959: 251)

Understanding the ethical entrepreneur as a merchant of morality presents a paradox. We have established that action based upon trust is one way for cooperation to emerge under conditions of uncertainty and bounded rationality. We have also argued that to be perceived as trustworthy, entrepreneurs must be competent actors. The more accomplished as actors, the more trustworthy they will appear. However, these are exactly the people who are most capable of deception.

Of course, one way to put on a good performance is to internalize the set of socially constructed norms. To the extent that this is achieved, we might call someone 'truly trustworthy'. Furthermore, given our limited cognitive capabilities, some internalization may be cost effective and consistent with the maxim of purely self-interested behaviour, even for an individual who places no value on 'doing the right thing'. Since there are positive returns associated with trust-worthiness, it may be most efficient to adopt standard 'trustworthy' responses rather than trying continually to determine when it is best to cooperate or to defect. While such a strategy may result in some suboptimal decisions, these losses are covered by reduced cognitive demands. As the late Senator Sam Ervin said: 'The problem with lying is that you have to have a perfect memory for what you said.'[3] In the long run, it may be more cost effective to commit to the principle of always telling the truth.

The fact that it is rational for individuals who value only instru-mental payoffs to develop routine behavioural responses that suggest otherwise, makes it difficult to assess a person's true character. For such individuals, internalization is not absolute, otherwise they forgo opportunities to defect when it is in their pure self-interest to do so (huge payoff, zero chance of detection, need to remember only one lie). Instead, it is possible to conceive of an optimal level of inter-nalization which is high enough to enable the individual to give authentic responses with minimal cognitive effort in most situations, but is not so high as to prevent the individual from ever defecting. Again, while there may be individuals who will never defect (i.e. saints), it seems an inappropriate assumption upon which to explore relationships in entrepreneurial contexts.

TRUST AND COMPETENCE

So far the discussion has focused on trust as a means to overcome the dangers of opportunism. This section examines the issue of compe-tence and how it relates to trust.

Economic theories of organization, and in particular principal-agency theory, have focused on issues of opportunism and paid less attention to the issue of competence (for an exception see Walsh and Steward 1990). However, when performance is less than expected, it is often difficult to know whether the cause is opportunism, lack of ability, or some exogenous factor. An assessment of competence is an essential precondition for willingness to have another individual act on one's behalf, or in the current context, a precondition for committing support to an entrepreneur. Assessing competence poses difficulties similar to those of assessing trustworthiness. Individuals vary in ability, and it is not a matter of them being either competent or not. Competence varies by context. A surgeon is not competent to do the work of a car mechanic and vice versa. And as the nature of the work becomes more ambiguous, determining competence becomes more difficult.

The willingness to commit support to an entrepreneur is a function of a stakeholder's assessment of the entrepreneur's trustworthiness and competence, as shown in Figure 4.1. In the low competence/ low trustworthiness cell, overall confidence in the entrepreneur is below an acceptable threshold. In the high competence/high trustworthiness cell, support is easily given. In the off-diagonal cells, it may be possible to secure stakeholder support through additional monitoring and/or the provision of guarantees in the case of low trustworthiness, or by the acquisition of additional competence through training or recruitment in the case of low competence. While a strength in one dimension may to some extent compensate for a weakness on the other, a minimum level is required on each dimension.

In common usage, when we say we 'trust' someone, we are usually

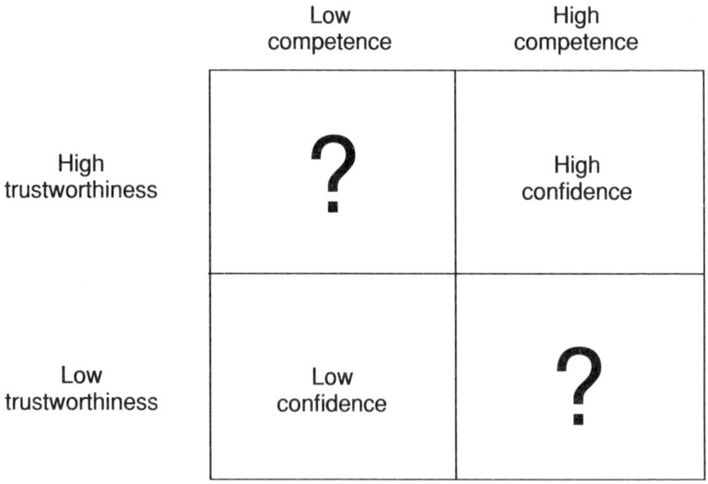

	Low competence	High competence
High trustworthiness	**?**	High confidence
Low trustworthiness	Low confidence	**?**

Figure 4.1 Confidence as a function of trustworthiness and competence

making a statement about both (lack of) opportunism and competence. I take my car to Harry and Joe's garage because I believe they will do a good job (competence) and not overcharge me (lack of opportunism). However, in this paper we use the term 'confidence' to indicate a simultaneous belief in trustworthiness and competence. In the next section we examine mechanisms for building confidence.

CONFIDENCE-BUILDING MECHANISMS

Mechanisms for building confidence fall into two categories, formal and informal. Both can be used to build a belief in trustworthiness and competence.

Formal mechanisms include accreditation, licensing, performance bonds, legal contracts, guarantees, and so on. These mechanisms are typically invoked through the use of a third party and represent institutionalized trust (Zucker 1987). Often the same mechanism helps to build confidence in both trustworthiness and competence. For example, the MD designation indicates that an individual has successfully completed studies in medicine (competence) and is to some extent bound by professional ethics as a result of socialization and/or threat of censure (trustworthiness). A written guarantee signals both trustworthiness and competence since it increases the cost of both defection and incompetence.

Informal mechanisms involve direct personal exchange and third-party reputation. Personal exchange is a process of mutual adjustment through which each party learns to accommodate and anticipate the behaviour of the other (Weick 1979). Information about these relationships travels through personal networks and results in third-party reputation. For example, if every time I take my car to Joe and Harry's garage, the work is done correctly and the price never exceeds the estimate, I develop a belief in their competence and trustworthiness. Furthermore, I tell my friends about it.

Often the greatest opportunities for building confidence arise when problems occur and trustworthiness and competence are brought into question. If upon investigation it is determined that the problems are attributable to factors other than opportunism or incompetence, then confidence is increased for having been tested. By observing multiple exchanges over time, it is possible to develop a much more precise understanding of the person's utility function, as well as a more precise understanding of their areas of greater and lesser competence.

Formal and informal mechanisms are complementary. Each may be sufficient by themselves for some kinds of transactions; however, as risk and the size of the stakes increase, there is increased need for both. In keeping with the metaphor of confidence building as drama, one might consider the formal mechanisms and third-party reputation as the stage and props, and interpersonal exchange as the performance.

A PROCESS MODEL OF CONFIDENCE BUILDING

Figure 4.2 illustrates a descriptive process model of confidence building. The process is initiated at stage one with a willingness between two relative strangers to engage in an exchange. This willingness is based upon the recognition of a potential return from cooperation and the presence of a minimum level of confidence based upon third-party reputation and formal mechanisms.

At stage two, the first outcome is known. If the outcome is successful, positive attributions are made about trustworthiness and competence and a positive feedback loop is created, increasing confidence and the likelihood of further exchange. If the outcome is unsuccessful or uncertain, attributions are made about causal factors. The outcome may be attributed to opportunism, incompetence, some exogenous factor, or some combination thereof.

In stage three, a response is made to the outcomes at stage two. Three responses are possible: do nothing; retaliate; and probe. There are costs and benefits associated with each option. The 'do nothing'

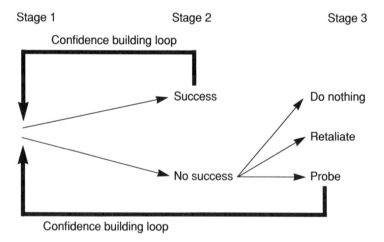

Figure 4.2 A process model of confidence building

option costs the least but reduces the likelihood of future exchange. Given that the first exchange was unsuccessful, if no attempt is made to determine the reasons for the poor performance, the net result will be a loss of confidence.

The 'retaliate' option involves a further investment in the relationship. However, it replaces cooperation as the dominant assumption governing the relationship with competition. If the cause of the poor performance was opportunism, and if future transactions are expected, then this may be an appropriate strategy. However, if the problem was not opportunism and the retaliation is perceived as unjustified, it may be difficult to rebuild a spirit of cooperation.

The 'probe' option has the most potential to build confidence. It also requires the greatest effort. In this case further information is sought to determine the cause of the poor performance. The probe may reveal negative information and lead to retaliation or severing of the relationship, or it may lead to a greater understanding of the situation and improved communication between parties. It is during a probe that trust-detecting and trust-signalling skills are most required.

An investor's recent experience in providing seed capital to an entrepreneur provides a useful illustration. The investor agreed to fund the development of a prototype as the first step in developing a new manufacturing business. The costs were to include materials and labour. The entrepreneur had been highly recommended to the investor by several reliable sources, and the two had several cordial meetings over a two-month period that resulted in the agreement to build the prototype.

When the investor received the bill for the prototype, both the materials and labour were fifty per cent higher than the estimate. The investor suspected the entrepreneur of opportunism. A call to a local supplier suggested that the entrepreneur was billing the materials well above the retail price. Furthermore, the investor had a good idea of what was involved in the task and thought it doubtful that the work had taken as many hours as were billed. Was the entrepreneur inflating the costs? If the entrepreneur was not cheating, his competence was certainly in question. Did the entrepreneur pay too much for the materials? If the hours were accurate, why did the job take so long? Did the entrepreneur know what he was doing?

The investor's first reaction was to retaliate and not pay the bill, or only to pay the estimated amount. The problem with this option was that the entrepreneur might threaten legal action and might even win, costing the investor additional time and money. Also, the entrepreneur might spread the word that the investor did not live up to his agreements, causing him embarrassment and making it difficult to engage in similar transactions in the future. Finally, it would mean the investor would have to abandon the project, which he still found attractive.

So the investor considered doing nothing, and simply paying the bill. The problem with this option was that if his suspicions were correct and he did not challenge the entrepreneur, he would surely be cheated in the future. It would set a very bad precedent. Paying the bill would fulfil his obligation to the entrepreneur and enable him to withdraw gracefully from the venture. But without resolving the issue, it would not be possible to proceed any further.

So in the end, the investor decided to probe. He explained to the entrepreneur that he was surprised at the amount of the bill and laid out his concerns, asking the entrepreneur for his side of the story. The entrepreneur provided technical details about why the job took longer than expected, but acknowledged that he should have anticipated the problem as part of his estimate. He also explained that the materials used were not comparable to those the investor had priced at the local supplier. He apologized for the estimating error and offered to reduce the bill by charging only the number of hours originally estimated, but requested that the cost of the materials be reimbursed fully. The investor agreed to the compromise, asking the entrepreneur to provide him with documentation showing the cost of the materials. Both expressed regret about the 'misunderstanding' and indicated their continued enthusiasm for the venture.

This simple example contains all the basic elements of a confidence-building loop. Each party stood to benefit from the transaction. Numerous factors, both formal (e.g. access to legal recourse) and informal (e.g. third-party reputation, previous exchange), contributed to a level of mutual confidence sufficient for the transaction to proceed. These factors set the stage. When a problem arose during the course of the exchange, it was unclear whether the cause was opportunism, lack of competence or some other factor. The problem provided the actors with the opportunity to demonstrate both confidence-detecting and confidence-signalling skills.

The issue was settled successfully because both actors implicitly agreed that the issue would be resolved by appealing to certain moral standards. For example, by raising the issue of the discrepancy between the estimate and the bill, the investor was appealing to the moral principles of 'fairness' and 'living up to one's commitments'. The entrepreneur might have challenged these principles by saying that the original costing was only an estimate and not binding. But he did not. Instead, he chose to provide information suggesting that even though the estimate was wrong, the appropriate work was done and the charges were fair. By doing so he was able to appeal to the same principles and argue that it was the investor's responsibility to pay for work which was properly done and fairly priced. While signalling his trustworthiness by providing information about hours worked and the cost of materials, he was also testing the investor's trustworthiness. Was the investor simply trying to find an excuse to default on his obligation to pay?

This story has an interesting epilogue which illustrates the ongoing and dynamic nature of confidence building. The entrepreneur submitted a revised bill, including a detailed breakdown of the materials costs. However, he failed to provide copies of the actual invoices, which was what the investor had expected as evidence that the prices had not been inflated. The investor replayed the conversation in his own mind and considered it possible that the entrepreneur had misunderstood what he wanted. Uncertain as to whether this was the case, or whether the entrepreneur could not provide the invoices because he had lied about his costs, the investor nevertheless paid the bill. He felt he had sufficiently demonstrated his trust-detecting skills and the entrepreneur had sufficiently demonstrated his trust-signalling skills, and that it was not in either's best interest to push the issue further and risk a confrontation. However, when he paid the bill, the investor included a note asking the entrepreneur to forward copies of the invoices in order to 'clear the paperwork'. And so, the confidence-building and detecting process continued.

CONFIDENCE BUILDING IN AN ENTREPRENEURIAL SETTING

So far this paper has explored issues of confidence building as it might apply in many contexts. In this section we explore these issues specifically in an entrepreneurial setting. An entrepreneurial context is interesting for two reasons. First, founding a new business is often associated with high stakes, and a great deal of uncertainty and risk. Therefore, it is an appropriate context for the study of confidence building. Second, a successful start-up usually requires resource commitments from a variety of stakeholders. Before committing to a venture, stakeholders need to have confidence in the entrepreneur at two levels. They must have confidence with respect to their own transaction, as well as a belief that the entrepreneur is able to build the same confidence with the other essential stakeholders. Achieving confidence at these two levels is difficult because stakeholders have divergent interests and need to be appealed to on the basis of different moral sentiments.

For example, assume that there are just two stakeholder groups, employees and investors, and that employees are only concerned about job security and investors are only concerned about financial returns. In order to win the confidence of each group, the entrepreneur needs to send different messages. To gain the confidence of employees, the entrepreneur needs to signal his moral commitment to continued employment, even if this means lower profits. To investors he needs to signal his moral commitment to the principle of maximizing returns for shareholders. What is the entrepreneur to do?

One possibility is for the entrepreneur to give a different performance for each stakeholder group. This is a risky strategy for several reasons. First, employees and investors might get together and discover the inconsistency. Second, in at least one, if not both, situations, the entrepreneur will have to give a dishonest performance, making it less likely that the performance will be convincing. Third, to the extent that each group recognizes that the commitment of the other is critical for the success of the venture, an overly solicitous performance will not be credible. For example, if the entrepreneur represents himself to investors in a manner that would jeopardize support from employees if they were to witness the performance, investors are forced to come to one of two conclusions, depending on whether they believe the performance is authentic. If they believe the performance is authentic, they will doubt the entrepreneur is capable of securing the support of employees. If they believe the performance is not authentic, they will judge the entrepreneur a chameleonic figure who changes his story with every context. In either case being overly solicitous will destroy rather than build confidence. So again, what is the entrepreneur to do?

The solution to this riddle lies in the fact that all players recognize the untenable position faced by the entrepreneur. For stakeholders to have confidence, they must believe that the entrepreneur's performance is authentic. However, because stakeholders recognize they have divergent interests and need to be appealed to on the basis of conflicting moral sentiments, they know it is not possible for the entrepreneur to give authentic performances in all circumstances. They might choose to believe that the entrepreneur is being authentic with them and deceptive with the other stakeholder groups. However, rather than judge the entrepreneur on the basis of what they impute to be his true character, they are more likely to judge him on the quality of his performance.

A good performance has a number of elements. First, the entrepreneur must demonstrate the ability to correctly identify the nature of a stakeholder's utility function, including relative values assigned to various instrumental and non-instrumental payoffs. Understanding what is important to stakeholders is a precondition for living up to their expectations, even if it is clear that the entrepreneur's own preferences are very different. By correctly diagnosing one stakeholder's utility function, the entrepreneur is demonstrating his likely ability to do the same thing for other stakeholder groups.

Second, the entrepreneur must demonstrate his ability to determine the level of confidence required to secure the stakeholder's support. In cases where stakeholder interests are not aligned, building confidence consumes scarce resources and constrains flexibility. Again, to use the example of employees and investors: the entrepreneur needs to signal sufficient commitment to a policy of continued employment to gain the confidence of employees, and sufficient commitment to generating financial returns to gain the confidence of investors. If an entrepreneur either under- or overestimates the level of required confidence, he is not using resources as effectively as possible. While each stakeholder individually prefers more confidence to less, this preference is mitigated by the recognition that the entrepreneur needs to balance the interests of the various groups.

In cases where stakeholder interests are aligned, building confidence does not consume scarce resources or flexibility and may have the opposite effect. For example, building confidence that the venture will be successful will assist in relations with all stakeholder groups. In giving an effective performance, the entrepreneur needs to demonstrate an understanding of when confidence building is zero sum, and when it has a positive multiplier effect. Third, the entrepreneur must demonstrate his ability to build confidence. This involves being sensitive and responsive to specific stakeholder concerns of trustworthiness or competence. In building confidence the entrepreneur can draw upon the range of formal and informal mechanisms discussed earlier. The appropriate choice of mechanisms or combination of mechanisms will depend on the circumstances. For example, spending time developing positive affect may be appropriate for employees, but less appropriate for lending institutions that base their decisions upon predetermined criteria. As with the other elements of a good performance, the demonstrated ability to build confidence with one stakeholder in a cost-effective manner will increase that stakeholder's confidence that the entrepreneur is capable of doing the same with other stakeholders.

Fourth, and finally, the entrepreneur must demonstrate his trust- and competence-detecting skills. If stakeholders feel the entrepreneur has not correctly diagnosed trustworthiness or competence in their own case, they will have no reason to believe that the entrepreneur will do better with others. Consequently the stakeholder will fear that the venture will fail, because someone is bound to cheat.

A common theme runs throughout these elements of a good performance. In each case the entrepreneur must manage a dyadic relationship such that it leaves a positive impression about the chances of success for the venture as a whole. The need to gain the commitment of stakeholder groups with divergent interests is both a major problem and a source of opportunity for the entrepreneur. It is a problem because the entrepreneur needs to be all things to all people, an impossible mission. It is an opportunity, because stake- holders recognize that this is the case, thus enabling the entrepreneur to implicitly play one group off against another. Stakeholders will allow this to happen as long as they anticipate a positive return from their participation.

RESOLVING THE PARADOX

Earlier in the paper, we argued that under conditions of bounded ratio- nality and uncertainty, trust is required for cooperation to emerge. We further argued that trustworthiness is not an innate characteristic of individuals, but rather a socially learned behaviour. Regardless of their true character, it is in an individual's self-interest to learn how to signal trustworthiness. Hence the paradox that those most capable of signalling trust are also those most capable of deception. Again, to quote Goffman:

> To use a different imagery, the very obligation and profitability of appearing always in a steady moral light, of being a socialized character, forces one to be the sort of person who is practised in the ways of the stage.

> (1959: 251)

So how is the paradox to be resolved? What does it mean to trust an entrepreneur? The answer is that stakeholders put their faith not in what they impute to be the entrepreneur's true character, but rather in the entrepreneur's demonstrated ability as a performer. While the former may be correlated with the latter, it is ultimately unknowable with any degree of certainty. Furthermore, it is the entrepreneur as performer who will lead the venture to success or failure. While the danger of being cheated always exists, a much greater danger is that the entrepreneur will fail to secure sufficient support to make the venture successful. To some extent, all ventures are self-fulfilling prophesies. Ventures only succeed because participants are willing to suspend their doubts and proceed on the expectation that success will materialize. To secure support, the entrepreneur needs to be 'practised in the ways of the stage'. Stakeholders recognize this, and if the expected returns from participating are sufficiently large, they will join in the drama, essentially becoming co-conspirators in the enactment of the successful venture. Once the decision has been made to cooperate, the role of the stakeholder is not to try and make the entrepreneur flub his lines, but rather to contribute to a successful performance.

RESEARCH IMPLICATIONS

This paper has combined the ideas of confidence building and impression management in an effort to understand better how cooperative relationships develop. While these issues are fundamental to most social activity, they are particularly salient in entrepreneurial contexts, where risk and uncertainty are high, self-interest and instrumental payoffs are typically dominant, and cooperation is required among multiple constituencies which often have divergent interests. This approach suggests several sets of propositions as the focus of future research.

First, the ideas in this paper provide an orienting framework for comparing the confidence-building skills of successful versus unsuccessful entrepreneurs:

Proposition 1: Successful entrepreneurs will be more skilled than unsuccessful entrepreneurs at each of the four elements of a good performance:
  (i)   diagnosing and signalling understanding of a stakeholder's preferences.
  (ii) determining and signalling understanding of the level of confidence required to secure a stakeholder's commitment.
  (iii) signalling trustworthiness and competence.
  (iv) demonstrating trust-detecting and competence-detecting skills.

Part of an effective performance is using the most cost effective confidence-building mechanisms for each stakeholder group. Consequently:

Proposition 2: Compared to unsuccessful entrepreneurs, successful entrepreneurs will use a greater variety of confidence-building mechanisms.

While a good performance will be tailored to each stakeholder group, the content will not be so different that the entrepreneur might be accused of dishonesty. This fact combined with the recognition that confidence is built through a series of exchanges over time, suggests:

Proposition 3: Compared to unsuccessful entrepreneurs, successful entrepreneurs will make fewer specific promises to different stakeholder groups, and instead will secure commitments by establishing and maintaining open lines of communication.

Second, the ideas in the paper suggest some propositions about stakeholders:

Proposition 4: Stakeholders will make attributions about the entrepreneur's ability to secure the commitment of others based on their own experiences.

The recognition that entrepreneurs must satisfy multiple stakeholders with diverse and sometimes divergent interests leads to:

Proposition 5: Stakeholders will perceive extremely solicitous performances as not credible.

Third, the paper provides an interesting perspective for conducting comparative studies of entrepreneurship in different cultures. Since trustworthiness is adherence to socially constructed norms and values, the process of trust signalling and trust detection will vary across cultures.

Proposition 6: Trust-detecting and trust-signalling mechanisms differ across cultures.

While this last proposition may seem obvious, it has important implications, particularly for entrepreneurship in a cross-cultural context. It is much more difficult to determine the trustworthiness of someone from a different culture. Since foreigners have likely internalized a somewhat different set of norms and values, it is more difficult for them to give an 'authentic' performance. Therefore:

Proposition 7: Building trust in cross-cultural entrepreneurial contexts is more difficult than in the context of a single culture.

Finally, by examining confidence-building as a primary determinant of successful transactions, and by considering how formal mechanisms and institutional structures can facilitate this process, the line of reasoning in this paper has the potential to contribute to our understanding of effective economic development strategies. For example, governments can encourage economic activity by putting in place institutional structures that enable transaction parties to develop confidence in one another. While this will include the development of efficient legal and accounting systems, it might also include finding ways to increase the amount of information available about potential transaction parties, such as through the establishment of credit-reporting agencies. Therefore:

Proposition 8: The establishment of institutional structures that increase the ability of transaction parties to develop confidence in one another has an important positive effect on facilitating economic development.

In the post-communist world, as newly established political entities with limited resources seek to rebuild their economies in a capitalist mode, it seems an idea worthy of serious consideration.

In conclusion, this paper has examined the complex process by which entrepreneurs develop cooperative relations with stakeholders. Developing cooperative relations is essential for all enterprise, but is particularly salient in entrepreneurial contexts where risks are high. In addressing this issue we explored issues of trustworthiness and competence and painted a picture of the entrepreneur as an amoral actor. This may appear a less than flattering portrait, but it is not intended as such. Rather, the intention is to distinguish between the entrepreneur's character and the entrepreneur as a character and a facilitator of cooperation, deeply embedded in a social context.

NOTES

1 Those not familiar with the prisoner's dilemma game and the research it has spawned may consult Rapoport and Chammah 1965.
2 Axelrod's (1984) discovery of the success of the TIT for TAT strategy is interesting in this context in that it suggests that in an ongoing game, credible commitments can be signalled through strategic behaviour.
3 Quoted in Thaler 1992: 14.

REFERENCES

Arrow, K. (1974) *The Limits of Organization*, New York: Horton.

Axelrod, R. (1984) *The Evolution of Cooperation*, New York: Basic Books.
Berger, P. and Luckmann, T. (1966) *The Social Construction of Reality*, New York: Doubleday.
Frank, R.H. (1983) *Passions within Reason: The Strategic Role of the Emotions*, New York: Norton.
Gambetta, D. (1988) *Trust: Making and Breaking Cooperative Relations*, New York: Basil Blackwell.
Goffman, E. (1959) *The Presentation of Self in Everyday Life*, New York: Doubleday.
MacMillan, I.C. (1983) 'The Politics of New Venture Management', *Harvard Business Review*, 61 (6): 8–17.
Rapoport, A. and Chammah, A. (1965) *Prisoner's Dilemma*, Ann Arbor: University of Michigan.
Thaler, R.H. (1992) *The Winner's Curse: Paradoxes and Anomalies of Economic Life*, New York: Free Press.
Walsh, J.P. and Steward, J.K. (1990) 'On the Efficiency of Internal and External Corporate Control Mechanisms', *Academy of Management Review*, 15 (3), 421–458.
Weick, K. (1979) *The Social Psychology of Organizing*, 2nd edn. New York: Random House.
Zucker, L.G. (1986) 'Production of Trust: Institutional Sources of Economic Structure, 1984–1920', in B.M. Staw and L. Cummings (eds), *Research in Organizational Behavior*, vol. 8, Greenwich, CT: JAI Press, 53–112.

5 Global dimensions of new competencies

Creating a review and research agenda

Rita Gunther McGrath, Ian C. MacMillan
and S. Venkataraman

INTRODUCTION

Prahalad and Hamel note that 'the essence of strategy lies in creating tomorrow's competitive advantages faster than competitors can mimic the ones you possess today' (1990: 69). A firm's array of competitive advantages is seen as a result of its ability to generate 'distinctive' competence, where distinction represents a firm's areas of superiority with respect to competition (McKelvey and Aldrich 1983; Selznick 1957). Increasingly, globalization of markets, products, and channels of distribution (Levitt 1983) imply that firms must understand not only the processes involved in the creation of new competences, but also the complexities introduced into these processes when a firm operates across borders. Cross-border issues manifest themselves under two circumstances: (1) when a firm faces competition from firms rooted in a different national origin (whether at home or across borders); and (2) when people in a firm seek to cooperate with those from another country (whether by direct foreign investment, joint venture, strategic alliance, or otherwise making an attempt to forge some common destiny).

The purpose of this paper is to offer a review of what we know about the international dimensions of new competence creation and to suggest areas in which future research into this process may fruitfully incorporate an international perspective. The article comprises three parts. First we offer an operational look at competence, identifying three processes that lie at the core of its development. Next we consider ways in which the literature suggests these processes will differ depending on the national origin of the firm attempting to develop new competence. From this, we offer a framework to identify some of the more interesting research issues which arise from the review, and list these at the end of the paper.

THE PROCESS OF NEW COMPETENCE CREATION

The idea of organizational competence has recently excited consider-able enthusiasm among strategy researchers (Mahoney and Pandian 1992; Amit and Shoemaker 1993; Prahalad and Hamel 1990; Barney 1991; Teece, Pisano, and Shuen 1991). Despite a rapidly growing body of literature, however, there has not yet emerged a precise and consistent definition of competence which would render the construct operationalizable. Much of the difficulty, we submit, comes from the important distinction which the many attempts to define competence in the literature have overlooked. This is the distinction between 'a competence' in the noun sense, and 'being competent' in the adjective sense.

Definitions of 'a competence' in the noun sense give rise to three major issues. First is the inability to clearly distinguish between the factors which yield competence and those which do not. Under these definitions, it is often difficult to distinguish between the concepts of competence, resources, and competitive advantage. Second is the problem that the elements which comprise a particular competence tend to be situation-specific, making it difficult to generalize about them (see Conner 1991 and Ghemawat 1991 for commentary on the difficulty of generalizing about particular 'success factors'). Finally, although a content approach to competence does allow us to begin to capture path-dependent and technologically cumulative features of the concept it does not allow the researcher to make an *ex ante* prediction of what advantage a particular competence will yield, which is often known only in retrospect.

This paper takes a rather different approach. We define competence here in the sense of 'a competent organization' (following McGrath 1993). We further suggest that the extent to which an organization is competent can be assessed by the extent to which it achieves what it sets out to do. Thus, the level of an entity's competence can be measured by the extent to which *ex ante* objectives are realized by *ex post* results. Organizational competence is defined therefore as the ability of an organization to reliably and consistently meet its objectives.

This definition has three major advantages over the definition of competence in the noun sense. First, it allows a precise distinction to be made between competence and competitive advantage. Thus, we can see that firms might have very high levels of competence, in the goal-attainment sense, yet not obtain from this competence an advan-tage, since other players are equally competent. Firms may also have relatively low levels of competence, yet achieve advantage in cases in which the competition is also not very competent. Second, this definition of competence is broadly generalizable, and does not depend upon a microscopic comparison of the particular elements of 'a competence' in competition. Finally, this definition opens the opportunity to study *ex ante* the processes underlying the emergence of competence, rather than limiting us to an *ex post* analysis of what particular factors eventually made the difference in a given competitive setting.

A focus on *ex ante* analysis complements the emphasis in this paper on the processes by which firms create new competence, rather than on the content of those competences. This follows the encouragement of many writers, both in academic- and practitioner-oriented outlets who have urged scholars to focus their attention more on the process side of new competence creation, and less on the content side (Ghemawat 1991; Burgelman 1983; Venkataraman, MacMillan, and McGrath 1992). Such a focus hearkens back to Simon's (1976) argument, in which he suggests that understanding procedural issues (or understanding the rationality of the 'how' of things in organizations) is at least as, and possibly more, important than understanding substantive issues, (or understanding the 'what' of things in organizations).

With this definition in hand, let us consider next how organizations become competent. This can be considered in the light of three fundamental processes:

1 processes through which objectives are formed;
2 processes through which the organization learns what will allow it to meet these objectives; and
3 processes through which the organization executes against this understanding.

Consider first the process of *objective formation*.[1] The formation of objectives can be thought of as culminating in the organization's decisions to do what it considers *worthwhile*. An organization seeking to develop new competence must establish what it feels is worthwhile for purposes of resource allocation. This can be thought of as the 'firm worth' component of the objective set, and will tend to guide where the firm will allocate resources and attention. Similarly, the firm must set objectives for how it will ensure a continuing flow of resources to it from outside its boundaries, or how it will provide worth to an external market. This can be considered a 'market worth' component of the objective set – to the extent that external players find benefit to themselves from what the firm has to offer which exceeds the price they must pay for it, this worth can be considered to be established. We might conclude that the outcome of the objective-formation process is the generation of an objective set which will yield worth both to the firm and the markets in which it participates (McGrath, Venkataraman, and MacMillan 1992 discuss the issues of firm and market worth in some depth).

Next, consider *learning processes*. A central problem for an organization trying to create new competence is that it faces uncertainty which simply cannot be eliminated until it understands causality with respect to the internal and external variables affecting achievement of its objectives (Nelson and Winter 1977). Until cause and effect are at least somewhat understood, it will be very difficult for the organization to become competent, in the sense of meeting its objectives, since it will quite literally not know what to do. A useful perspective on this process is offered by March (1991). March describes an organization's external reality as having *m* dimensions, independent of beliefs about it. At any period in time, he suggests, beliefs about each dimension are held both by individuals and by the organization within what he calls an 'organizational code of received truth' (1991:74). The organizational code can be thought of as a simplified model of reality, which members rely upon to give order and meaning to information which otherwise would be uninterpretable (Daft and Weick 1984). To the extent that the code is rich, the organization's understanding of reality is well advanced. To the extent that the code is sparse, as will be inevitable in an early stage endeavour, the organization must operate on the basis of guesses and assumptions, rather than on causal understanding. If a rich code is central to becoming competent, it follows that associated learning processes are also central to competence.

Finally, let us think about *task execution processes*, where these are defined as 'those behaviours aimed at organizing members to get work done as opposed to those that influence affect or the team's ability to maintain itself as a group' (Ancona and Caldwell 1992: 323). A new term shall be introduced to capture the level of effectiveness of these processes, which is organizational 'deftness'.[2] To the extent that an organization is deft, processes such as search, coordination, problem identification, and problem solution will require a minimum of effort and resources. Deftness can be thought of as the way in which the interpersonal processes in an organization help it to overcome agency and transaction problems to allow effective joint effort. To the extent that these problems are not overcome, additional resources will need to be deployed to provide incentives and monitor the behaviour of agents, and to provide a structure for the flow of information and transactions.

Thus, the pace at which the firm will become competent will be related to the rate at which it is able to forge and articulate a set of objectives that capture firm and market worth, learn what cause and effect relations shape the possibilities of meeting objective sets, and overcome the problems of uncertainty, agency and transactions costs in executing against this understanding.

We may now contemplate the likely effects of introducing cross-border and cross-cultural dynamics into this framework. Firms seeking to participate in other economies are likely to be faced with organizations utilizing different competence-creation processes. This has highly significant competitive implications. For example, one after another American industry (automobiles, small electronics, computer chips) has been faced with Japanese competitors who utilized very different processes to formulate objectives, learn about causality with respect to these objectives, and work together to achieve them (Imai, Nonaka, and Takeuchi 1985). These *process* differences are commonly cited as the major reason Japanese firms have achieved considerable success against American competitors in American markets (for example, Kagono, Nonaka, Sakakibara, and Okumura 1985). Similarly, process differences appear to explain the bulk of the variance firms experience when seeking to cooperate with partners from different national origins (Cusumano and Takeishi 1991).

This discussion allows us to create a framework for summarizing the likely international issues with respect to new competence creation (see Table 5.1). With this framework as background, we will now review what the literature tells us about the likely effects of differences between countries upon the processes of new competence creation.

GLOBAL DIFFERENCES IN OBJECTIVE-SETTING PROCESSES

In a market in which all players are from the same background, it is likely that the processes through which organizations attempt to create competence will be substantially similar, since their members will tend to share the same basic belief structures (Hofstede 1980; 1991). We would expect, however, to find differences in the approach to competence creation taken by firms from different national cultures. Considerable evidence suggests that this is indeed the case.

The literature reveals a number of areas in which objectives and objective-setting processes will tend to differ between firms of different

Table 5.1 Key challenges of new competence creation in an international frame of reference

Under conditions of competition	Process	Under conditions of cooperation
Challenge: Goal alignment in the face of different objective sets	Objective formation	Challenge: Formulating strategies which reflect the 'built in' advantages and disadvantages of opponents' objective formation process.
Challenge: Creating a shared frame of reference for information	Learning	Challenge: Recognition of and compensation for blind spots in absorptive capacity
Challenge: Managing agency and transaction problems created by expectations, communications patterns, and reward structures	Task execution	Challenge: Redesign of taskexecution processes in the face of more deft competition

national origins. Four of the most frequently mentioned are: (1) processes which underlie the basic purposes for which economic activity is undertaken and the results which are sought; (2) time horizons within which goals are to be achieved; (3) the urgency with which activities are undertaken; (4) the way in which organizations are designed to produce objectives.

Perhaps the most important difference between companies from different countries is that they differ on the nature of the results that they expect to obtain. Firms may, for example, focus on shareholder wealth (the commonly understood objective of most organizations in the United States), on the creation of jobs, on the generation of high cash flows, on family well-being, on ecological or other social welfare objectives, and so on. The idea that differences in national origin correspond to differences in national objective sets receives considerable support in the literature.

Several studies suggest that people from different national origins want to achieve different ends from their engagements in economic activity, and will undertake quite different activities in response to these objectives (Hofstede 1991; Schneider and De Meyer 1991). For instance, Japanese firms have been found to seek market presence and global brand identification in the short term, and profitability only in the long term, while American firms seek primarily short-term profit maximization and individual (or shareholder) gain (Hamel and Prahalad 1985). Latin European managers, on the other hand, are reported to seek support for an improved quality of life and relationships from the organizations for which they work, and are relatively unlikely to emphasize 'business ideology' (Schneider and De Meyer 1991). Chinese managers were different yet again, placing relatively little emphasis on personal and family life, greater emphasis on collective (as opposed to individual) challenges, and actively avoiding individual recognition (Shenkar and Ronen 1987: 572). This conclusion is echoed by Boisot and Child (1988) who remark that 'Chinese firms pursue a broader and vaguer, less codified, set of objectives than profit-maximizing Western enterprises' (p. 516).

Hurry, Miller, and Bowman (1992) offer a detailed study comparing the objectives of American venture capitalists with their Japanese counterparts, a comparison which highlights the potential economic effects of differences in goal formation processes. They find that American venture capital investments tend to be evaluated on the basis of financial returns, specifically on return on initial investment earned by the investing company after an initial public offering allows them to dispose of their holdings. The mindset is not one which attempts to exploit any of the other assets the funded firm may have created. These authors found that Japanese venture capital invest-ments, in contrast, are judged on the basis of their ability to 'obtain new technologies and new business opportunities' (1992: 87), and their study found strong support for the idea that Japanese investors were far more likely to use these investments to build new compe-tence as opposed to simply obtaining financial returns for them.

A second oft-cited area of distinction between countries concerns the relevant time horizon for which objectives are developed. It seems that patience levels vary significantly across national origins. Research has shown, for example, that American industry in general tends to be focused upon returns in the short term, while Japanese competitors focus more heavily upon opening new opportunities for the long term (Kester 1991). Chinese managers are known for their willingness to allow the passage of considerable time before seeking results from their activities (Adler, Brahm, and Graham 1992), perhaps in partial response to a view of time as circular and plentiful, rather than linear and limited (Lockett 1987).

Another construct related to time is reported by Schneider and De Meyer (1991), who find that cultural differences strongly affect perceived sense of urgency in strategic conduct. Differences in urgency are likely to affect the amount of time allowed for an activity to occur and the amount and type of resources allocated to it. Similar differences in urgency are reported by Lockett (1987), who finds considerably less urgency to conclude negotiations among Chinese managers than among Westerners.

Finally, a rich literature tackles the issue of how firms from different countries organize themselves internally to set their goals. Perhaps the most comprehensive of such efforts was undertaken by Hofstede (1991). Hofstede describes four archetypes for organizations: pyramids, machines, markets, and families, suggesting that the way in which the organization is structured in terms of authority and decision-making substantially affects the goals subsequently derived. For example, he reports that senior managers in firms from the United Kingdom occupy themselves more with strategic problems, and less with day-to-day operations, while in France and Germany managers take far more interest in the executional aspects of their jobs. Such a focus on the part of management will necessarily shape the precision and directness of organizational objectives, arguably in a consistent way.

From this discussion, we may draw two major conclusions. First, that it is highly likely that the national origin of a firm will significantly affect both the nature of the objectives which it formulates, and the process by which it arrives at these objectives.

GLOBAL DIFFERENCES IN THE APPROACH TO LEARNING

A variety of arguments support the idea that a firm's ability to understand cause and effect, or its approach to learning, has a substantial impact upon its ability to become competent in new areas. There appears, for example, to be a distinct difference in the learning processes required to be successful in a purely domestic situation as opposed to an international one. Hamel and Prahalad (1985) make the point that understanding competitors in global competition requires 'a different set of concepts and tools than is normally used to assess competitors and competitive advantage' (p. 145). Levitt (1983) suggests that increasing homogeneity of consumer attribute preferences requires firms to use different processes to identify customer needs and niches and to create offerings for those niches.

A strategic question is whether national or cultural differences in the approach to learning appear to yield predictable areas of superiority as well as predictable blind spots among firms from those national origins. The literature would seem to support such a position. For example, we are told that the ability of Italian executives to leave behind the baggage of national tradition is a major contributor to an 'Italian invasion' of direct foreign investment, joint ventures, and exports overseas (Bruce 1987). The literature points to three differences in learning processes which seem to be strategically relevant. These seem to be whether learning is a visceral or an analytical exercise; whether firms maintain a high or low 'absorptive capacity', and whether information flows and information interpretation are handled differently.

The literature offers strong evidence that people from different countries are quite literally taught to learn differently (Hofstede 1991). Take the contrasting cases of Japanese versus German orientation to obtaining a 'visceral' understanding of phenomena. Japanese firms are described as learning through a principle which Imai, Nonaka, and Takeuchi (1985) term 'information redundancy' involving significant time and effort spent on horizontal information flows and direct, personal contact with phenomena of interest (see also Aoki 1986). Germans, in contrast, are seen to focus their efforts upon the technical and technological analysis needed to execute programmes which fall within the purview of highly specialized training, and are very comfortable obtaining new information which is highly codified and abstract. Indeed, Hofstede (1991) notes that German students are inclined to feel that anything they can understand easily has little educational value.

Firms from different countries are also seen to invest differently in the maintenance of different levels of 'absorptive capacity' (Cohen and Levinthal 1990). A way to think about this is the extent to which firms from a given country are apt to suffer from the 'not invented here' syndrome in trying to obtain new information. Many Asian companies, Japanese in particular, are seen to have a well-developed absorptive capacity which allows them to readily adopt and utilize knowledge originated by others. Japanese companies are thought to be excellent and aggressive imitators, while American firms have difficulty with any idea which they did not originate (Hurry, Miller, and Bowman 1992; Westney and Sakakibara 1986; Mansfield 1988; Shan and Hamilton 1991). The facility with which Japanese firms are seen to adopt innovations and accept new ideas originating elsewhere has actually been the source of some tension in relations among firms from Japan and the United States (Reich and Mankin 1986), and illustrates how differences in national origin can lead to completely different views of the legitimacy of one or another approach.

A final important distinction in learning processes between firms from different national origins concerns how they go about identifying legitimate sources of information and how this information is interpreted. Chinese firms, for example, are seen to rely very heavily upon interpersonal communication as sources of valuable information (Adler, Brahm, and Graham 1992). Such a stance is consonant with a collectivist, uncertainty-avoiding attitude toward new ideas, in which the legitimacy of information is assured through group linkages and group interaction (Hofstede and Bond 1988). Indian managers are seen to rely very heavily upon the opinions and ideas of those in positions of authority, irrespective of others kinds of 'hard' data to the contrary (Hofstede 1991). Schneider and de Meyer (1991) further find that national origin influences the interpretation of *identical* events.

In summary, the literature suggests that differences in national origin can lead to differences in a firm's characteristic approach to learning, in particular to its overall approach (analytical vs. visceral), to its investments in and acceptability of absorptive capacity, and to differences in the sources for and interpretations of information that it receives.

GLOBAL DIFFERENCES IN DEFTNESS

The way in which organizations undertake task processes intended to facilitate new competence creation can be thought of as a reaction to three enduring and relatively insoluble issues. The first is the problem of uncertainty, an unavoidable condition facing those who seek to innovate (Nelson and Winter 1977). The second is the agency problem, in which some way must be identified to align goals and ensure behaviour in accordance with those goals, and the third is the issue of transaction costs. National origin appears to have influenced the ways in which firms cope with these problems.

Let us begin by considering the question of how task groups in organizations deal with the problem of uncertainty. One of the fundamental purposes of organizations is thought to be the creation of mechanisms by which sub-groups can avoid becoming paralysed by uncertainty, or uncertainty absorption mechanisms (Cyert and March 1963). Organizations based upon different national origins appear to use different uncertainty-absorption mechanisms to facilitate the emergence of deftness.

Schneider and De Meyer (1991) suggest that Japanese firms adopt a 'requisite variety' (Ashby 1956) stance toward uncertainty, by including sufficient variety and information in their processes to understand uncertainty. For instance, in executing against their objectives, Japanese firms organize their teams differently. They operate on a 'logic' of overlapping, lean production systems which use peer management processes to absorb uncertainty and handle agency and transactions costs. Schneider and De Meyer report that Western cultures, on the other hand, appear to deal with uncertainty by attempting to reduce it or to minimize the extent to which it is felt (1991: 316). Americans are seen to operate on a 'mass production' logic, in which the system, not the team, provides buffers, offers incentives and sanctions, and provides the antidote to market costs, a logic of 'mass production' (MacDuffie and Krafcik 1991). Chinese groups, in contrast, are seen to rely upon Confucian philosophy and traditions, which absorb uncertainty through kinship affiliations (Shenkar and Ronen 1987). Indeed, in describing the typical commercial patterns of Chinese living abroad, Hofstede (1993) notes that the size of their organizations tends to be limited by the availability of trusted family members to act in a managerial capacity. Thus, problems of both uncertainty and agency are dealt with in a Chinese context by containing important responsibility and decisions within a close family circle.

Turning to the agency problems in task execution, we find that a relatively clear-cut difference among firms from different national origins can be seen in the extent to which the management system (or the individual manager) puts in place incentive and monitoring systems as opposed to other means of control. Hofstede (1993) suggests that the appeal of F. W. Taylor's scientific management approach was immense in the United States, in which 'large numbers of workers with diverse backgrounds and skills had to work together' (p. 83), while firms from national origins without such diversity had little need for such a stringently controlled structure.

Similarly, American concepts of manager control of incentives and rewards are unknown in Japan and Germany, where the locus of effort is on worker groups and those who have survived an apprenticeship rather than on relatively undifferentiated raw material. The locus for the creation of deftness may be peer oriented, as in Japan; generated as part of a comprehensive and universal training and apprenticeship programme, as in Germany; or tending to rely upon the behaviour of a 'manager' or coordinator, as in the United States (Hofstede, 1993). American theories of group effectiveness tend to glorify the group leader and focus on decision-making, but there is no evidence to suggest that either of these should correlate with deftness across national origins.

Finally, consider the problem of the transaction costs which organizations mitigate. Operations which are deft minimize such costs by establishing a communication frame, within which information may flow and be consistently acted upon by group members. The problem of creating an effective communication frame is intensified in a situation in which group membership is diverse. Working jointly with people from other national origins may require that communications utilize different languages, different emphases, and different levels of elaboration (Davidson 1987; Hall 1985). Thus, Adler, Brahm, and Graham (1992) document in painstaking detail a series of minute differences in the negotiating style and communication patterns of Americans negotiating with individuals from the People's Republic of China (see also Bond 1986; Hofstede and Bond 1988; Redding 1980). They also describe a number of culturally embedded difficulties which may exist when the communications patterns considered appropriate in one national origin rub up against those of another national origin. Thus, the constant questioning interruption of discussion by Brazilian managers, lack of eye contact from Japanese discussants and repeated questioning of the same points on the part of Chinese participants are all 'potential sources for friction and misunderstanding' (1992: 463).

Transaction costs may be further exacerbated when systematically different interpretations of the same information are created as a result of cultural factors. Schneider and De Meyer (1991), for example, find that managers from different national origins experience the identical strategic situation (as presented in a case) very differently. Some experience it as a threat, some as a crisis, and some as neither of these. Similarly, some see the situation as provoking a need for immediate action, while others do not. They conclude that there is a 'need to present issues in different ways' (1991: 317) if the organization is to act in a unified manner. This has important implications for deftness – until a group can achieve some consensus about when an event is a crisis and about how urgent it is that something be done about it, it is likely to experience significant difficulty in achieving a sensible response to the situation.

A final important point in considering deftness is to contemplate the malleability of the practices and behaviours which generate deftness in different national origins. Evidence suggests serious limitations to this malleability. McGrath, MacMillan, Yang, and Tsai (1992) find, for instance, that despite fifty years of exposure to very different ideologies, people from Taiwan, the Republic of China, and Mainland China continue to prefer collective, as opposed to individual, action and to share similar attitudes towards work. Similarly, Turnbull,

Oliver, and Wilkinson (1992) report on the problems created when the vehicle industry in the United Kingdom attempted to emulate Japanese interactions with suppliers. The powerful negative effect upon deftness of different cultural approaches is further supported by Chatterjee, Lubatkin, Schweiger, and Weber's (1992) findings that mergers between firms, even of identical national origin, were unsuccessful to the extent that they did not share a common organizational culture. Problems of culture clash thus do not even appear to be confined to cases of different national origins. In contrast, Cusumano and Takeishi (1991) find that although it does take time, Japanese management practices with respect to supplier relationships could be effectively 'transplanted' to the United States.

In summary, the literature suggests that depending on differences in national origin, there will tend to be characteristic approaches toward dealing with the joint problems of uncertainty, agency, and transactions costs.

COMPETENCE CREATION: COMPETITION VERSUS COOPERATION

We have stated above that competence creation is driven by three major processes: objective formation, learning, and group task execution, and that these processes differ fundamentally in different countries. So, in attempting to develop new competences in a cross-national context, it is important to take into account how national origin moderates these three processes. We now systematically turn to the issues which need to be taken into account when attempting to build competence in a cross border context.

To begin, consider the fundamentally different challenges of two different settings in which competence must be created. In the first situation the firm is in a competitive mode, either attempting to venture into a new country and build the competences to compete there, or is attempting to fend off the onslaught of a foreign competitor entering its markets. In the second situation, the firm is in cooperative mode, attempting to forge a relationship with a foreign firm in a joint venture, strategic alliance, or other such common effort to capitalize on the strengths of the two disparate parties. Let us consider each in turn.

Competence creation and foreign competition

The first challenge of creating new competence in the face of foreign competition is to simultaneously develop objectives which render a firm competitive and to understand the objective set developed by competitors. An issue of some importance here is that firms from different countries have 'built-in' advantages and disadvantages arising from different objective-formulation processes and differential resource endowments (Porter 1990).

The first competitive issue in forming objectives stems from the twin processes of path-dependency and technological accumulation, which both enable and constrain the potential objective set of a firm. Thus, the kinds of initiatives undertaken in the first place are likely to reflect differences in constraints faced by firms from different countries with different resource endowments. Hence, Cantwell (1989) finds that the current array of technologies in a given location or in a given national group of firms reflects past technological accumulation. Davidson (1976) finds that firms will tend to introduce innovations to a market which are perceived to economize the relatively most scarce (expensive) factor of production in the local economy. He finds that there are significantly different patterns in the objectives for which process innovations were undertaken in Japan, the United States, Europe and the United Kingdom. Thus, in Japan, only 16 per cent of process innovations in the data he reports were intended to be labour saving, while in the United States, some 61 per cent of process innovations were intended to be labour saving. Differential availability of input factors suggests that we will see differential emphasis on desirability of different attributes in different regions.

In essence, historical and current national resource endowments shape the objectives likely to be associated with a given national origin for a firm. National endowments and path-dependency shape what is perceived as worthwhile by both the firm and the markets in which it participates. In addition, national resource endowments tend to shape what innovations will be emphasized. This may explain a focus in the United States on labour saving and its embrace of Taylorism. The United States is a society rich in natural resources and needful of ways to mobilize a relatively scarce and highly diverse workforce. On the other hand Japan, Korea and Taiwan have limited resources and (until recently) an abundance of labour. Deming, rather than Taylor, appeared to more adequately address the issues they faced, encouraging a focus on making the most of scarce resources through quality engineering, utilizing people well, and systematically improving everything that was done.

Over time, in the absence of outside intervention, there can be seen to emerge in each country's economic structure a balance between market worth and firm worth objectives which reflect the society's particular circumstances and trade-offs. An important process is mutual accommodation between firms and their markets, accompanied by rich, co-evolved sets of supporting institutions. Suppliers, distributors, regulators, and politicians all develop objectives which reflect a mutually acceptable set of 'rules of the game' (McGrath, MacMillan, and Tushman forthcoming; Tushman and Rosenkopf 1992). Firms whose objectives fail to suit those of societal stakeholders eventually come under serious selection pressures, as they are hampered in their ability to obtain resources and secure other kinds of support from their environment. Witness, in the United States, the difficulty experienced by tobacco companies, whose products have become increasingly unacceptable to American cultural and social norms.

Firms operating in their own home bases thus reflect both the complete set of objectives and the weighting of this set which has emerged as the norm in their countries. The content of competences developed by such firms may be quite idiosyncratic, in that they are developed partially in response to the concerns of nations. A topical example is reflected in high demand for 'green' products in Europe. In the future, it is likely that non-European firms will be at a disadvantage in being able to deliver products that satisfy the environmental requirements to which many European countries are now subscribing.

Consider now a firm which decides to enter a foreign market. It is faced with the following daunting challenges:

- incumbent players who are competent at competing against others on the basis of the scarcest resource inputs in their markets;
- incumbent players who have developed a fine-grained understanding of the objective preferences of the society within which they are imbedded;
- a co-evolved set of institutional players who have developed mutual understanding and agreements on the rules of the game: this includes suppliers, distributors, agencies and legislators who may operate in competition with one another, but who all agree and sympathize with the current rules of competition.

A number of dynamics become interesting when firms pit their competences against one another in such a setting. Two in particular appear to be relevant to the process of competence creation. These are (1) the balance between a disadvantageous position with respect to foreign markets of an incumbent, and the potential for advantage which stems from different 'firm worth' requirements than those which constrain incumbents; and (2) processes by which firms attempt either to defend or reconfigure their competences when the entry of a newcomer shifts the competitive environment.

The first challenge for a firm seeking to enter a foreign market is to determine how to provide worth to a large enough segment of the target market to justify entry in the first place. Evidence suggests that the only way a foreign entrant can tempt customers away from existing suppliers is by offering far superior value or far lower cost for products which are desirable to that market (Levitt 1983). Clearly the venturing firm needs to enter the market with an offering carrying considerable market worth, as only superior market worth will crack the 'incumbency' advantage. Thus, in formulating its objectives, a new entrant must understand what constitutes market worth from the perspective of the foreign market, not of the entering firm.

Many of the most lamentable failures experienced by firms going beyond the bounds of their own country stem from the failure to understand what constitutes worth to the new market. A much publicized case is that of the no-alcohol policy of the Disney Corporation's 'Euro-Disney' theme park near Paris, France. In the United States, a ban on alcoholic beverages is considered quite acceptable, and desirable in family-oriented settings. Part of Disney's corporate ethos is to stringently avoid 'unwholesome' alcoholic beverages on its various properties. Europeans, in contrast, have an entirely different perspective. Beverages such as wine and beer are acceptable in virtually all social settings, and are felt to be pleasant accompaniments to family holiday life. Disney's unwillingness to relent (so far) and permit alcohol sales is often cited as a factor which discourages European visits to the theme park.

While it is often very difficult to understand what constitutes market worth to people from another country, competing against established firms in another setting simultaneously opens unusual opportunities. These stem from the ability of the entrant to use different objectives for firm worth than are used by incumbents in pursuing business goals. Thus, Japanese ability to be very patient in entering American markets is in itself a distinct competitive advantage. The ability of Mexican firms to operate in a low-cost position with respect to labour reflects in part an advantage over American competitors whose 'firm worth' constraints require that employees be paid a wage consistent with those throughout its operations.

The behaviour of Samsung in building its competences at computer chip manufacture nicely illustrates this point. Americans were astonished to find that the company pursued a very subtle strategy to do this quite literally over years. Samsung first invested in the training of Ph.D.

candidates in electrical engineering at top United States institutions, then supported them in becoming placed in top research posts. This allowed them to create considerable know-how about cutting edge American technology. Then, in some cases after a decade or more away from home, the company 'summoned' those it had supported back to Korea. Not all came, but those who did brought with them invaluable skills and technological know-how, which the company arguably could have obtained no other way. Such a long-term strategy for knowledge acquisition would be virtually inconceivable to an American CEO, and was probably a public policy surprise to American policymakers.

Of course, because the firm is no longer competing against players with similar objective preferences, it may also be blind to idiosyncratic weaknesses that pertain only to its foreign competitors. Failure to understand where the competition is vulnerable may lead a firm to overlook a source of potential advantage, and opens it to the risk of being blindsided by an unanticipated competitive move.

International competition may in the extreme case result in an evaporation of the previously 'safe' domestic market, with its well-understood market worth parameters. Once the competition moves from national to global level, there is a need for what Prahalad and Hamel (1990) refer to as a global logic. Competition moves from direct and bi-directional to diffuse and multidirectional. The firm that maintains a national logic runs the risk of being outmanœuvred by competitive moves on multiple fronts.

Entry of new players can have the effect of dramatically changing the competitive ground rules in a country's markets. Exactly such a challenge is faced by DuPont, which is finding itself suddenly in global competition with firms from Asian countries who have both lower labour costs and more modern technological facilities. The Asians can achieve unprecedented efficiencies in production. Firms such as DuPont are now faced with the problem of dismantling years of co-evolved structures, both internally in terms of massive investments in plant, equipment and routines, and externally in terms of relationships with other organizations. Such firms may even have to call into question deeply held objective preferences.

The major disadvantage faced by incumbent firms that have achieved dominance is that their very dominance gives rise to a reduction in variety for them. In such situations, they lose absorptive capacity and become capable of adaptive learning only over a narrow band of variety (Miller 1993). Within this band their ability to adapt may be awesome, but beyond that band their capacity to learn and adapt becomes impaired.

Once an entrant achieves a foothold in a new market, incumbents may find that the understanding of causality which they thought they had is suddenly and dramatically undermined. Thus, the common wisdom of American auto manufacturers that there was no demand in the US for small cars suffered serious setbacks as the energy crisis and the emergence of Japanese imports as a viable alternative demonstrated that this was simply incorrect.

Incumbents don't know the newcomer or how the newcomer intends to compete. They may not be able to understand effects stemming from fundamental differences in objective sets. This creates problems not only for the process of objective formulation, but also for learning and task execution as well. Not only does the organization begin to become aware that its code no longer accurately reflects a changed reality, but it is likely to experience a drop in task effectiveness. When the world suddenly becomes a more hostile place, it is very difficult to sustain the mutual confidence and smooth information flows which are characteristic of deft teams.

These challenges characterize the situation of the firm entering and competing in a foreign market. Obviously, the mirror image of these problems pertains if the firm is facing the entry of a foreign competitor in its own markets.

Competence creation and cooperation with foreign firms

An entirely different set of challenges is posed when people from different cultural backgrounds seek to cooperate. Fundamental differences in the processes through which objectives are set, in how information is obtained and interpreted, and in how people work together can create havoc in an organization's efforts to become jointly competent with partners from another country. This, despite an acknowledgement of the potential mutual benefit of working in a cooperative relationship, whether due to potential national advantage or otherwise (Porter 1990; Shan and Hamilton 1991).

Once again the extent to which the firm can create competence in a cooperative relationship is a function of the three processes of objective formation, learning and group deftness.

With cooperation as the mode, the basic objective is to capitalize on the mutual benefits of working together with the foreign firm so that both parties can derive their own benefits from the relationship.

The first and most fundamental obstacle to successful cooperation is failure on the part of both parties to understand their 'cooperator's' objective set. Hofstede (1991) lists many examples of situations in which even well-meaning partners are simply unable to comprehend the goals and methods by which foreigners operate. Cooperative arrangements run a real risk of failure if both parties fail to understand the objective preferences of their partners.

A second and equally serious risk is the failure of both parties to capture firm worth, which may be quite different for each of them. Developing mutual understanding of the partner's idea of firm worth appears to be essential to the continuation of joint ventures or other cooperative arrangements (Kogut 1989). Issues which both parties need to address include what constitutes mutually acceptable results, and what timing and urgency will pertain to these results. Failure to build mutual understanding of these issues will have the inevitable effect of decreasing deftness, thus increasing distrust and escalating agency and transaction costs.

A third challenge for both parties is to attempt to use differences between them to advantage, by neutralizing the weaknesses and blind spots of one with the strengths of the other and vice versa. If this does not occur, the partnership is likely to be hindered in its ability to develop new competence because the two parties are unable to surmount each of their mutual weaknesses. In such a situation, the whole may add up to less than the sum of its parts.

The final risk associated with cooperative objective formation is the failure to recognize that associated with incumbency advantages are also incumbency constraints, and that the network of agreements and understanding which the partner has created in its own domain also placed limits on the actions the partner can undertake. This failure to understand incumbency restraints can lead to unnecessary expectations, causing partnership failure.

A second set of risks in cooperative arrangement across borders stem from differences in learning processes identified above. First there is a danger that the partners will fail to share their learning frames or processes and thus will fail to share what each party is learning as the cooperative relationship unfolds. In particular, if one partner has not adjusted its learning processes to match the increased variety that accompanies the entry into this new, cross-national relationship, there is a danger that it simply will not 'learn'. The pooling of learning approaches and the communication of differential learning taking place adds to requisite variety and enhances absorptive capacity needed to match the new variety.

Finally, there is a danger that the parties will not share and debate their different interpretations of the information that they are receiving. This means that both parties will proceed to make decisions and e actions on the basis of very different interpretations of the same data. If enough of this differential interpretation takes place, the inability to learn from one another will give rise to a third set of risks associated with cross border cooperation, and that is the failure to develop deftness. Mutual misunderstanding or differences in interpretation, unarticulated differences and objectives, and incomprehensible actions on the part of the partner give rise to fears of opportunistic behaviour which can rapidly escalate into uncontrolled agency and transaction costs which wipe out the benefits of the partnership.

The challenges of cross-national cooperation are no less daunting than those of cross-border cooperation, although they are perhaps less widely discussed. Differences in objectives, in learning processes, and in the ability to create deftness will tend to mitigate against the effective establishment of cooperative relations among firm members from different national origins.

CONCLUSION AND RESEARCH QUESTIONS

This paper has examined the problem of new competence creation from an international perspective. Clues from extant literature tell us that there are real challenges for competence creation when an international dimension is introduced. These challenges have to do with three processes, those of developing an objective set, organizational learning, and task execution. In an international context, national differences in the way these processes are pursued become important predictors of outcomes in two conditions. These are firstly, conditions of competition with firms from other national origins than one's own, and secondly cooperative environments in which it becomes essential to work with people from other nations.

An objective of this exercise has been to identify research questions raised by the discussion. If the above logic is reasonable, it raises a number of intriguing questions for future research, some of which have been addressed to some extent and many which have not been addressed at all. We will conclude by presenting a summary list of these new research questions.

Research questions with respect to objective formation

1 Do initial resource endowments lead to national preferences in objectives, and if so to what extent do these influence firm objective preferences and market worth objective preferences in specific national situations?

2 What differences are there in objective sets among different nations?
3 What differences are there in objective preferences in markets among different nations?
4 Are market objective preferences idiosyncratic to specific nations or universal?
5 Does sustained success in national markets really lead to specific national competences?
6 To what extent does sustained success of firms in national markets lead to co-evolved institutional structures?
7 Do these co-evolved institutional structures lead to incumbency advantages for national firms?
8 Does sustained success by national firms lead to reduction in absorptive capacity over time, and does this in turn reduce adaptive band width?
9 If invaders succeed in cracking national markets, does the 'reversal of incumbent fortunes' phenomenon occur, and in what circumstances does this occur?

Research questions with respect to organizational learning

1 Do nations have different learning processes, and if so to what extent do these processes influence development of idiosyncratic national strength and idiosyncratic national blind spots?
2 Does globalization raise variety enough to call for a higher level global logic, rather than a national logic for learning?
3 Under what conditions does this occur?

Research questions with respect to deftness

1 Do different nations have idiosyncratic processes for developing deftness?
2 What burden does a move to global or cross-border competition place on deftness?
3 To what extent do idiosyncratic deftness processes differentially affect this burden?
4 To what extent are deftness processes in different nations malleable?
5 Under what conditions does deftness collapse under conditions of competition or cooperation? In other words, are some nations' deftness processes more robust than others?

NOTES

1 This discussion does not imply that objective formation is a purely rational or even a conscious process. We take the perspective that organizations are 'myopically purposeful' (Levitt and March 1988) and that much that occurs within them happens by accident.
2 *Webster's New Collegiate Dictionary* defines deft as 'marked by facility and skill'. This is the sense in which the term is used here.

REFERENCES

Adler, N.J. (1986) *International Dimensions of Organizational Behavior*, Boston, MA: Kent Publishing.
Adler, N.J., Richard Brahm, and John L. Graham (1992) 'Strategy Implementation: A Comparison of Face-to-Face Negotiations in the People's Republic of China and the United States', *Strategic Management Journal*, 13: 449–466.
Amit, R. and P. Schoemaker (1993) 'Strategic Assets and Organizational Rent', *Strategic Management Journal*, 14(1): 33–46.
Aoki, Masahiko (1986) 'Horizontal vs. Vertical Information Structure of the Firm', *American Economic Review*, 76 (5): 971–983.
Ancona, D.G. and David F. Caldwell (1992) 'Demography and Design: Predictors of New Product Team Performance', *Organization Science*, 3 (3): 321–341.
Anderson, Erin (1990) 'Two Firms, One Frontier: On Assessing Joint Venture Performance', *Sloan Management Review*, Winter: 19–30.
Barney, Jay B. (1991) 'Firm Resources and Sustained Competitive Advantage', *Journal of Management*, 17 (1): 99–120.
Baumol, William J. (1985) 'Rebirth of a Fallen Leader: Italy and the Long Period Data', *Atlanta Economic Journal*, 13 September: 12–26.
Boisot, M. and J. Child (1988) 'The Iron Law of Fiefs: Bureaucratic Failure and the Problem of Governance in the Chinese Economic Reforms', *Administrative Science Quarterly*, 33: 507–527.
Bond, M.H. (1986) *The Psychology of the Chinese Mind*, London: Oxford University Press.
Bowman, Edward H. (1974) 'Epistemology, Corporate Strategy and Academe', *Sloan Management Review*, 15: 35–50.
Bruce, Leigh (1987) 'The Italians: The Best Europeans?', *International Management*, May 1987: 24–31.
Burgelman, R. A. (1983) 'A Process Model of Internal Corporate Venturing in the Major Diversified Firm', *Administrative Science Quarterly*, 28: 223–244.
Buzzell, R. D. (1968) 'Can You Standardize Multinational Marketing?', *Harvard Business Review*, November–December: 102–113.
Cantwell, J. (1989) 'Historical Trends in International Patterns of Technological Innovation', in *Technological Innovation and the Multinational Corporation*, Oxford: Basil Blackwell.
Chatterjee, S., M.H. Lubatkin, D.M. Schweiger, and Y. Weber (1992) 'Cultural Differences and Shareholder Value in Related Mergers: Linking Equity and Human Capital', *Strategic Management Journal*, 13 (5): 319–334.

Clark, K., W. Bruce Chew, and T. Fujimoto (1987) 'Product Development in the World Auto Industry', *Brookings Papers on Economic Activity*, 3: 729–782.

Cohen, Wesley M. and Dan A. Levinthal (1990) 'Absorptive Capacity: A New Perspective on Learning and Innovation', *Administrative Science Quarterly*, 35: 128–152.

Cole, Robert E. (1990) *Strategies for Learning: Small-Group Activities in American, Japanese and Swedish Industry*, Berkeley, CA: University of California Press.

Collis, David J. (1991) 'A Resource-Based Analysis of Global Competition: The Case of the Bearings Industry', *Strategic Management Journal*, 12: 49–68.

Conner, Kathleen R. (1991) 'A Historical Comparison of Resource-Based Theory and Five Schools of Thought within Industrial Organization Economics: Do We Have a New Theory of the Firm?', *Journal of Management*, 17 (1): 121–154.

Cusumano, Michael A. and A. Takeishi (1991) 'Supplier Relations and Management: A Survey of Japanese, Japanese-Transplant, and US Auto Plants', *Strategic Management Journal*, 12: 563–588.

Davidson, W.H. (1976) 'Patterns of Factor-Saving Innovation in the Industrialized World', *European Economic Review*, 8: 207–217.

Davidson, W.H. (1987) 'Creating and Managing Joint Ventures in China', *California Management Review*, 29(4): 77–94.

Dierickx, Ingmar and Karel Cool (1989) 'Asset Stock Accumulation and Sustainability of Competitive Advantage', *Management Science*, 35 (12): 1504–1511.

D'Iribarne, P. (1989) *La Logique de l'Honneur*, Paris: Seuil (as cited in Schneider and De Meyer, 1991).

Dougherty, Deborah (1992) 'Interpretive Barriers to Successful Product Innovation in Large Firms', *Organization Science*, 3 (2): 179–202.

Fiol, C. Marlene (1991) 'Managing Culture as a Competitive Resource: An Identity Based View of Sustainable Competitive Advantage', *Journal of Management*, 17 (1): 191–211.

Ghemawat, Pankaj (1986) 'Sustainable Advantage', *Harvard Business Review*, Sept.–Oct.: 53–58.

Ghemawat, Pankaj (1991) *Commitment: The Dynamic of Strategy*, New York: Free Press.

Hall, J.L. (1985) *The International Joint Venture*, New York: Praeger.

Hamel, Gary and C.K. Prahalad (1985) 'Do You Really Have a Global Strategy?', *Harvard Business Review*, July–Aug.: 139–148.

Hofstede, Geert (1980) *Culture's Consequences*, Beverly Hills, CA: Sage Publications.

Hofstede, Geert (1991) *Cultures and Organizations: Software of the Mind*, Cambridge: McGraw-Hill Book Company (UK) Ltd.

Hofstede, Geert (1993) 'Cultural Constraints in Management Theories', *Academy of Management Executive*, 7 (1): 81–94.

Hofstede, G. and M.H. Bond (1988) 'Confucius and Economic Growth: New Trends into Culture's Consequences', *Organizational Dynamics*, 16: 4–21.

Huber, G. B. (1991) 'Organizational Learning: The Contributing Processes and the Literatures', *Organization Science*, 2 (1): 88–115.

Hurry, D., A.T. Miller, and E.H. Bowman (1992) 'Calls on High Technology: Japanese Exploration of Venture Capital Investments in the United States', *Strategic Management Journal*, 13 (2): 85–102.

Imai, I. Nonaka, and H. Takeuchi (1985) 'Managing the New Product Development Process: How Japanese Companies Learn and Unlearn', in *The Uneasy Alliance: Managing the Productivity-Technology Dilemma*, eds K.B. Clark, R.H. Hayes, and C. Lorenz, Boston: Harvard Business School Press, 1985.

Kagono, T., I. Nonaka, K. Sakakibara, and A. Okumura (1985) *Strategic vs. Evolutionary Management: A US – Japan Comparison of Strategy and Organization*, Amsterdam: Elsevier Science Publishers B.V.

Kester, W.C. (1991) *Japanese Takeovers: The Global Quest for Corporate Control*, Boston: Harvard Business School Press.

Laurent, A. (1983) 'The Cultural Diversity of Western Conceptions of Management', *International Studies of Management and Organizations*, 13: 75–96.

Levitt, Barbara and James G. March (1988) 'Organizational Learning', *Annual Review of Sociology*,14: 319–340.

Levitt, Theodore (1983) 'The Globalization of Markets', *Harvard Business Review*, May–June.

Lieberman, Marvin B. (1989) 'Learning, Productivity and US – Japan Industrial "Competitiveness"', in *Managing International Manufacturing*, ed. K. Ferdows, 215–238.

McGrath, R.G. (1993) *The Evolution of New Competence in Established Organizations: An Empirical Investigation*, Ph.D. dissertation, the Wharton School, University of Pennsylvania.

McGrath, R.G., Ian C. MacMillan, and Michael L. Tushman (forthcoming) 'The Role of Executive Team Actions in Shaping Dominant Designs: Towards the Strategic Shaping of Technological Progress', *Strategic Management Journal*.

McGrath, R.G., I.C. MacMillan, E. Yang, and W.M.H. Tsai (1992) 'Does Culture Endure or Is It Malleable? Issues for Entrepreneurial Economic Development', *Journal of Business Venturing*, 7: 441–458.

McGrath, R.G., S. Venkataraman, and I.C. MacMillan (1992) 'Outcomes of Corporate Venturing: An Alternative Perspective', *Academy of Management Proceedings*, August.

McKelvey, Bill and Howard Aldrich (1983) 'Populations, Natural Selection and Applied Organizational Science', *Administrative Science Quarterly*, 28: 101–128.

Mahoney, J.T. and J.R. Pandian (1992) 'The Resource-Based View within the Conversation of Strategic Management', *Strategic Management Journal*, 13: 363–380.

Mansfield, E. (1988) 'The Speed and Cost of Industrial Innovation in Japan and the United States: External vs. Internal Technology', *Management Science*, 34 (10): 1157–1168.

Miller, Danny (1993) 'The Architecture of Simplicity', *Academy of Management Review*, 18 (1): 116–138.

Nelson, R. and Winter, S. (1977) 'In Search of a Useful Theory of Innovation', *Research Policy*, 6: 36–76.

Nonaka, Ikujiro (1991) 'The Knowledge-Creating Company', *Harvard Business Review*, Nov.–Dec.: 96–104.

Penrose, Edith T. (1959) *The Theory of The Growth of the Firm*, White Plains, New York: M.E. Sharpe, Inc.

Porter, Michael (1980) *Competitive Strategy*, New York: Free Press.

Porter, Michael (1985) *Competitive Advantage*, New York: Free Press.

Porter, Michael (1990) *The Competitive Advantage of Nations*, New York: Free Press.

Prahalad, C.K, and Gary Hamel (1990) 'The Core Competence of the Corporation', *Harvard Business Review*, May–June: 79–91.

Redding, S.G. (1980) 'Cognition as an Aspect of Culture and its Relation to Management Processes: An Exploratory View of the Chinese Case', *Journal of Management Studies*, 17: 127–148.

Reed, Richard and Robert J. DeFillippi (1990) 'Causal Ambiguity, Barriers to Imitation, and Sustainable Competitive Advantage', *Academy of Management Review*, 15 (1): 88–102.

Reich, R.B. and E.D. Mankin (1986) 'Joint Ventures with Japan Give Away our Future', *Harvard Business Review*, 64: 78–86.

Rumelt, R.P. (1987) 'Theory, Strategy and Entrepreneurship', in *The Competitive Challenge: Strategies for Industrial Innovation and Renewal*, ed. D.J. Teece, Cambridge, MA: Ballinger Publishing Co., 137–158.

Schneider, S.C. and A. De Meyer (1991) 'Interpreting and Responding to Strategic Issues: The Impact of National Culture', *Strategic Management Journal*, 12 (4): 307–320.

Selznick, Philip (1957) *Leadership and Administration*, New York: Harper and Row.

Senge, Peter M. (1990) *The Fifth Discipline: The Art & Practice of the Learning Organization*, New York: Doubleday.

Shan, Weijian and William Hamilton (1991) 'Country-Specific Advantage and International Cooperation', *Strategic Management Journal*, 419–432.

Shenkar, O. and S. Ronen (1987) 'Structure and Importance of Work Goals Among Managers in the People's Republic of China', *Academy of Management Journal*, 30 (3): 564–576.

Simon, H. (1976) 'From Substantive Rationality to Procedural Rationality', *Method and Appraisal in Economics*, ed. S. J. Latsis, Cambridge: Cambridge University Press, 129–148.

Teece, D.J. (1981) 'The Multinational Enterprise: Market Failure and Market Power Considerations', *Sloan Management Review*, Spring: 3–19.

Teece, D.J., Gary Pisano, and Amy Shuen (1991) 'Dynamic Capabilities and Strategic Management', Working Paper, revised, November 1991.

Turnbull, Peter, Nick Oliver, and Barry Wilkinson (1992) 'Buyer–Supplier Relations in the UK Automotive Industry: Strategic Implications of the Japanese Manufacturing Model', *Strategic Management Journal*, 13: 159–168.

Tushman, M. and L. Rosenkopf (1992) 'Organizational Determinants of Technological Change: Toward a Sociology of Technological Evolution', *Research in Organizational Behavior*, JAI Press, pp. 311–347.

Venkataraman, S., Ian C. MacMillan, and Rita Gunther McGrath (1992) 'Progress in Research on Corporate Venturing', ch. 19 in *State of the Art in Entrepreneurship Research*, ed. D.L. Sexton, Boston: PWS-Kent Publishing Co.

Wernerfelt, Birger (1984) 'A Resource-Based View of the Firm', *Strategic Management Journal*, 5: 171–180.

Wernerfelt, Birger (1989) 'From Critical Resources to Corporate Strategy', *Journal of General Management*, 14 (3): 4–12.

Westney, D.E. and K. Sakakibara (1986) 'The Role of Japan-Based R&D in Global Technology Strategy', in *Technology in the Modern Corporation*, ed. M. Hurowitch, London: Pergamon Press, 217–232.

Zimmerman, M. (1985) *How To Do Business With the Japanese*, New York: Random House.

Part II

Empirical findings in entrepreneurship

Section I
Networks

6 Networking and entrepreneurship in Japan

Mitsuko Hirata and Akihiro Okumura

RESEARCH OBJECTIVES

This research explores the networking and personal traits of Japanese entrepreneurs. The results of this analysis are expected to lead to several proposals for defining entrepreneurship in further research. The rationale for this research is as follows:

1 The manner and the characteristics of the entrepreneur may be different from the non-entrepreneur in the homogeneous society of Japan. If so, how are they different?
2 The specific characteristics of entrepreneurship in Japan may be different from those in other countries; this will be studied in future research.

The purpose of the paper is to identify the personal traits that characterize entrepreneurs in Japan. These characteristics should be such that they allow us to differentiate between self-employed entrepreneurs and salaried managers by their personalities.

One of the main objectives is to determine the personal traits of Japanese entrepreneurs from the psychological viewpoint, by comparing them with non-entrepreneurs.

The historical definition of entrepreneurship was first elucidated by Schumpeter (1934, 1961) who stated that the role of entrepreneurship was to create a new market and set up a process of destruction for its further development. Then, Penrose (1959) defined entrepreneurship by comparing it with the attitude of managers as follows:

Entrepreneur	*Manager*
• new market creation	• implementation of entrepreneur's idea
• to create an enterprise	• ordinary control activity

In Japan, Yoshimori (1989) also compared entrepreneurial attitude with managerial attitude:

Entrepreneur	*Manager*
• adaptability to business environment	• adaptability to organization
• proactive adaptation	• reactive adaptation
• non-continuity in change	• continuity in change
• strategic mind	• management (control) mind
• target emphasis	• process emphasis
• utility	• efficiency
• progress or innovation as target	• stability or profitability
• risk-taker as individual	• risk-taker as organization

These definitions, however, characterize the functional aspects of entrepreneurship/management. As such, we consider them manifestations of personality, and therefore ask further: What are the underlying personality traits that transform into different attitudes as described?

The second focus of this research is to study entrepreneurs' networking. Mueller (1986) noted that an important activity for an entrepreneur is human networking in addition to management activity. Of course, non-entrepreneurs such as people in an organization can also participate in networking activity. There may, however, exist differences between them in how often and which type of networking they are participating in. We expect to classify entrepreneur networking activities, determine the specific type of networking, and compare them with that of the non-entrepreneur.

This research then aims at finding out how the interaction of networking and personal traits influences the entrepreneur. We assume neither networking nor the personal traits alone, but the interaction of both factors might explain the creativity which is a major characteristic of entrepreneurship.

This research is also expected to develop a way to measure entrepreneurship. Because Japanese society is considered to be homogeneous, we have to thoroughly study which variables in the form of personal traits make the difference between the entrepreneur and the non-entrepreneur. Such traits may not appear in behaviour; in other words, they cannot be observed.

RESEARCH FRAMEWORK

Our research framework includes factors describing networking activities and personal traits, including their relationships, as shown in the following chart.

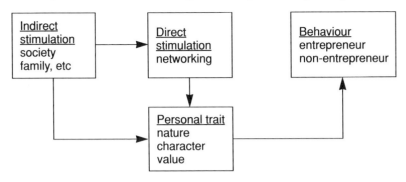

Figure 6.1 Relationships of networking activities and personal traits

The key question in this framework is how the interaction of direct stimulation and personal traits affects the behaviour of an entrepreneur. Moreover, indirect stimulation may also influence behaviour through personal traits.

Regarding direct stimulation, we selected networking as a source of communication and information as mentioned above. The detailed questions were designed based on the following two attributes:

1 distribution of time for communication with family, employees and other people
2 networking behaviour
   (a) number of networking groups which the entrepreneurs and the non-entrepreneurs belong to
   (b) the kind of people associated with in the networking group

For personal traits, we covered those aspects of personal nature which cannot be controlled by individuals, such as observable character, behavioural variables, and behaviour toward value. The detailed items are as follows. The research respondents evaluated themselves on a seven-point scale.

1 *nature:* health, vitality, verbal intelligence, practical intelligence, emotion
2 *observable character:* happy-go-lucky, adventurous, competitive, persistent
3 *behavioural variables:* extroversion, self-objectification, self-assurance, altruism, social intelligence
4 *behaviour to value:* theoretical interest, economic interest, artistic interest, religious interest

DATA

Research subjects

We randomly selected business-founders and those who had taken over existing businesses. The office managers in some large Japanese companies participated in this research as non-entrepreneurs. The final sample consisted of 18 entrepreneurs and 32 non-entrepreneurs. The sample characteristics are shown in Tables 6.1 and 6.2.

Table 6.1 Gender of sample

	Entrepreneurs	Non-entrepreneurs
Male	10	30
Female	8	2
Total	18	32

Table 6.2 Age of sample

Age	Entrepreneurs	Non-entrepreneurs
–29	0	3
30–34	0	6
35–39	9	13
40–44	2	7
45–49	1	3
50–54	1	0
55-	5	0
Total	18	32

Research method and analysis

Questionnaires designed on the basis of the above research framework were distributed to each respondent. The collected data were analysed by factor analysis and analysis of variance.

Major findings

We obtained data, as shown in Table 6.3, on the difference in communication patterns between entrepreneurs and non-entrepreneurs. The findings from Table 6.3 are as follows :

1 Entrepreneurs tend to spend more time with external people (non-employees) rather than with internal ones (employees). On the other hand, non-entrepreneurs tend to take more time with internal people.

2 Entrepreneurs tend to communicate less with their family. However, half of the non-entrepreneurs spend more time than average with their family.

Table 6.3 Time allocation by entrepreneurs and non-entrepreneurs (no. of people)

	Internal	*External*	*Total*
Entrepreneurs			
Home-oriented	2	3	5
Not home-oriented	4	9	13
Total	6	12	18
Non-entrepreneurs			
Home-oriented	7	4	11
Not home-oriented	7	3	10
Total	14	7	21

The number of networking groups in which the surveyed participants were involved are presented in Table 6.4. Entrepreneurs participate in networking groups much more than non-entrepreneurs.

Table 6.4 Number of networking groups

Number of networking groups	*Entrepreneurs (no. of persons)*	*Non-entrepreneurs (no. of persons)*
0	1	15
1	2	10
2	2	4
3	4	1
4	3	1
5	4	1
6	2	0
Average number per person	3.44 groups	0.94 groups

The types of people whom entrepreneurs associate with in their networking activities are more varied than those of non-entrepreneurs, as shown in Table 6.5. For instance, entrepreneurs associate with researchers and scholars, whereas non-entrepreneurs in this survey do not have frequent communication with such groups of people.

After trying to compare pairs of various combinations, three pairs showed a clear difference in variables in their personal traits as shown in the list below. These are the entrepreneurs versus non-entrepreneurs, the networker versus non-networker, and two groups and more versus less than two groups. The full comparison tables of

Table 6.5 Types of networking associates

Networking associates	Entrepreneurs	Non-entrepreneurs
Female entrepreneurs	6	0
Entrepreneurs in the same business	10	1
Business people	23	12
Colleague of previous company	0	0
Alumni	4	4
Researchers/scholars	6	0
Governmental people	3	2
Others	12	11
Total	64 groups	30 groups

each pair based on the F-test are shown in Appendixes 1 to 3 at the end of this chapter.

Entrepreneurs vs. Non-entrepreneur
   I have strong vitality. (Q2)
   I have a strong spirit of independence. (Q13)
   I am thoughtful and creative. (Q26)
   I have religious beliefs. (Q35)
   (I become emotional easily over various subjects and in various situations. (Q7))
   (I am patient and I persevere. (Q17))

Networker vs. Non-networker
   I have strong vitality. (Q2)
   I become emotional easily over various subjects and in various situations. (Q7)
   I have a strong spirit of independence. (Q13)
   (I can observe others objectively. (Q20))

2 groups and more vs. less than 2 groups
   I can endure stress. (Q3)
   I have a strong spirit of independence. (Q13)
   I am patient and I persevere. (Q17)

The structure of personal traits can be determined by factor analysis (Table 6.6). Among the 35 questions, five factors can be extracted from this analysis : 'patronage', 'idealism and dogmatism', 'vitality and independence', 'social skills' and 'creativity'. We emphasize that the third factor, 'vitality', includes characteristics of independence, self-sufficiency, and extrovertism. These may be contradictory.

In examining the differences between factor scores in the five factors which were extracted by factor analysis (Table 6.6), we found 'vitality' was the most important factor that differentiates entrepreneurs from non-entrepreneurs.

From the results of the analysis of variance with various combinations, we obtain the following two findings:

1 The entrepreneurs who have high scores in the 'idealism and dogmatism' factor also have higher scores in the 'creativity' factor.
2 The entrepreneurs who participate in two networking groups or more also have higher scores in the 'creativity' factor.

Table 6.6 Factor analysis of personal traits

Factors	I	II	III	IV	V	Commu
Factor I: Patronage (pct. of var. 20.3 %)						
12 I like taking the role of leader.	0.774	0.068	0.260	0.073	–0.096	0.686
29 I can fully understand other people's emotion.	0.734	0.137	0.114	0.186	0.041	0.607
16 I often speak of myself and my opinion.	0.733	0.222	0.121	–0.064	–0.001	0.605
4 I have good linguistic ability.	0.733	–0.024	–0.161	0.189	0.193	0.636
23 I have a sense of humour.	0.715	–0.059	–0.019	–0.264	–0.126	0.601
25 I am self-confident.	0.622	–0.244	0.341	0.135	0.226	0.632
18 I express myself frankly.	0.595	0.186	–0.118	0.449	0.158	0.629
34 I have artistic sense.	0.526	0.179	0.229	–0.004	0.482	0.594
3 I can endure stress.	0.492	–0.047	0.346	0.333	–0.070	0.480
5 I like listening to others.	0.474	0.037	0.062	–0.012	0.028	0.308
15 I have a strong sense of responsibility.	0.451	–0.080	0.121	0.079	0.130	0.247
19 I am very interested in others.	0.407	0.314	0.080	–0.085	0.287	0.360
Factor II: Idealism and dogmatism (pct. of var. 9.9 %)						
22 I am often dogmatic.	–0.077	0.752	–0.027	–0.129	0.170	0.618
9 I often indulge in my day dreams.	0.167	0.725	0.156	0.142	–0.207	0.640
7 I become emotional easily.	0.187	0.698	0.082	0.046	0.047	0.534
8 I am very emotional.	0.066	0.609	–0.311	0.009	–0.195	0.511
31 I know how I am expected to behave in front of others and do so.	0.299	–0.503	0.227	–0.038	0.003	0.395
35 I have religious belief.	0.210	0.434	0.361	–0.087	0.342	0.488
Factor III: Vitality (pct. of var. 7.5 %)						
2 I have strong vitality.	0.154	–0.237	0.702	–0.054	0.191	0.611
13 I have a strong spirit of independence.	0.435	0.178	0.584	0.227	0.198	0.653

Factors	I	II	III	IV	V	Commu
11 I am bold and like adventures.	0.242	0.374	0.531	0.081	–0.104	0.497
27 I prefer spending time with others.	0.065	0.212	0.550	0.008	–0.093	0.360
17 I am patient and I persevere.	0.317	–0.216	0.509	–0.064	0.464	0.626
6 I have good ability in business operations.	0.415	–0.381	–0.420	0.360	0.189	0.658
1 My physical condition is good.	0.132	–0.071	0.413	0.133	0.143	0.231
10 I am unconcerned and am happy-go-lucky.	–0.056	–0.093	0.274	0.216	–0.237	0.190
14 I am obedient.	–0.056	–0.128	0.274	–0.258	–0.018	0.161
Factor IV: Social skills (pct. of var. 7.2 %)						
28 I believe others.	0.008	0.029	0.162	0.705	–0.290	0.609
24 I acknowledge my faults frankly.	0.274	–0.134	–0,104	0,704	–0.037	0.602
33 I think a sense of economy is very important.	–0.071	0.192	0.107	0.590	0.096	0.411
20 I can observe others relatively objectively.	0.185	–0.041	0.044	0.515	0.273	0.378
30 I understand social rules and observe them.	–0.370	–0.101	0.395	0.471	0.034	0.526
Factor V: Creativity (pct. of var. 6.3 %)						
21 I observe myself critically.	0.017	–0.043	–0.071	0.117	0.803	0.666
26 I am thoughtful and creative.	0.152	0.021	0.184	–0.005	0.771	0.652
32 I prefer theoretical discussions.	0.033	–0.267	–0.046	0.472	0.500	0.547

DISCUSSION

It is found that 'vitality', 'independence', and 'creativity' are key variables to distinguish entrepreneurs from non-entrepreneurs. The key words for networkers including both entrepreneurs and non-entrepreneurs were 'vitality' and 'independence'. Consequently, the most significant word for explaining entrepreneurship from the viewpoint of personal traits is 'creativity'.

Therefore, we should examine further the difference between entrepreneurs and non-entrepreneurs in their networking. The entrepreneurs' manner of networking is quite different from that of the non-entrepreneurs' in terms of the numbers of networking groups and the types of networking members.

It may be possible that networking adds to 'creativity' of entrepreneurs. Of course the networking activity should be more thoroughly studied, in addition to the number of networking groups and the types of people in the networking groups described earlier.

The 'vitality and independence' factor includes the attributes of independence and spending time with others rather than staying alone. Although 'independence' and 'gathering', generally speaking, are contradictory, 'gathering', is thought to be the primary characteristic of networkers and 'gathering' as used here can be understood as 'gathering' of independent people. This type of 'gathering' is typical human networking.

Networking behaviour has two characteristics. One is the opportunity of interaction. The participants share information, experience, values, and so on, and thus stimulate each other. This kind of situation relies on independent people. If the participants were dependent types, communication would be one-way only.

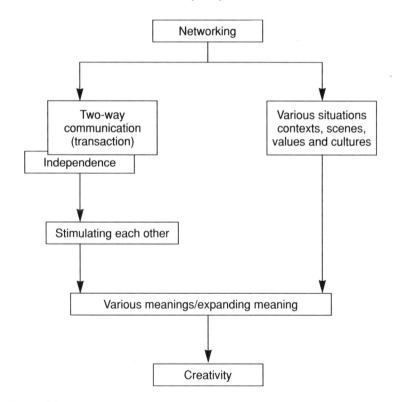

Figure 6.2 Networking and creativity

The other characteristic of human networking is face-to-face communication. Face-to-face communication tends to bring meaningful information, as Nonaka (1988) noted. Furthermore, the field of cognitive science suggests that meaning depends on the situation. In other words, unless one can imagine the situation from the information, that information would be syntactic information which will not be internalized. On the other hand, if one understands the situational context or scene which lies behind the information, the information content becomes more meaningful and contextual. In order to understand the situation, the context or scene behind the information, the abstract and quantitative information is limited (Nonaka 1988). The qualitative information, in which the information sender can explain his experience, situations, context or scene and share them with the information receivers, tends to be meaningful information. This is the reason why face-to-face communication in the networking is important.

Another use of information is its application to new situations. This is a kind of creative activity. In order to obtain more meaningful information and expand the meaning itself, it is important to communicate with people with different experiences, with different knowledge, with different values, and with different cultures. By meeting them and communicating with each other, meaningful information will be the information that has more varying meanings for each member than when it is received by documents or one-way announcements. Thus, we believe that networking as a meaningful information source is effective for 'creativity'.

FURTHER RESEARCH

The following should be considered in order to develop the study of entrepreneurship in Japan:

1 It is necessary to examine whether 'vitality', 'independence', and 'creativity' are common key variables for entrepreneurs to distinguish them from non-entrepreneurs in other countries. It is also necessary to study personal traits which occur in specific countries or cultures.
2 The impact of networking on entrepreneurship should be studied in Japan as well as in other countries in broader terms.
3 Business-founders and business-successors may be different in their networking and personal traits. Although this research was conducted by combining them as one category of entrepreneurs, we expect to find a different pattern between them.

4 The questionnaire of the personal traits should be examined more thoroughly to determine whether it is adequate for comparing entrepreneurship in foreign countries with that in Japan.

APPENDIX

Table 6.7 Mean comparison between entrepreneurs and non-entrepreneurs (two groups or more, and less than two groups)

		Two groups or more (18)		Less than two groups (32)	
		Mean	Std D	Mean	Std D
I.	Number of specialities	1.778	1.555	0.875	1.314 *
II.	Number of hobbies	2.944	1.798	3.438	1.645
III.	Number of networking groups	3.444	1.756	0.938	1.243 **
IV.	Personal traits				
1	My physical vitality.	5.333	1.414	5.281	0.924
2	My condition is good.	5.778	0.808	5.219	0.906 *
3	I can endure stress.	5.056	1.514	4.938	1.045
4	I have good linguistic ability.	4.722	1.487	4.719	1.420
5	I like listening to others.	5.556	0.922	5.406	1.073
6	I have good ability in business operations.	4.889	1.231	5.094	1.146
7	I become emotional easily over various subjects and in various situations.	5.444	1.097	4.843	0.954
8	I am very emotional. (degree)	4.278	1.320	4.496	1.103
9	I often indulge in day-dreams.	4.944	1.349	4.344	1.289
10	I am unconcerned and am happy-go-lucky.	3.556	1.381	3.750	1.136
11	I am bold and like adventures.	4.389	1.501	4.219	1.260
12	I like taking the role of leader.	4.556	1.149	4.469	0.950
13	I have a strong spirit of independence.	5.556	0.922	4.906	0.995 *
14	I am obedient.	4.167	0.857	3.938	1.134
15	I have a strong sense of responsibility.	5.778	0.647	5.500	0.981
16	I often speak of myself and my opinion.	5.278	1.320	5.063	0.948
17	I am patient and I persevere.	5.444	1.149	4.813	1.378 †
18	I express myself frankly.	4.944	1.305	5.094	1.228
19	I am very interested in others.	4.833	0.857	4.938	1.076
20	I can observe others relatively objectively.	5.167	0.707	5.188	0.998
21	I observe myself critically.	4.222	1.353	4.063	0.914
22	I am often dogmatic.	4.167	1.098	4.063	1.162
23	I have a sense of humour.	4.667	1.138	4.938	1.134

	Two groups or more		Less than two groups	
	Mean	Std D	Mean	Std D
24 I acknowledge my faults frankly.	5.333	0.907	5.313	0.780
25 I have self-confidence.	5.278	0.895	4.844	0.954
26 I am thoughtful and creative.	4.944	0.725	4.313	1.230 *
27 I prefer gathering with others to staying alone.	4.833	1.249	4.219	1.431
28 I believe others.	4.889	1.079	4.875	0.793
29 I can fully understand other people's emotions.	5.056	0.998	4.969	0.861
30 I understand social rules and behave naturally based on them.	5.167	0.924	4.938	0.716
31 I know how I am expected to behave in front of others and do so.	4.944	0.938	4.906	0.734
32 I prefer theoretical matter to practical matter.	5.000	1.372	5.000	0.950
33 I think a sense of economy is very important.	5.611	0.778	5.250	0.950
34 I have artistic sense.	4.667	1.940	4.000	1.566
35 I have religious beliefs.	4.444	1.866 **	2.875	1.362

Note: *** < 0.0001, ** < 0.001, * < 0.05, † < 0.1

Table 6.8 Mean comparison between networker and non-networker (two groups or more and less than two groups)

		Two groups or more (32)		Less than two groups (17)	
		Mean	Std D	Mean	Std D
I.	Number of specialities	1.406	1.500	0.882	1.364
II.	Number of hobbies	3.488	1.741	3.000	1.581
III.	Number of networking groups	1.250	0.984	0.235	0.664 ***
IV.	Personal traits				
1	My physical vitality.	5.406	1.160	5.117	1.054
2	My condition is good.	5.658	0.627	5.059	0.899 *
3	I can endure stress.	5.156	1.370	4.706	0.849
4	I have good linguistic ability.	4.844	1.417	4.588	1.460
5	I like listening to others.	5.656	0.937	5.235	0.970
6	I have good ability in business operations and in various situations.	4.875	1.238	5.294	1.047
7	I become emotional easily over various subjects	5.281	1.085	4.706	0.849 *
8	I am very emotional. (degree)	4.313	1.230	4.412	1.121
9	I often indulge in day-dreams.	4.588	1.281	4.412	1.417

	Two groups or more (32)		Less than two groups (17)	
	Mean	Std D	Mean	Std D
10 I am unconcerned and am happy-go-lucky.	3.656	1.234	3.824	1.185
11 I am bold and like adventures.	4.500	1.344	3.882	1.317
12 I like taking the role of leader.	4.594	1.043	4.353	0.998
13 I have a strong spirit of independence.	5.375	1.100	4.765	0.664 *
14 I am obedient.	4.084	0.893	3.824	1.286
15 I have a strong sense of responsibility.	5.500	0.950	5.765	0.752
16 I often speak of myself and my opinion.	5.219	1.070	5.000	1.173
17 I am patient and I persevere.	5.225	1.244	4.588	1.417
18 I express myself frankly.	5.094	1.353	4.059	0.966
19 I am very interested in others.	5.063	0.914	4.588	1.121
20 I can observe others relatively objectively.	5.375	0.783	4.882	0.993 †
21 I observe myself critically.	4.125	1.238	4.118	0.781
22 I am often dogmatic.	4.063	1.105	4.294	1.105
23 I have a sense of humour.	4.719	1.170	5.059	1.086
24 I acknowledge my faults frankly.	5.375	0.907	5.235	0.664
25 I have self-confidence.	5.000	0.984	5.000	0.935
26 I am thoughtful and creative.	4.625	1.008	4.353	1.320
27 I prefer gathering with others to staying alone.	4.531	1.270	4.353	1.618
28 I believe others.	4.938	0.914	4.882	0.781
29 I can fully understand other people's emotions.	5.031	0.967	5.000	0.791
30 I understand social rules and behave naturally based on them.	5.094	0.856	4.882	0.687
31 I know how I am expected to behave in front of others and do so.	4.875	0.871	5.000	0.707
32 I prefer theoretical matter to practical matter.	4.966	1.257	5.000	0.791
33 I think a sense of economy is very important.	5.500	0.984	5.177	0.728
34 I have artistic sense.	4.531	1.704	3.765	1.715
35 I have religious beliefs.	3.625	1.718	3.059	1.784

Note: *** < 0.0001, ** < 0.001, * < 0.05, † < 0.1

Table 6.9 Mean Comparison Between Two Groups or More
and Less Than Two Groups in Networking

		Two groups or more (22)		Less than two groups (28)	
		Mean	Std D	Mean	Std D
I.	Number of specialities	1.364	1.529	1.071	1.412
II.	Number of hobbies	3.364	1.891	3.179	1.565
III.	Number of networking groups				
IV.	Personal traits				
1	My physical vitality.	5.409	0.959	5.214	1.228
2	My condition is good.	5.636	0.727	5.250	1.005
3	I can endure stress.	4.455	1.299	4.607	1.031 *
4	I have good linguistic ability.	4.773	1.343	4.679	1.517
5	I like listening to others.	5.682	0.945	5.286	1.049
6	I have good ability in business operations.	4.046	1.214	5.000	1.155
7	I become emotional easily over various subjects and in various situations.	5.227	1.055	4.929	1.016
8	I am very emotional. (degree)	4.318	1.323	4.393	1.066
9	I often indulge in day dreams.	4.909	1.306	4.286	1.301
10	I am unconcerned and am happy-go-lucky.	3.682	1.323	3.679	1.156
11	I am bold and like adventures.	4.500	1.336	4.107	1.343
12	I like taking the role of leader.	4.882	1.171	4.357	0.870
13	I have a strong spirit of independence.	5.300	1.012	4.857	0.932 *
14	I am obedient.	4.091	0.888	3.864	1.170
15	I have a strong sense of responsibility.	5.818	0.733	5.429	0.959
16	I often speak of myself and my opinion.	5.364	1.036	5.984	1.136
17	I am patient and I persevere.	5.591	0.959	4.607	1.423 **
18	I express myself frankly.	5.318	1.249	4.821	1.219
19	I am very interested in others.	5.955	0.999	4.857	1.008
20	I can observe others relatively objectively.	5.364	0.648	5.036	0.922
21	I observe myself critically.	4.182	1.259	4.071	0.940
22	I am often dogmatic.	4.000	1.024	4.177	1.219
23	I have a sense of humour.	4.682	1.211	4.964	1.071
24	I acknowledge my faults frankly.	5.500	0.913	5.179	0.723
25	I have self-confidence.	5.227	0.869	4.821	0.983
26	I am thoughtful and creative.	4.773	1.020	4.357	1.162
27	I prefer gathering with others to staying alone.	4.500	1.263	4.393	1.499
28	I believe others.	4.955	0.999	4.821	0.819

	Two groups or more (22)		Less than two groups (28)	
	Mean	Std D	Mean	Std D
29 I can fully understand other people's emotions.	5.182	1.053	4.857	0.756
30 I understand social rules and behave naturally based on them.	5.136	0.941	4.929	0.663
31 I know how I am expected to behave in front of others and do so.	5.046	0.785	4.821	0.819
32 I prefer theoretical matter to practical matter.	5.273	1.241	4.786	0.957
33 I think a sense of economy is very important.	5.591	1.008	5.214	0.787
34 I have artistic sense.	5.000	1.690	3.643	1.521 **
35 I have religious beliefs.	4.046	1.838	2.964	1.503 *

Note: *** < 0.0001, ** < 0.001, * < 0.05

REFERENCES

Johnson-Laird, P.N. (1988) *The Computer and the Mind: An Introduction to Cognitive Science*, London: Willam Collins Sons & Co., Ltd.

Mueller, R.K. (1986) *Corporate Networking – Building Channels for Information and Influence*, New York: Macmillan.

Nonaka, Ikujiro (1988) 'Creating Organizational Order Out of Chaos: Self-Renewal in Japanese Firms', *California Management Review*, Spring, 57–73.

Penrose, E. (1959) *The Theory of the Growth of the Firm*, Oxford: Blackwell.

Schumpeter, J. A. (1934, 1961) *The Theory of Economic Development*, London: Oxford University Press.

Yoshimori, Masaru (1989) (in Japan) *A Study of Decreasing Entrepreneurship*, Tokyo: ToyoKeizai-sinposha.

7 Entrepreneurial networks and business performance

A panel study of small and medium-sized firms in the research triangle[1]

Pat Ray Reese and Howard E. Aldrich

New businesses are founded when motivated entrepreneurs gain access to resources and find niches in opportunity structures. Networking allows founding entrepreneurs to enlarge their span of action, save time, and gain access to resources and opportunities otherwise unavailable. But are networks also important in the ongoing operations of a business? Perhaps the demands of running a business in modern capitalist societies are so high that differences in networking generate little advantage for an owner, net of skill, experience, and resources controlled. Few observers are likely to accept such a claim, and we certainly would seem like the last investigators to put forward such an argument!

None the less, almost all claims about the importance of networking rest on inferences made from cross-sectional data, obtained from active and potential entrepreneurs at only one point in time (Aldrich 1991). Cross-sectional studies have allowed us to paint a fairly complete picture of the basic structure of entrepreneurs' personal networks and to document the amount of time and effort entrepreneurs put into expanding their circle of strong and weak ties to others. By comparing entrepreneurs who are at different points in their careers and at different points in the life cycle of their businesses, investigators have been able to make pseudo-dynamic analyses of networking from cross-sectional studies. Some interesting and provocative arguments have been drawn from such analyses, but they are no substitute for actual longitudinal studies of entrepreneurs in action.

We set out, in 1990, to design a study that would allow us to test hypotheses about business networking with data collected over time on the same owners and their businesses.

BUSINESS NETWORKS

The starting point for studying entrepreneurship through social networks is a relationship or transaction between two people. A personal network, or role set, consists of all those persons with whom an entrepreneur has direct relations. For example, we could think of partners, suppliers, customers, bankers, and family members as part of an entrepreneur's personal network. Typically, these are persons whom entrepreneurs meet on a face-to-face basis and from whom they obtain services, advice, and moral support. Personal networks are constructed from the viewpoint of a particular individual, but the concept of a 'social network' is much broader – it can include the local community, a region, or an industry. It may even span national boundaries.

This way of thinking about networks alerts us to the way personal networks interconnect, overlap, or stand in isolation from one another. People might enjoy extensive connections within a limited region of a total network, but lack the indispensable relation needed to discover essential information in another region. Information and resources can be thought of as mapping onto networks, and networks can be thought of as the thread or channel along which information and resources flow.

The simplest kind of personal network includes direct ties linking people with persons with whom they have direct contact. When we use the term 'networking' as a verb to describe behaviour, we are usually thinking of special kinds of relations within personal networks – a network built on *strong ties*, relations entrepreneurs can 'count on.' By contrast, *weak ties* are superficial or casual, and people typically have little emotional investment in them (Granovetter 1973). The strength of ties depends on the level, frequency, and reciprocity of relations between persons, and ties can vary from simple, one-purpose relations to multiplex, all-purpose relations.

Networking is often mentioned because people feel the need to distinguish networking behaviour from ordinary business behaviour. Picture behaviour at two extremes: first, one-of-a-kind, short-term, non-sustaining transactions between people who never expect to see each other again (e.g., buying a magazine at a corner news-stand in Lyon), and second, contact between two persons who expect to see each other frequently, interact meaningfully, and who are in a relation for the long term (e.g., taking a plant manager in Paris to lunch to discuss specifications for a new type of equipment you would like her to consider buying).

The first behaviour is a straightforward pragmatic transaction between people whose personal characteristics are rarely important; in many circumstances, it can be an efficient way of doing business. However, there are three problems associated with these short-term, market-mediated transactions: competition, uncertainty, and exit. First, *competition* is always a possibility. In short-term, non-sustaining relationships, competitive behaviour makes perfect sense. Second, this problem is exacerbated under conditions of *uncertainty*, quite akin to the prisoner's dilemma. It may be impossible to predict all the conditions under which a contract will have to be carried out, or to know precisely all the specifications a piece of equipment will have to meet. Third, when problems crop up, the other party may simply *exit*. Whereas you might like to collaborate, the other party may simply walk out, leaving you in the lurch.

'Networking', by contrast, refers to the expectation that both parties are investing in a long-term relationship. Consider three benefits that follow from creating a social context in which people expect to deal with each other frequently over an extended period: trust, predictability, and voice. First, regardless of what popular fiction says about business, *trust* – assured reliance on the character or truthfulness of someone – is an important component of business dealings. Trust is enhanced – purely through self-interest – under conditions when people feel there is a good chance of dealing with each other again. Self-interest is involved because a reputation for reliability and keeping one's word raises the probability that other people will continue to deal with you.

Second, *predictability* is increased when long-term relations are established. Predictability, to some extent, depends on trust. If trust exists in a relationship, then behaviour tends to be predictable. The inherent uncertainty in a situation is not reduced. However, based on that trust, what *is* reduced is the uncertainty about whether the other party will do something to assist you when things do not go according to plan. Uncertainty is also reduced when your network contacts tell you where to go for assistance and provide information or resources you might not otherwise obtain.

Third, people are more likely to use *voice* rather than exit in response to problems in long-term relations. *Voice* means making one's complaints known and negotiating over them, rather than sneaking silently away – an example of good problem-solving techniques.

Thus, 'networking' with one's direct ties to turn them into strong ties is first and foremost a way of overcoming the liabilities inherent in purely market-like transactions with other people. *'Networking' involves expanding one's circle of trust.* In network terms, relations of trust are strong ties, as opposed to casual acquaintances, who are weak ties.

Direct ties, especially strong ones, are significant not only for the persons directly linked to an entrepreneur, but also for the indirect access they provide to people beyond an entrepreneur's immediate contacts. Through indirect ties, entrepreneurs can leverage their direct connections by judicious use of contacts who have access to others. In our project, we set out to investigate the extent to which entrepreneurs who had more extensive networks, and who spent more time on networking, gained an advantage over others.

We focus only on entrepreneurs who were actually running a business when we first interviewed them, rather than on the start-up process itself. Our analysis focuses on the extent to which networking activity at time one is associated with various measures of business performance at time two.

STUDY DESIGN

We wanted to study individuals in the early stages of organizational formation, as well as established organizations with a transaction history, and so in an exploratory phase of our project we located voluntary and non-profit organizations of interest to entrepreneurs in the Research Triangle area of North Carolina, in the United States. This area includes Raleigh, Durham, Cary, and Chapel Hill, and is well known because of the more than 40 large firms and research institutes located in the Research Triangle Park, including IBM, Northern Telecom, Glaxo, BASF, the Environmental Protection Agency, Research Triangle Institute, and the SAS Institute. Organizations differed in gender composition, purpose, and membership interests, but they all focused on entrepreneurial or business activity: (1) the Council for Entrepreneurial Development (CED), based in Durham, included both entrepreneurs and service providers; (2) six networking organizations, all of which included both entrepreneurs and employees; (3) participants at Wake Tech Small Business Center classes, including entrepreneurs in very early stages of business start-up; and (4) the National Association of Women Business Owners (NAWBO), which is restricted to women entrepreneurs. We added another sub-sample, randomly selected from business start-ups, to use as a reference. This sample was selected from new businesses that filed registration forms in Wake County, which includes Raleigh.

We collected the initial (Time One) data in two phases. Phase I was a short questionnaire, which could be completed in about five minutes; Phase II involved in-depth, 30–45 minute telephone interviews that included structured and open-ended questions. We collected Time One questionnaires and conducted interviews during a nine-month period in 1990 and 1991.

Combining all sub-samples, we distributed 659 questionnaires and received 444 in a usable format, for an average response rate of 67 per cent, as shown in Table 7.1. Response rates across the sub-samples ranged from 41 per cent to 78 per cent. We conducted a total of 353 telephone interviews, yielding completed interviews for 54 per cent of those who received questionnaires and 80 per cent of those who returned a questionnaire.

Our response rates compare favourably with other efforts to study entrepreneurs. Birley, Cromie, and Myers (1990), using records similar to those we used in the business sample, achieved a 24 per cent response rate; Cooper and Dunkelberg (1987) reported a 29 per cent return; Aldrich, Rosen, and Woodward (1987) achieved less than 41 per cent return in a study of CED members; and Kalleberg (1986), using phone interviews which traditionally have a higher response rate than questionnaires, reported response rates between 55 per cent and 68 per cent, although he excluded non-working phone numbers in his calculation, whereas our rates include such cases as non-responses. Our response rates, and tests of non-response bias (Reese 1992), increase our confidence in our findings.

In June and July of 1992, we contacted respondents who had returned questionnaires two years earlier. Of the 444 returned questionnaires, we removed 13 cases from the Time Two sample for a variety of reasons: six respondents had moved between the first and second phase of the Time One data collection and could not be tracked two years later, four questionnaires contained large amounts of missing data, and two people had explicitly notified us that they did not want to participate in any future studies. We mailed questionnaires to the remaining sample of 431.

We used a two-phase approach much like our Time One contact: we began with a short questionnaire and conducted short follow-up telephone interviews. We repeated several of our networking measures: we asked about the entrepreneur's business, whether they had made specific changes in their business, their use of resources, information about their business strategy and environment, their reasons for starting their business, and their business performance, as well as information on new businesses that entrepreneurs had begun in the two years since our initial contact.

Table 7.1 Sample size and response rates

Sample source	Time 1				Time 2		
	Questionnaire		Follow-Up phone interviews	Question-naire	Questionnaire and phone interview		
	Number distributed	Per cent returned	Per cent of return completing interview	Number mailed	Fully completed	Partially completed	Combined completion
CED members	339	76%	82%	250	53%	37%	90%
Networking organization members	67	78%	83%	49	43%	43%	86%
Wake Tech students	78	68%	79%	52	25%	58%	83%
Business sample	150	41%	64%	61	39%	45%	84%
NAWBO sample	25	76%	84%	19	63%	32%	95%
Total per cent	–	67%	80%	–	64%	24%	88%
Total number	659	444*	353	431*	203	177	380

Note: *The difference between the 444 questionnaires returned at Time 1 and the 431 respondents followed up at Time 2 is due to people who refused to participate further at the end of Time 1 or who were lost to the sample during interviewing for Time 1 for other reasons.

We had a very good response from our second round of contacts, as shown in the four right-hand columns of Table 7.1. Of the 431 mailed questionnaires, we received questionnaires from 246 entrepreneurs and completed a short follow-up interview with 175 of them. We collected full information on an additional 28 respondents by asking the questionnaire and interview questions during a long telephone interview. We collected information on 106 other cases during a short, abbreviated telephone interview. Thus, we have extensive data on 64 per cent of the sample and complete or partial information on 88 per cent of the Time One participants.

Because few researchers have attempted this kind of panel study of entrepreneurs, we have few comparisons for our response rates. Kalleberg and Leicht (1991), in the second wave of their panel study of small businesses in Indiana, completed interviews with 70 per cent of their original businesses. They obtained information that 34 companies were out of business, giving them information about 78 per cent of their original sample. For our study, collecting information on 88 per cent of the sample respondents after a two-year period of time gives us increased confidence in our results.

In this paper we restrict our data analysis to those entrepreneurs who were business owners at our initial contact in 1990. We are concerned about the continuance of their business and their business's performance, and whether entrepreneurs' networking characteristics are associated with their businesses' performance.

Measurement of independent variables

Our independent variables in this paper are various measures of networking activity, as reported by our respondents at the time of the first interview.

Network activity

Patterning our research after previous work (Aldrich, Rosen, and Woodward 1987), we measured networking efforts by asking respondents to estimate their time spent developing and maintaining business contacts. The actual wording of the questions was: 'In a typical week, how many hours do you spend: developing contacts (meeting new people) with whom you can discuss business matters?; maintaining contacts (talking to people you already know) about business matters?' In our initial interview, business owners estimated an average of 5.7 hours (s.d. of 8.8) spent *developing* business contacts in a typical week. When contacted two years later, the same respondents reported significantly fewer hours developing contacts, estimating an average of 4.8 hours (s.d. of 6.1). In 1990 business owners estimated they spent an average of 7.5 hours (s.d. of 8.0) *maintaining* business contacts in a typical week whereas in 1992, estimates by these same respondents had increased, although not significantly, to 9.5 hours per week (s.d. 10).

Efforts to develop and maintain business contacts yield a business network, a group of people with whom entrepreneurs discuss business matters. We measured network size by having respondents estimate the number of people they talk to about business matters in a month. The actual question was: 'From time to time, most people discuss important business matters or business plans with other people. Looking back over the past month: Please estimate the number of people with whom you have discussed aspects of starting a new business or operating your current business.' In our first interview, business owners estimated an average network size of 8.8 (s.d. of 18.9). In their second interview, they estimated 10.3 (s.d. 19.4) people – a modest increase but one that did not reach statistical significance.

We broke the networking variables into thirds to form high, medium and low values of network size, and hours spent developing and maintaining business networks. Network size values are low (0–2.9), medium (3–6.9) and high (7 or more). Hours developing business network values are low (0–1.4), medium (1.5–3.9) and high (4 or more). Hours maintaining business network values are low (0–2.9), medium (3–7.9) and high (8 or more). We chose cut-off values which approximately divided the sorted variable into thirds. We also examined age, education, marital status, industry, and sample source, as shown in Table 7.2.

RESULTS

Our analysis focuses on two general outcomes: business survival and business performance. We defined business survival as the continuation of the same business under the same owner from Time One until Time Two. If the business was sold to another owner, for whatever reason, we defined that event as the non-survival of the original business.

Business survival

One of the first things we wanted to know was: How many businesses survived? Even without economic recession, about 10 per cent of all

Table 7.2 1990 business owners in 1992

	Survival % (N)	Increased revenues % (N)	Financial performance				Performance compared to others			
			Profit %	Break even %	Loss %	(N)	Better %	Same %	Worse %	(N)
All	79 (281)	82 (200)	55	28	17	(201)	47	45	8	(177)
Sex										
Men	77 (206)	83 (142)	55	25	20	(143)	49	43	8	(129)
Women	86 (74)	79 (58)	55	36	9	(58)	42	50	8	(48)
	p=.08									
Marital Status										
Single	83 (42)	79 (38)	50	29	21	(38)	50	41	9	(32)
Married	78 (224)	83 (162)	56	28	16	(163)	46	46	8	(145)
Other	92 (13)									
Education										
Less than college degree	78 (58)	70 (43)	35	49	16	(43)	40	47	13	(38)
College degree	79 (121)	87 (89)	57	26	17	(89)	53	43	5	(80)
Masters/law degree	76 (71)	86 (49)	67	16	16	(49)	48	50	2	(42)
PhD/MD	90 (29)	79 (19)	60	20	20	(20)	35	41	24	(17)
Group										
Business sample	82 (38)	73 (22)	39	48	13	(23)	30	65	5	(20)
CED	80 (181)	82 (135)	59	22	19	(135)	53	38	9	(118)
NAWBO	82 (17)	67 (12)	58	25	17	(12)	30	70	0	(10)
Networking org.	82 (28)	96 (22)	59	36	5	(22)	48	48	5	(21)
Wake Tech students	59 (17)	89 (9)	22	56	22	(9)	13	63	25	(8)
Industry										
Construction	71 (14)	71 (7)	43	43	14	(7)	43	43	14	(7)

Finance, ins. & real estate	85 (26)	80 (20)	45	35	20	32 (20)	68	0	(19)
Manufacturing	74 (35)	96 (23)	57	22	22	65 (23)	35	0	(20)
Retail	70 (23)	71 (14)	21	57	21	42 (14)	50	8	(12)
Service	82 (163)	82 (61)	59	26	15	47 (123)	44	9	(107)
Other	74 (19)	79 (14)	71	7	21	50 (14)	33	17	(12)
Business age (years)									
0–.9	65 (37)	95 (21)	43	29	29	50 (21)	40	10	(20)
1–1.9	76 (50)	82 (34)	40	31	29	32 (35)	50	18	(28)
2–2.9	69 (36)	88 (25)	56	32	12	48 (25)	48	4	(21)
3–3.9	84 (38)	83 (29)	76	24	0	44 (29)	48	8	(25)
4–9.9	87 (84)	73 (63)	56	29	16	49 (63)	46	5	(57)
10+	86 (36)	86 (28)	61	21	18	58 (28)	38	4	(26)
	p=.04								
Network size in 1990									
Low (0–2.9)	79 (119)	80 (80)	51	36	14	43 (81)	51	6	(72)
Medium (3–6.9)	81 (78)	80 (60)	60	20	20	43 (60)	51	6	(51)
High (7 or more)	78 (86)	87 (60)	57	25	18	56 (60)	31	13	(54)
Hrs/wk developing business networks									
Low (0–1.49)	78 (88)	78 (59)	54	27	19	44 (59)	44	12	(48)
Medium (1.5–3.9)	79 (77)	88 (56)	67	26	7	47 (57)	45	8	(53)
High (4 or more)	80 (118)	81 (85)	48	29	22	49 (85)	46	5	(76)
Hrs/wk maintaining business networks									
Low (0–2.9)	74 (84)	84 (50)	60	34	6	37 (50)	58	5	(43)
Medium (3–7.9)	78 (102)	79 (76)	56	23	21	52 (77)	37	10	(67)
High (8 or more)	85 (97)	84 (74)	51	28	20	48 (74)	45	8	(67)

Note: Unless otherwise noted, none of the differences between subgroups in the above panels attained statistical significance at the 0.10 level

businesses are disbanded each year. Some fail with losses to creditors – the classic bankruptcy situation – but most are shut down because of low profitability, the owner's retirement, a chance to take a better opportunity elsewhere, and so on. When we contacted the entrepreneurs in our second wave of data collection, about two years after the first interview, we found that slightly over three-fourths (79 per cent) of those running a business at our first contact were still running the same business, as shown in Table 7.2. This is about what we expected, based on other studies. Kalleberg and Leicht (1991), for example, found that about 84 per cent of their sample was still in business after two years.

We checked to see whether our result for business survival might be inflated because of non-response bias in our second wave of data collection. Because we were concerned that our non-respondents might be disproportionately those whose businesses had failed, thus inflating business success, we calculated the business success rate as if all non-responses were business disbandings. When all non-responses are counted as disbandings, the rate of business success is reduced to 73 per cent. Thus, we can say with some confidence that between 73 per cent and 79 per cent of the businesses survived. Taking the economic recession into account, the entrepreneurs in our study did fairly well over the interval between interviews, in part because the Research Triangle was less harshly affected than other areas.

As a further sign of entrepreneurial health, we found that 15 per cent of business owners with continuing businesses had started another business, and 23 per cent of those with non-continuing businesses had started another business. Having so many entrepreneurs starting additional businesses in a two-year period of time reminds us of the importance of looking at entrepreneurial careers rather than focusing only on one entrepreneurial event. Our findings also highlight the importance of distinguishing between a business disbanding and a business failure. Some of the entrepreneurs shut down businesses they felt were under-performing and started up new ones, whereas others not only dissolved their businesses but also moved out of the area. In this paper, we have been conservative in labelling all non-surviving businesses as 'disbandings', rather than failures.

How did women fare? Because women in general have higher rates of business dissolutions than men (Small Business Administration 1986; Brush 1992) and women frequently report difficulties in obtaining business financing (Butner and Rosen 1988), we expected to find fewer women business owners with surviving businesses. Instead, we found that woman were slightly more likely than men to have their business continue, although the difference was not statistically significant: 86 per cent of women business owners were running the same business at our second contact compared to 77 per cent of men business owners. We found that women were less likely to have started an additional business (9 per cent) than their male counterparts (18 per cent). The women in our sample tended to be beginning their entrepreneurial careers, whereas more of the men had previously owned businesses.

Our results for women business owners in the Research Triangle match those of Kalleberg and Leicht (1991). They also found that there was no statistically significant difference between business closing rates for men and women, even before controls were introduced for differences in work experience and involvement in other businesses.

We also explored the effects of marital status, age, educational level, industry and sample group on business survival, as shown in Table 7.2. We found that single business owners were slightly more likely to have surviving businesses, although the difference is not significant: 83 per cent of single business owners compared to 78 per cent of married business owners. We checked to see if this might be due to age differences between married and single entrepreneurs, and found no association between owners' ages and business survival rates. We also checked to see if marital status might be measuring a level of commitment to the business. We found that business owners with surviving business reported devoting more time to the business (54.8 hours per week) compared to those whose business had been disbanded (41.6 hours per week). When we compared the amount of time that single and married business owners devoted to the business, we found no differences.

Educational level had little effect on whether a business survived, although Ph.D.s and M.D.s seemed to have higher rates of survival, a difference that may be due to industries which attract those with different educational levels. We found the lowest rates of business survival for retail (70 per cent) and construction (71 per cent) businesses and the highest rates for finance, insurance and real estate businesses (85 per cent) and service businesses (82 per cent). Industries which have higher educational requirements for business owners fared better than those with lower educational requirements, but until we conduct further analyses, we cannot assess the relative importance of industry effects versus educational levels.

We also compared the rates of business survival for each of the sub-samples. We found almost identical rates for all the sub-samples, except the Wake Tech students, who had a dramatically lower rate of survival. Because Wake Tech students tended to be the least experienced and in the earliest stages of business ownership, it is likely that their different outcome reflects these characteristics, rather than some aspect of their training or group membership.

Finally, we examined the association between business age and survival, because research has shown strong evidence for a liability of newness in organizational survival. Our results show a liability of newness for young businesses, as the survival rate of businesses under one year old was lower than for subsequent ages. The survival rate increased from 65 per cent to 76 per cent for one- to two-year-old businesses, dropped at 2 to 2.9 years, and then increased through the remaining age categories. Almost 9 in 10 businesses over ten years old survived, compared to only about 2 in 3 businesses under one year old. As shown in the other columns of Table 7.2, the association between business age and survival is not a simple function of economic performance, as younger businesses were more likely to report revenue increases than older ones, but also more likely to report a loss.

Networking and survival

In our phone interviews, business people told us that networking is essential to survival, but preliminary results do not support their views. As shown in the last three panels of Table 7.2, none of our three measures of network size or activity are significantly related to business survival.

We divided respondents into three groups: those having low, medium, and high rates of reported network activity. We found that those with higher rates of network activity were not more likely to have surviving businesses, and all the differences we found were minor. For network size, the difference between the 'low' and the 'high' categories was only 79 per cent versus 78 per cent. For hours spent developing business networks, the difference between 'low' and 'high' was only 78 per cent versus 80 per cent. Finally, the difference between business owners who invested the most time in maintaining their business networks versus those who had invested the least was the largest we found, but it was still not statistically significant: 85 per cent compared to 74 per cent.

Although our results are tantalizing in their suggestion of a possible association between network activity and business survival, a conservative reading requires that we accept the null hypothesis that, over the two-year period we studied, business survival was simply not dependent on an entrepreneur's network size or direct effort. Perhaps 'survival' is too crude a measure of networking's impact; perhaps so many other factors affect business survival that, in the short run, networking's impact is masked by more immediate economic considerations.

If so, then an examination of the performance of only those businesses that survived through our second interview might reveal differences within this group that support our initial expectation that networking activities give an entrepreneur an advantage.

Networking and financial outcomes

Questions about increased revenues, financial performance, and economic performance compared to other businesses are only relevant to the survivors in our sample, and so the rest of the columns in Table 7.2 refer only to them. We asked business owners with continuing business if their business's revenues had increased between 1990 and 1992. The majority (82 per cent) told us that revenues had increased. We also asked them to describe the financial performance of their business for the past six months before the interview: 55 per cent reported they had made a profit, 28 per cent reported they had broken even, and 17 per cent reported a loss. Finally, we asked owners to compare their business to others like theirs in the area, and to assess whether they were doing better, the same, or worse than the rest: after excluding the 24 owners who did not know how they stood with respect to competitors, we found that 47 per cent thought they were doing better, 45 per cent the same, and only 8 per cent worse.

None of our three network measures showed a statistically significant association with a reported increase in revenues since the last interview. Similarly, none of the network measures was systematically related to changes in financial performance, although for two of three measures, businesses in the middle of the distribution were the most profitable. It is possible that entrepreneurs who spend too much time on networking do as poorly as those who spend too little time on networking. As in so many other things in life, the golden mean may lie somewhere in the middle. We will explore this relationship further in subsequent analyses. Finally, our three network measures did not significantly affect how owners compared their businesses' performance to others in their area, although for all three network measures, owners at the 'low' end were the least optimistic.

Having found that neither survival nor general economic performance was significantly related to our three global measures of networking activity, we were understandably disappointed. Perhaps there were just many other factors affecting these businesses' fates and confounding the real effects of networking. Or, perhaps the global measures were just too crude to capture the effects we sought. Thus, we turned to one last analytic strategy: an assessment of the extent to which particular personal network connections, linked to specific business resources, had affected business performance.

Resource pathways

During our first interviews with respondents, we asked them a series of questions about people they could contact if they needed a particular type of help. We asked 'do you know someone you could go to for: (1) legal assistance in business matters; (2) financial or accounting assistance (such as taxes, records, capital flow); (3) assistance in obtaining business loans or investors; and (4) help from someone who has several years of experience in your line of business?' Information was recorded separately for each type of assistance. We also asked if they had contacted that person within the past year. Then, at our second interview, at Time Two, we asked if they had sought such assistance during the past year.

In Table 7.3, we show the association between the extent to which a resource pathway existed at the time of the first interview and actual use of the resource in the intervening period prior to Time Two. We measured resource pathways using a three-category breakdown: (1) a respondent did not know anyone who could provide this (legal, financial, etc.) source; (2) a respondent knew someone but had not asked them for advice or assistance in the past year; and (3) a respondent knew someone and had asked them for advice or assistance within the past year.

Almost everyone knew someone they could ask for legal, financial, or accounting advice, and most also knew someone they could turn to for help with a loan or advice from an experienced business owner. As can be seen from the number of respondents at each of our three levels of knowledge, given in parentheses in Table 7.3, most people had also asked for advice in each of these realms. For example, of the 223 people interviewed at Time One, 15 did not know anyone who could provide legal advice, 31 knew someone who could provide legal advice but had not asked them, and 177 both knew someone who could provide legal advice and had asked them for such advice. Thus,

Table 7.3 Resource pathways, business disbanding, and resource use

Time 1: Extent to which resource Pathway existed	Legal advice		Financial or Accounting advice		Help with a loan		Contact with experienced owner	
	Business survived	Resource used Time 2	Business survived	Resource used Time 2	Business survived	Resource used Time 2	Business survived	Resource used Time 2
R did not know anyone who could provide this source	73%(15)	50%(14)	70%(10)	50%(8)	77%(44)	36%(36)	88%(33)	67%(27)
R knew someone *but* had not asked them for advice or assistance	84%(31)	73%(22)	82%(22)	75%(16)	83%(41)	36%(28)	86%(7)	83%(6)
R knew someone *and* had asked them for advice or assistance	78%(177)	61%(140)	80%(191)	77%(154)	79%(137)	48%(113)	77%(178)	72%(138)
	78%(223)	62%(176)	80%(223)	76%(178)	79%(222)	44%(177)	79%(218)	71%(171)

Note: None of the differences within a column are statistically significant

a picture emerges of a group of entrepreneurs who were quite active during the period when we first interviewed them.

Business survival was not significantly affected by the extent to which respondents had access to any of these four resource pathways, as the per cent surviving across the three levels of access is about the same. Similarly, whether a respondent actually had sought advice or assistance in one of these areas over the year prior to our last interview is also not significantly associated with how active they had been at Time One with regard to that pathway.

What are we to make of these results? Most entrepreneurs knew someone who has the information or experience they needed, in the four areas we examined in Table 7.3, and most had actively sought such advice within the past year, both at Time One and Time Two. Their propensity to seek such advice is apparently not affected by whether they knew someone previously or whether they had actually used such advice a few years ago. We will explore this issue further in subsequent papers, but for the moment, it seems that people are not seriously constrained in their advice or information seeking behaviour by social inertia. Networking, in this sense, may be triggered more by immediate circumstances – needing legal advice, needing more capital – than by patterns of relationships laid down years before.

A CAVEAT: VOLATILITY IN BUSINESS GROWTH AND DECLINE

As we mulled over our results, especially our inability to find any significant impact of networking activity on survival or performance over our study period, we thought again about the situation of the businesses in our sample. About one-third were two years old or less at the time of the first interview, and almost 58 per cent were less than four years old. Thus, it is possible that the tremendous stress and turmoil associated with the early years of business start-up and growth has muddied the waters and interfered with our ability to gain a clear picture of networking's importance.

We looked at changes in the number of full-time employees and in the number of part-time employees to gain some idea of how volatile this population had been in the years we were following it. Obviously, this means we had to restrict our focus to those business owners who have continuing businesses at our second contact.

Our sampled businesses had added an average of 3.1 full-time employees and an average of 1.4 part-time employees. However, the standard deviations around these numbers were very large, as we found considerable variation in business owner's experiences with full-time employees, ranging from a loss of 50 to an increase of 297 employees (although 72 per cent have a range between –2 and +2), and also considerable variation in changes in part-time employees, ranging from a loss of 30 to a gain of 200 people (although 85 per cent have a range between –2 and +2). Only two cases added more than 100 employees: a business that manufactures women's apparel added 297 full-time employees and a restaurant chain added 200 part-time employees.

Correlations between number of employees at Time One and Time Two were strong but not perfect. The number of full-time employees at Time One was correlated 0.68 with the number of full-time employees at Time Two, and part-time employment was correlated 0.86 between the two periods. Taking the logarithm of numbers of employees raised the correlation even further for full-time employees, 0.89, but lowered it for part-time employees, 0.66.

Some swings in numbers employed were extremely striking. There were six businesses that employed at least 25 workers full time in 1990–1 which had essentially collapsed by the summer of 1992. Of the six, four were out of business by the time of our second interview. One business had dropped from 43 to 4 employees, and the other had fallen from 32 to 5 employees. At the other extreme, there were nine businesses that had grown to 25 or more employees at Time Two that started with less than 25 employees at Time One. Five of these firms were less than five years old in 1990. Consider these changes: from 31 to 120, 35 to 85, 3 to 300, 20 to 40, and 34 to 51.

Part-time employees also showed some volatility. Of the six firms with more than 25 part-time employees in 1990–1, two had increased and two had decreased significantly: from 100 to 300, from 150 to 200, from 25 to 0, and from 70 to 40. The other two were fairly stable. Three businesses grew from less than 25 to more than 25 part-timers over our study period: from 1 to 68, from 6 to 25, and from 12 to 30.

With such turbulence in this set of firms, as businesses encounter disaster or good fortune in a few years, perhaps our methods of analyzing business performance should be more fine-grained. We may need methods that are more sensitive to how entrepreneurs deal with very immediate, short-term problems in their businesses.

DISCUSSION

Our panel study of entrepreneurs in the Research Triangle Area of North Carolina was designed to test the proposition that networking pays off in business success, through increasing a firm's chances of survival and improving its economic health. Most prior studies of entrepreneurial networking have been cross-sectional and thus not well-suited to drawing causal inferences about the consequences of networking. By using a short time interval between contacts with our respondents and by vigorously pursuing non-respondents, we achieved one of our objectives, which was to assemble a high-quality data set of start-ups and young businesses (almost three in five of our sampled firms were under four years old).

We found no evidence, using three fairly standard measures of networking activity, that the size of an entrepreneur's personal network or the amount of time invested in developing and maintaining a network, affect business survival or performance. Although all the analyses reported in our paper are extremely simple, with no multivariate analyses or controls added, the almost total absence of any hint of a relationship between our networking measures and our dependent variables makes us sceptical that any further data manipulations would 'save' our initial hypotheses.

Why did network activities not predict performance? We have identified three possible factors that bear further scrutiny: (1) the many difficulties in measuring business performance; (2) the too-easy equating of personal networking with business networking; and (3) the gap between general measures of networking and the immediate context in which networking is carried out.

First, business survival is conditional on many forces, only some of which are under an entrepreneur's control. In many industries, especially highly competitive ones like business and personal services – which represent a large proportion of our sample – market forces are the dominant feature in the life of a business. Demands for services rise and fall with the economy, and many businesses struggle just to keep up. The early years of a firm's existence are also fraught with peril, and rapid shifts in fortune produce the kinds of volatility in business size we have seen in our data. In the face of such large swings in performance, networking will not be able to explain very much. In addition, many entrepreneurs with non-continuing businesses are not 'business failures' but went on to run other, sometimes bigger, businesses. Thus, our look at non-continuing businesses includes both business failures and people who have 'moved on' with their entrepreneurial careers.

Second, many of the entrepreneurs we studied have created firms in which they are not the only people responsible for business networking. We have only measured the business owner's networking activities, and we have used the performance of the entire business as our outcome variable. Perhaps we need to measure the networking activity of all the people involved in making and maintaining a business's contacts, and then assess their effect on a business's performance outcomes.

Third, in this paper we have examined mostly global measures of networking and performance. Perhaps we need to take a more micro-level view of networking, exploring an entrepreneur's use of specific network ties to people who control particular resources needed in the business. The immediate context for highly focused actions may well be influenced by an entrepreneur's personal network, and so we will turn to that level of analysis in future papers.

NOTE

1 We acknowledge the helpful assistance of Rory McVeigh and James Moody in gathering data for this paper. Deborah Tilley shaped the manuscript into its final form.

REFERENCES

Aldrich, H.E. (1991) 'Methods in Our Madness? Trends in Entrepreneurship Research', in D. Sexton and J.D. Kasarda (eds), *The State of the Art of Entrepreneurship*, Boston: PWS-Kent Publishing, 191–213.

Aldrich, H., Rosen, B, and Woodward, W. (1987) 'The Impact of Social Networks on Business Foundings and Profit: A Longitudinal Study', Babson Entrepreneurship Conference.

Birley, S., Cromie, S, and Myers, A. (1990) *Entrepreneurial Networks: Their Creation and Development in Different Countries*, SWP 24/90, Bedford, UK: Cranfield School of Management.

Brush, C. (1992) 'Research on Women Business Owners: Past Trends, a New Perspective and Future Directions', *Entrepreneurship, Theory and Practice*, 16, 5–30.

Butner, E.H. and Rosen, B. (1988) 'Bank Loan Officers' Perceptions of the Characteristics of Men, Women, and Successful Entrepreneurs', *Journal of Business Venturing*, 3, 249–58.

Cooper, A. and Dunkelberg, W. (1987) 'Old Questions, New Answers and Methodological Issues', *American Journal of Small Business*, 11: 11–23.

Granovetter, M. (1973) 'The Strength of Weak Ties', *American Journal of Sociology*, 78: 1360–1380.

Kalleberg, A. (1986) 'Entrepreneurship in the 1980s: A Study of Small Business in Indiana', in G.D. Likecap (ed.), *Entrepreneurship and Innovation, vol. I*, Greenwich, CT: JAI Press.

Kalleberg, A.L. and Leicht, K. (1991) 'Gender and Organizational Performance: Determinants of Small Business Survival and Success', *Academy of Management Journal*, 34: 136–161.

Reese, P.R. (1992) 'Entrepreneurial Networks and Resource Acquisition: Does Gender Make a Difference?', Ph.D. dissertation, University of North Carolina, Chapel Hill, NC.
Small Business Administration (1986) *A Report to the President: Self-employment as Small Business*, Washington, DC: USGPO.

Section II
Initial public offerings

8 IPO long-term performance in the United Kingdom

A dynamic beta reappraisal

Benôit F. Leleux and Daniel F. Muzyka

INTRODUCTION

Recent studies have stressed the importance of rapid-growth entrepreneurial businesses to both economic development and employment. These businesses are supported by risk capital investments made with the expectation that the financial value created by the business may be realized through many mechanisms, including public offerings. Over the last five years, though, European primary equity markets have all but dried up, significantly reducing the choice of exit mechanisms available to entrepreneurs.

This paper summarizes the latest empirical evidence on the post-issue performance of IPO markets in the UK after 1987. Using comparable methodologies, the study extends recent US evidence of significant under-performance in the secondary market for IPO shares to the largest European IPO market. It highlights the overall negative returns for IPO investments, with UK shares under-performing the market average by more than 50 per cent in the 36 months after the initial offering, as opposed to 30 per cent for the US.

In the second section, we reexamine the abnormal returns and systematic risk profiles of the IPOs in an attempt to validate the standard market-adjusted event-study methodology used in the literature. Using time series of cross-sectional regressions with robust estimation procedures, we outline the sensitivity of the reported abnormal returns to the actual specification of the residual returns. In particular, the cross-sectional systematic risk of IPO shares in secondary trade appears much lower than generally assumed, especially when using estimation procedures robust to departures from the Gaussian assumptions. A dynamic market model adjustment for systematic risk significantly reduces the reported under-performance. The evidence is interpreted as indicating that a significant portion of the observed under-performance is due to methodological inadequacies and a general misunderstanding of the true nature of the risks involved in high-growth firms.

EXECUTIVE SUMMARY

In a period when European financial integration is more than ever the subject of impassioned talks and discussions, it is discomfiting to observe just how little is actually known about some of the most important aspects of capital markets in Europe. Despite their importance to the entrepreneurial and venture capital communities, European IPO markets have received only limited academic interest. This is due to the lack of consistent, integrative, long-term sources of information. Partly to blame for this lack of data is the fragmentation of the markets, the coexistence of numerous going-public procedures (first-price auctions, underwritten or best-effort fixed-price introductions, repeated auctions, etc.) and the absence of some centralizing 'authority' to keep track of the developments in the different countries.[1]

If most empirical aspects of IPO pricing have basically been analysed in the American markets, with Ritter (1991) and Loughran and Ritter (1992) adding the latest perspective on the topic with long-term performance investigations, no such picture can be drawn for their European counterparts. Apart from anecdotal evidence and the occasional initial price reaction analysis (with time horizons of days or weeks, not months) with limited samples, very little has been done so far on long-term performance studies and even less on multi-country comparisons. This paper is an attempt to address the need for European IPO performance information. Two fundamental objectives are to be fulfilled: First of all, there has been anecdotal evidence presenting European markets as being much less easily subject to fads and other 'herd' behaviours than their American cousins. At the same time, the nature of the firms going public in terms of the stage of development may very well vary between the two environments. So a first objective of this study is to test whether IPO shares in the UK exhibit less extreme reactions than American shares in the seasoning period. This hypothesis is tested using long-term data on IPO performance in the last four years (1988–1992) and a combination of event study and arbitrage portfolio approaches.

The paper highlights the extreme similarity in post-issue performance across methods of issue, markets on which the shares are issued, the year in which the firm went public and in comparison to the US experience. Contrary to the usual belief, the performance of

UK IPO shares in the secondary market, with the exception of some privatization programmes, is as dismal as that of American IPO shares. In the first three years following their listing, shares lose on average more than 50 per cent of their value after adjusting for market effect. This is to be compared with the 30 per cent loss observed on average in the US over the period 1974–1984.

A second objective of the study therefore is to investigate the possible limitations of the return adjustment procedures used in the literature. In particular, we show on the UK sample that the seasoning pattern of systematic risk among IPO shares may induce a potentially invalidating negative bias in the reported abnormal performances. When specifically incorporating the systematic risk component into the model, the reported under-performance is significantly reduced. This leads us to conclude that a better understanding of the dynamics of the systematic risk in newly issued firms probably holds the key to a number of the IPO-related 'anomalies'.

LITERATURE REVIEW

Most of the empirical evidence and theoretical developments in IPO pricing have originated in the US. Among some of the reasons for this state of affairs are the overall availability of information and the dynamism of IPO markets in that country. Those two components are essential in enabling significant cross-sectional time-series analyses of initial public offerings.[2] When the centre of attention moves across the ocean, one is surprised by the paucity and sketchiness of IPO information across Europe. As illustrated in Table 8.1, nothing comes close to meeting the desirable standards of completeness for policy or longitudinal study purposes.

There is no need here to expand on the reasons for this situation. Obviously, the general difficulty in gathering information on such financial events does not help. In the following sections, we quickly introduce the methodologies used for the various country-specific and cross-market studies. We then present the overall findings of our analysis of the IPO performance in the UK over the period 1988–1992.

RESEARCH METHODOLOGIES

A combination of traditional event studies and cross-sectional regression methodologies is used in the analysis. First of all, all IPOs which took place in the UK were identified from stock-market published information or financial newspapers. In particular, specific

Table 8.1: European IPO studies: an overview of the evidence

Study authors	Country	Sample size	Study period	Results
Buckland *et al.* (1981)	UK	297	65–75	9.6 %
Davis and Yeomans (1976)	UK	174	65–71	8.5 %
McStay (1987)	UK	238	71–80	7.4 %
Merrett *et al.* (1967)	UK	149	59–63	13.7 %
Levis (1990)	UK	123	85–88	8.6 %
Keasey *et al.* (1991)	UK	249	84–88	18.5 %
Levis (1993)	UK	712	80–88	14.1 %
Rees (1992)	UK	489	84–91	NA
Jacquillat *et al.* (1978)	France	60	66–74	2.7 %
Husson and Jacquillat (1989)	France	131	83–86	11.4 %
Topsacalian (1984)	France	8	83	29.7 %
McDonald and Jacquillat (1974)	France	31	68–71	3.0 %
Jenkinson and Mayer (1988)	France	11	86–87	25.0 %
Wessels (1989)	Netherlands	46	82–87	5.1 %
Kunz and Aggarwal (1991)	Switzerland	42	83–89	35.8 %
De Ridder (1986)	Sweden	55	83–85	40.5 %
Keloharju (1992)	Finland	85	84–89	9.5 %
Dawson and Reiner (1988)	Germany	97	77–87	21.5 %
Hansson and Ljungqvist (1992)	Germany	163	78–91	12.0 %
Rogiers and Manigart (1992)	Belgium	28	84–90	10.1 %
Cherubini and Ratti (1992)	Italy	75	85–91	27.1 %
Rahnema, Fernandez and Martinez (1992)	Spain	71	85–90	35.0 %
Freixas and Inurrieta (1992)	Spain	58	86–90	22.3 %
Alpalhao (1988)	Portugal	62	86–87	54.4 %

characteristics of the issues, such as the offer price, the market on which the issue took place, the value of the shares issued, and the first trade day were collected. Using on-line Datastream services, the price, capital structure change, and dividend series are extracted for the individual stocks. Price series are collected on a monthly basis for the stocks and for the market index. The information is then used to build monthly continuously-compounded returns series for each stock in each month in the post-offering period. A traditional event study performance analysis is then conducted over a 36-month period after the issue (the seasoning period). The raw returns are adjusted for general market movements using a standard 'market' adjustment:

$$AR_{i,t} = R_{i,t} - R_{m,t} \tag{1}$$

where $AR_{i,t}$ is the adjusted or abnormal return on share i in post-IPO month t, $R_{i,t}$ is the raw return on share i in month t, and $R_{m,t}$ is the corresponding return on the market index during the same time period. An average abnormal return is next calculated for each event month following the IPO, using:

$$AR_t = \frac{1}{n_t} \sum_{i=1}^{n_t} AR_{it} \tag{2}$$

where n_t is the number of shares present in the cross-section in post-IPO month t. The cumulative abnormal returns are then calculated by summing up over time the AR_t.

The adjustment procedure for the returns implicitly assumes that IPO shares have a beta risk of 1 with respect to the market index used. The literature in this respect tends to indicate that on average the beta risk of IPO shares is significantly greater than one[3] in the secondary trade. Accordingly, negative abnormal returns are also fully compatible with IPOs having average betas greater than one and negative average market returns. To address the problem, cross-sectional regression methodologies, combined with estimation procedures robust to non-normalities in the distributions (such as the Trimmed Regression Quantile Method) are used to determine the systematic risk and abnormal returns of portfolios of IPO shares. The month-by-month RATS [4] procedure, equivalent to an arbitrage strategy consisting of buying IPO shares at the beginning of each seasoning month and selling them at the beginning of the next month of seasoning (for a one-month holding period), is used. The estimated betas of the strategies above provide indications of the validity of the adjustments made to the raw returns. In effect, betas close to one would vindicate the selected market adjustment procedure.

UNITED KINGDOM IPO MARKET PERFORMANCE, 1988–1992

Historical evidence

In November 1980, the Stock Exchange established the Unlisted Securities Market (USM) to promote financing of small growth companies. From its inception to 1991, more than 750 firms have obtained a listing on the USM. This success story unfortunately has to be tempered with the latest evolution of the issuing market. In particular, the USM has rapidly dropped into oblivion as a means of capital financing: companies raised £308m in 1988, but this figure dropped to £45m in 1990, £11.6m for 1991 and was only marginally higher in 1992, resulting in the pull-out of several market makers. After the collapse of the Third Market at the end of 1990, there have even been calls in the press and the Stock Exchange for the termination of the USM altogether, with transfer of the listed companies to the main market.[5]

A number of studies have been conducted recently to analyse the IPO scene in the UK. Keasey, Short, and Watson (1991) studied all firms achieving a flotation via the placement method during the period 1984–1988.[6] During the sample period, out of 444 flotations, 356 firms were floated on the USM using the placement method. On a sample of 249 firms, the authors observed the average initial price reaction of 18.48 per cent (market adjusted) to be related to a number of variables that may capture the *ex ante* uncertainty of an issue. Mario Levis (1990) analysed the winner's curse problem in a sample of 123 issues over the period January 1985 to December 1988, representing almost 85 per cent of the population on offer for sales, most of them on the Main Market. The abnormal first-day return, market adjusted, stands at 8.64 per cent and is shown to be explained almost entirely by the combined effects of the winner's curse problem and the particular nature of the settlement mechanism applicable in the UK new issues market.

The evidence so far on IPO pricing and performance in the UK is thus best described as patchy. In the next section, we use a large sample of post–1987 IPOs on all three markets (Main, USM, and Third) and all three issuing procedures (offer for sale, introduction, and placement) to investigate the post-IPO performance of initial public offerings in the UK.

Sample and methodologies

All forms of introduction on the UK markets were identified for the period from January 1988 to December 1991. All prices, capital structure changes, and dividend series are extracted from Datastream on-line services. 63.2 per cent of all IPOs which took place during the period are included in the sample, for a total of 220 IPOs analysed out of a possible 348. Given our main source of return information, there is an inherent bias in the sample towards larger, more liquid firms, although only 60 per cent of them would actually meet Ritter's (1991) lower benchmark for inclusion. As before, each IPO is tracked for at least 36 months after the issue date.

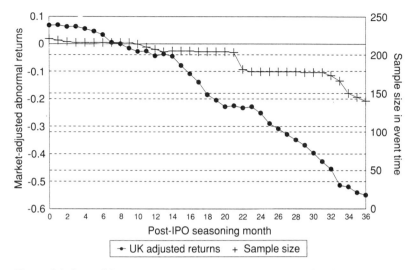

Figure 8.1 Overall long-run IPO average abnormal returns (UK)

Post-IPO performances

Overall post-IPO performance in the UK

Figure 8.1 illustrates the monthly cumulated abnormal returns on the whole sample of 220 firms which went public between 1988 and 1992. The initial positive performance turns around after 10 months into significantly negative abnormal returns.

Part of the overall results could be due to aggregation problems, with different forms of going-public procedures demonstrating very different performances through event time. This possibility is investigated next.

Long-run performance in the UK by method of introduction

Three major forms of initial public offering are used in the UK: the Placement, the Offer for Sale, and the Introduction.[7] We broke down the overall sample by going-public method. The post-IPO performance of the shares is presented in Figure 8.2.

It appears that Offers for Sale significantly depart from the overall reported pattern of under-performance. This departure can be traced back exclusively to shares introduced as part of the privatization programme of the electric utilities in 1990. Introduced through the Offer for Sale Procedure on the Main Market, electric utilities performed

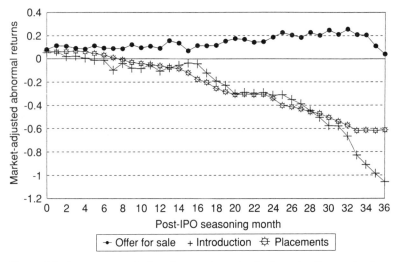

Figure 8.2 Average cumulative abnormal returns by introduction method used (UK)

abnormally well in the following 36 months, an element not unconnected to the brash press reports of 'fire sales' of public assets.

Another possible source of explanation could be related to the relative sample sizes in each of the sub-samples. In effect, the Offer for Sales figures may have been obtained over a limited cross-section of firms or could be clustered in calendar time. Figure 8.3 highlights the sub-sample sizes first by method of introduction, second by the markets on which the introduction took place, and finally by the year of issue.

Post-IPO performance in the UK by issue market

Three markets are available for going-public purposes in the UK: the Main Market, the Unlisted Securities Market (USM), and the Third Market. In this subsection, we investigate the post-IPO performance of shares issued on each of those markets. The sub-sample sizes are presented in Figure 8.3. The average and cumulative average abnormal performances of the shares issued on each market are presented in Figure 8.4. Shares issued on the Main Market seem to exhibit a better resistance over time. Caution is needed here again because of the influence of privatization programmes which took place in 1990. As mentioned above, the electric utilities introduced

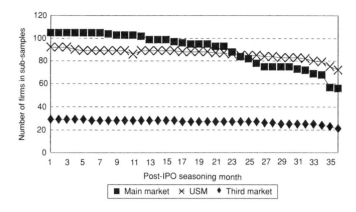

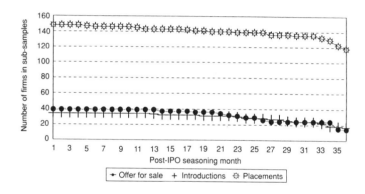

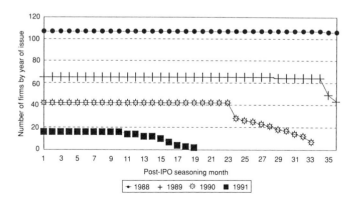

Figure 8.3 Evolution of sub-sample sizes in post-issue event time (UK)

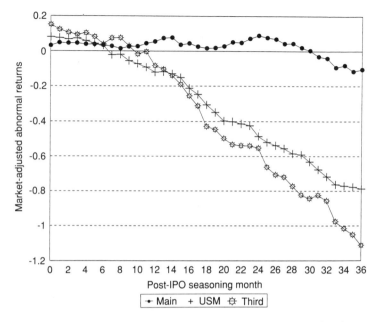

Figure 8.4 Long-run performance of IPO shares by issue market (UK)

then have exhibited superior performance over the years. The other markets' performances present the reversal after only a year. The same general pattern holds for all IPO markets.

Post-IPO performance in the UK by issue year

Figure 8.5 below graphically illustrates the evolution of the Financial Times All Shares Index over the period investigated here, in parallel with other European indices. It is also important to check if the overall performance observed is not due to issue clustering in calendar time around a period of declining market performance. This is done by disaggregating the sample by year of issue and running the same overall analyses. The results of the tests are presented graphically in Figure 8.6.

It shows essentially that the general under-performance observed is not specific to any particular year of issue. 1988 was characterized by a large number of introductions compared to the subsequent three years. This is normally referred to as a 'hot issue' market. But it does not seem to affect the general under-performance pattern. 1990 on

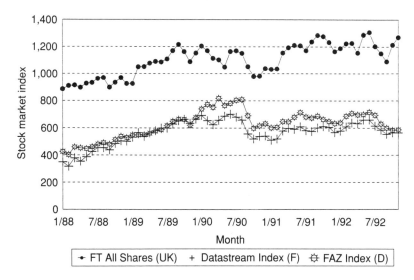

Figure 8.5 Evolution of the stock-market indices (UK, Germany, France)

Notes: All dates refer to the first trading date of the month. Stock index values are at closing on first trade day of the month.

the other hand was characterized by a lower number of issues, but among them was a wave of electric utilities privatizations.

Conclusion

For all useful purposes, the general pattern of under-performance of IPO shares seems to be robust to the type of introduction selected, the market on which the introduction took place, or the year of introduction. These findings are in line with the reports of Ritter (1991) and Loughran and Ritter (1992) in the United States.

APPRAISAL OF THE RISK-ADJUSTMENT PROCEDURES USED

The robustness of the under-performance results across countries, time periods, introduction methods, and markets on which the issues take place could be interpreted as the ultimate form of support for the fundamental importance of the phenomenon. More pragmatically, it also leads one to question the very methodology used by researchers to evaluate the post-IPO abnormal returns for the existence of systematic forms of biases.

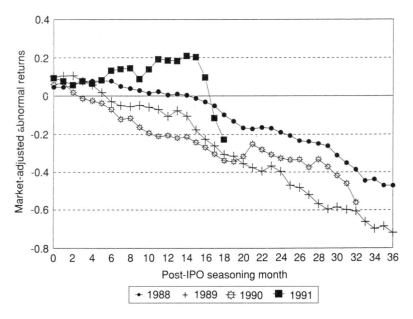

Figure 8.6 Long-run performance of IPO shares by issue year (UK)

One particularly disquieting, implicit[8] assumption is that the average beta of IPO shares in the secondary market is superior to one, hence the alleged conservative nature of the market adjustment when investigating post-IPO performances. If this is not the case, the market adjustment will lead to reports of significantly negative abnormal returns where there is only adequate compensation for the level of market risk involved.

There is actually ample evidence in the entrepreneurship literature focusing on the management of high-growth firms that most of the risk faced by growing businesses is actually firm specific, and hence diversifiable. In this context, the market-related component of the total risk may be much reduced, to the degree where it could actually be lower than for major established firms more subject to general market conditions. In other words, the implied 'high risk' in young, high-growth firms may not be reflected in systematic risks larger than one because of the diversifiable nature of most of the overall risk.

To test for such a possibility, we examine the dynamic evolution of the post-IPO betas using a cross-sectional regression methodology known as RATS (detailed in Appendix A). Previous evidence indicates that the systematic risk of newly issued shares drops rapidly in secondary trade, as in Cotter (1992) or Chan and Lakonishok (1992). The summary results from the latter, on a sample of 661 IPOs, are presented in Table 8.2 below. Although not stressed in the literature, those results seem to support rather low betas for IPO shares.

Table 8.2 IPO cross-sectional beta estimates, Chan and Lakonishok 1992

	One-day returns	
Trading day	OLS	TRQ
1	4.26	3.20
2	1.62	0.92
3	1.24	0.71
4	1.74	1.25
5	1.42	0.90
6	1.19	0.72
7	1.36	0.85
8	1.02	0.63
9	1.46	0.87

Note: OLS = Ordinary Least Squares; TRQ = Trimmed Regression Quantiles estimates

We show next that in the long-term, the cross-sectional systematic risk on our sample firms remains significantly below one. The tests are conducted on the UK sample using both standard OLS regressions and advanced robust regressions techniques such as the Trimmed Regression Quantile method at various levels of trimming.

Post-IPO dynamics of returns and systematic risk in the UK

OLS and robust beta estimation techniques

It falls outside the scope of this paper to review the econometrics literature regarding the estimation biases resulting from the use of OLS procedures when the distribution of stock returns departs significantly from normality.[9] Recent empirical evidence on IPO pricing, such as Ruud (1991), indicates that the problem may be material in post-issue performance studies. Accordingly, a combination of both OLS and robust estimation techniques are used on the post-IPO abnormal return estimations. In particular, Trimmed Least Square Regression Quantile[10] estimators are reported for two levels of trimming, respectively 5 per cent and 10 per cent, with corrections applied for the logarithmic specifications of both dependent and independent variables.

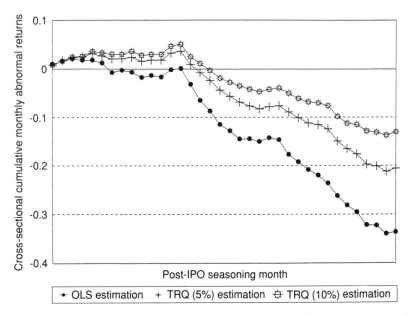

Figure 8.7 Cross-sectional abnormal returns estimates (UK)

Cross-sectional abnormal performance estimates

Table 8.3 below details the cross-sectional estimates of the one-month holding period IPO portfolios, where the estimations are conducted using both standard OLS and robust estimation procedures. For

Table 8.3 Cross-sectional post-IPO month-by-month abnormal performances (UK)

Event Month	Estimated Alpha	Standard Error	T-Ratio	Signif.	Event Month	Estimated Alpha	Standard Error	T-Ratio	Signif
Month 1	0.0103	0.0059	1.7568		Month 19	−0.0137	0.0077	−1.7826	
	0.0082	0.0049	1.6725			−0.0135	0.0101	−1.3348	
	0.0079	0.0048	1.6400			−0.0097	0.0071	−1.3658	
Month 2	0.0055	0.0062	0.8856		Month 20	−0.0172	0.0087	−1.9786	
	0.0088	0.0042	2.0769	*		−0.0122	0.0074	−1.6530	
	0.0088	0.0041	2.1277	*		−0.0077	0.0059	−1.3000	
Month 3	0.0052	0.0071	0.7332		Month 21	0.0007	0.0171	0.0420	*
	0.0064	0.0059	1.0969			−0.0085	0.0073	−1.1618	
	0.0081	0.0053	1.5185			−0.0079	0.0059	−1.3386	
Month 4	−0.0032	0.0057	−0.5584		Month 22	−0.0069	0.0079	−0.8701	
	0.0013	0.0043	0.2973			−0.0066	0.0070	−0.9400	
	0.0014	0.0042	0.3317			−0.0051	0.0066	−0.7694	

Event Month	Estimated Alpha	Standard Error	T-Ratio	Signif.	Event Month	Estimated Alpha	Standard Error	T-Ratio	Signif
Month 5	−0.0002	0.0066	−0.0326		Month 23	0.0080	0.0084	0.9465	
	0.0067	0.0054	1.2464			0.0049	0.0068	0.7142	
	0.0097	0.0052	1.8684			0.0046	0.0065	0.7104	
Month 6	−0.0066	0.0067	−0.9861		Month 24	−0.0045	0.0100	−0.4497	
	−0.0050	0.0054	−0.9256			0.0017	0.0080	0.2137	
	−0.0037	0.0049	−0.7468			0.0030	0.0073	0.4052	
Month 7	−0.0204	0.0115	−1.7673		Month 25	−0.0313	0.0223	−1.3999	
	−0.0061	0.0056	−1.0729			−0.0138	0.0079	−1.7561	
	−0.0033	0.0056	−0.5785			−0.0117	0.0063	−1.8511	
Month 8	0.0050	0.0113	0.4439		Month 26	−0.0157	0.0075	−2.0861	
	0.0004	0.0062	0.0651			−0.0129	0.0070	−1.8409	
	−0.0004	0.0057	−0.0780			−0.0114	0.0064	−1.7706	
Month 9	−0.0049	0.0068	−0.7307		Month 27	−0.0165	0.0087	−1.9085	*
	0.0030	0.0055	0.5419			−0.0119	0.0070	−1.7060	
	0.0059	0.0051	1.1509			−0.0076	0.0060	−1.2708	
Month 10	−0.0119	0.0068	−1.7437		Month 28	−0.0128	0.0125	−1.0288	
	−0.0089	0.0057	−1.5600			−0.0038	0.0087	−0.4403	
	−0.0084	0.0056	−1.5093			−0.0020	0.0083	−0.2343	
Month 11	0.0040	0.0085	0.4693		Month 29	−0.0164	0.0094	−1.7486	
	0.0022	0.0065	0.3377			−0.0091	0.0080	−1.1346	
	0.0016	0.0055	0.2879			−0.0066	0.0074	−0.8968	
Month 12	−0.0030	0.0080	−0.3788		Month 30	−0.0269	0.0103	−2.6047	
	−0.0005	0.0065	−0.0753			−0.0254	0.0088	−2.8995	
	0.0004	0.0060	0.0661			−0.0223	0.0079	−2.8027	
Month 13	0.0151	0.0090	1.6798		Month 31	−0.0198	0.0106	−1.8680	**
	0.0147	0.0066	2.2301	*		−0.0169	0.0071	−2.3813	**
	0.0163	0.0065	2.4941	**		−0.0140	0.0073	−1.9096	**
Month 14	0.0030	0.0072	0.4168		Month 32	−0.0143	0.0120	−1.1884	
	0.0036	0.0056	0.6328			−0.0111	0.0106	−1.0490	**
	0.0041	0.0049	0.8244			−0.0038	0.0084	−0.4485	
Month 15	−0.0332	0.0084	−3.9640	**	Month 33	−0.0279	0.0151	−1.8416	
	−0.0275	0.0070	−3.9604	**		−0.0214	0.0133	−1.6064	
	−0.0255	0.0061	−4.1838	**		−0.0138	0.0110	−1.2516	
Month 16	−0.0330	0.0120	−2.7565	**	Month 34	−0.0010	0.0145	−0.0708	
	−0.0171	0.0074	−2.3088	*		−0.0041	0.0110	−0.3716	
	−0.0141	0.0074	−1.9038	*		−0.0039	0.0092	−0.4266	
Month 17	−0.0224	0.0098	−2.2797	*	Month 35	−0.0170	0.0115	−1.4708	
	−0.0162	0.0077	−2.0865	*		−0.0118	0.0114	−1.0429	
	−0.0143	0.0068	−2.0892	*		−0.0062	0.0105	−0.5870	
Month 18	−0.0288	0.0103	−2.8071	**	Month 36	0.0036	0.0139	0.2582	
	−0.0208	0.0068	−3.0521	**		0.0061	0.0117	0.5233	
	−0.0164	0.0071	−2.3073	*		0.0070	0.0103	0.6819	

Notes: For the three lines of each Event month:

Line 1: OLS estimates of cross-sectional abnormal performance in event-time months 1 to 36

Line 2: trimmed regression quantile estimates, with 5 per cent trimming level

Line 3: trimmed regression quantile estimates, with 10 per cent trimming level

* indicates a *t*-ratio statistically different from 0 at the 10 per cent level

** at the 5 per cent level

*** at the 1 per cent level

easier interpretation, the cumulative abnormal returns are plotted in Figure 8.7 below for the sample as a whole and the three different estimation techniques. Appendix B reports the OLS estimates of the cross-sectional regression alphas by type of introduction method used. Appendix C reports the same results by market on which the issues took place.

The observed differences between estimation methodologies indicates a lack of robustness to the general normality-of-returns assumptions. In particular, once reasonable care is taken for distributive outliers, the reported post-IPO under-performance significantly drops. The results in Appendices B and C are consistent with the event-study methodology used previously, although the magnitude of under-performance is slightly reduced for all cases.

Cross-sectional systematic risk estimates

The beta coefficients of the cross-sectional regressions represent the systematic risk of one-month holding period arbitrage portfolios of IPO shares. The estimates are presented in Table 8.4 below.

Figure 8.8 below graphically illustrates the estimated cross-sectional systematic risk estimates under both OLS and Trimmed Regression Quantiles (with trimming levels of 5 and 10 per cent). No trend could be detected in the event-time pattern of betas.

Table 8.4 Cross-sectional post-IPO month-by-month systematic risks (UK)

Event Month	OLS Beta	TRQ Beta 5%	TRQ Beta 10%	Event Month	OLS Beta	TRQ Beta 5%	TRQ Beta 10%	Event Month	OLS Beta	TRQ Beta 5%	TRQ Beta 10%
1	0.58	0.55	0.51	13	0.51	0.42	0.35	25	−0.15	0.33	0.36
2	0.43	0.38	0.38	14	0.63	0.53	0.47	26	0.97	0.89	0.81
3	0.74	0.60	0.47	15	1.03	0.95	0.94	27	0.59	0.54	0.54
4	0.61	0.57	0.56	16	1.23	1.14	1.12	28	0.76	0.68	0.65
5	0.73	0.63	0.58	17	0.83	0.69	0.59	29	0.71	0.58	0.56
6	0.62	0.61	0.57	18	−0.00	0.13	0.17	30	0.30	0.34	0.35
7	0.61	0.64	0.62	19	0.67	0.55	0.53	31	0.30	0.36	0.36
8	0.52	0.52	0.51	20	0.41	0.27	0.26	32	0.35	0.48	0.40
9	0.31	0.33	0.29	21	1.39	0.58	0.53	33	0.19	0.32	0.25
10	0.96	0.88	0.83	22	0.56	0.51	0.50	34	0.82	0.65	0.60
11	0.79	0.79	0.82	23	0.68	0.58	0.57	35	0.77	0.67	0.65
12	0.53	0.56	0.53	24	0.05	0.07	−0.03	36	0.39	0.53	0.41

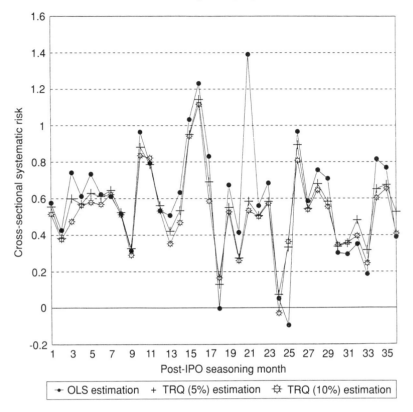

Figure 8.8 Cross-sectional systematic risk estimates (UK)

It appears clear that, similar to the evidence collected by Chan and Lakonishok (1992), the systematic risk of one-month IPO portfolio holding strategies is significantly below 1.0 in most of the periods following the issue date. Similarly, the use of robust estimation techniques seems to offer more consistent estimates of beta risk over event time.

In the next section, we attempt to evaluate the impact of a more adequate beta-risk specification on the reported post-IPO performance results.

Dynamic specification of systematic risk and post-IPO abnormal returns

To formally evaluate the impact of the misspecification of the systematic risk in the standard event-study methodology, we reexamine the results using a CAPM adjustment of the returns instead of the market adjustment, with estimated betas from the cross-sectional regressions under various estimation procedures (OLS and Trimmed Regression Quantile with 5 and 10 per cent trimming levels). We hypothesize that proper account of the dynamics of the systematic risk will result in reduced reported under-performance of IPO shares in the long term. The resulting abnormal returns are reported graphically in Figure 8.9 below.

As anticipated, adjusting the raw returns using a cross-sectional beta estimate significantly reduces the under-performance. For the first twelve-month post-IPO, no under-performance is actually detectable using either of the three cross-sectional beta estimation techniques. On the other hand, the long-term pattern remains, even though reduced by almost 40 per cent.

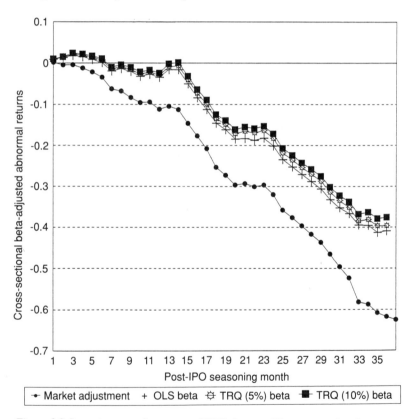

Figure 8.9 Long-term performance of IPO shares with cross-sectional systematic risk adjustments (UK)

It appears that overadjustment of the raw returns does lead to excessive reports of under-performance of IPO shares in the long run. On the other hand, this does not materially affect the very existence of the phenomenon itself or its troublesome nature. We need to recognize here the limitations inherent in the crude adjustment process used. In particular, adjusting the returns for a cross-sectional average of the systematic risk in event time is probably better than assuming *ex ante* a beta of one, but it is definitely less convincing than adjusting each firm individually for its own systematic risk.

Cotter (1992) introduces just such a method using daily returns and a 30-day rolling-window estimation procedure, where the systematic risk of each IPO firm at time t is estimated by regressing its returns over time $t + 1$ to $t + 30$ on the returns of a stock-market index over the corresponding period. The result is a time series of beta estimated for each stock, which is then averaged across firms to provide a risk profile in event time. The results he provides are consistent with the results of our cross-sectional approach. One additional advantage of his technique is the ability to dynamically adjust each stock return series for its own estimated risk over time. Without daily return information at our disposal, the methodology proposed here is clearly a compromise between the traditional market adjustment and the advantages provided by daily returns.

CONCLUSIONS AND IMPLICATIONS

We have presented above a comprehensive analysis of IPO long-term performances in the UK. In terms of the first overall objective of the study, it would appear fair to state that UK IPO shares *do not* exhibit less extreme reactions than American shares in their seasoning periods, when abnormal returns are evaluated using a standard market-adjusted event-study methodology. The results of this study, which involves comparatively recent data, underline the significant under-performance of IPO shares in secondary trading. Those general results are robust across type of issue, year of issue, or market on which the IPOs are being conducted. The long-run under-performance of IPO stocks is of the same general magnitude as that reported in the US by Ritter (1991) and others. Consistent with the second objective of the study, we now have a relatively clear picture of current trends in IPO performance.

When reexamining the systematic risk profile of IPO shares in secondary trading using robust estimates of cross-sectional regressions parameters and dynamically adjusting the residual returns for it, it appears that the reported under-performance is significantly reduced. This can be interpreted as evidence supporting an econometric component in the anomalous post-IPO results. In many cases, the assumption of an average systematic risk of 1.0 for post-IPO shares seems to lead to an overadjustment of the raw returns and the subsequent downward trending pattern in post-IPO abnormal returns. The market adjustment is definitely not conservative in this regard.

At least three sets of questions remain to be answered. First of all, why are IPO shares exhibiting such low systematic risks in the period following their introductions on the market? Can this be related to the extant literature on managing the growing firm that seems to indicate the firm-specific nature of most of the risk ? Most early studies in the finance literature focused on random samples of the largest firms, moving from the Dow Jones 30 to broader market databases when they became available. Is this change in the nature of the data available for research accompanied by a significant shift in the characteristics of the underlying returns distributions, with far-reaching implications in empirical finance? If underpricing is present, the question still remains of what caused this behaviour of IPO shares. Should we ascribe the phenomenon to fads, as Ritter did ? Loughran and Ritter (1992) show that the general trend persists beyond the original 36 months post-IPO. Is there a point at which the trend reverses itself? Is the trend the result of systematic overpricing of stocks due to a lack of sufficient information with which to set initial prices? Is there initial overpricing due to excessive 'packaging' of information? Are the abnormal returns due to a lack of understanding of the systematic problems which face all growing businesses? Finally, how can we explain the dramatic decline in the use of secondary stock markets for raising equity financing in the UK? Is this decline temporary or is it part of a long-term trend toward other sources of financing (banks, other financial intermediaries)? Can the decline in the number of issues brought to market be causally related to the under-performance, if any, of the IPO shares, seriously constraining the demand for such shares? In that case, how can we explain the fact that NASDAQ is thriving under apparently similar conditions in after-market performance?

We would suggest that a better understanding of the causes of this phenomenon are very important to the future of robust markets for initial public offerings in the UK and Europe in general. If investors cannot be confident that their investments in these firms will generally hold their value for even the medium term, it is unlikely the markets in Europe will be willing to absorb many further public offerings by fast-growing, entrepreneurial businesses. The observed decline in IPO share prices would block one of the key methods of capturing value for both entrepreneurs and risk capital investors.

APPENDIX A

The cross-sectional abnormal return and systematic risk methodology (RATS)

The analysis of the returns to the post-IPO arbitrage strategies is significantly complicated by the possible existence of temporal risk shifts and serial correlation in the returns.[11] The calculation of returns from IPOs is, therefore, not a straightforward matter.

Most useful for our purpose, Ball and Kothari (1989) developed a methodology to test market efficiency with respect to a trading rule in which controlling for relative risk changes is critical. In particular, when measuring event-time abnormal returns post-IPO, one would simultaneously like to check the extent to which the average beta risk is evolving. The RATS methodology is most handy in this case.

A cross-sectional regression model is formulated as

$$r_{i,n} - r_f = a_n + b_n \, [r_m - r_f] + e_{i,n} \tag{3}$$

where $r_{i,n}$ is the return of security i in seasoning month n, r_m is the return on the market index measured in the same calendar month as $r_{i,n}$, a_n is the regression constant interpreted as the average abnormal returns in seasoning month n, b_n is the systematic risk coefficient, $e_{i,n}$ is the stochastic disturbance term for asset i in seasoning period n, and finally r_f is the risk-free return measured on the same calendar month as $r_{i,n}$. Practically, there is thus one such cross-sectional regression for each seasoning period month n, where the cross-section is over all securities in the same stage of post-IPO seasoning.

A potential problem with the methodology is the sensitivity of standard estimation procedures, such as OLS, to non-normalities in the distributions. Although still unbiased, it is important to recognize the lack of efficiency of the least-square technique. Given that RATS is usually called upon in situations where fat-tailed stock return distributions are to be expected (as in common stock repurchases, corporate restructurings, or the announcements of major financial news), it becomes particularly important to use alternative, unbiased, and more efficient estimation techniques for the regressions. Without detailing here the technical sides of robust estimators,[12] they can be said to give relatively less weight to 'outlier' observations.

APPENDIX B

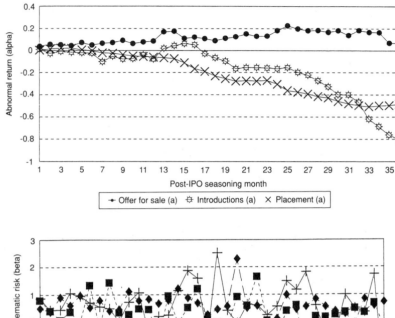

Figure 8.10 Cross-sectional abnormal performance by method of introduction used (UK)

APPENDIX C

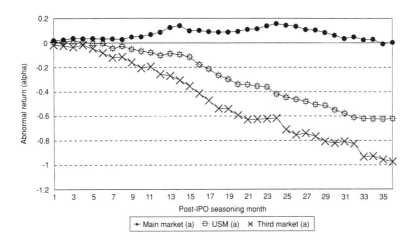

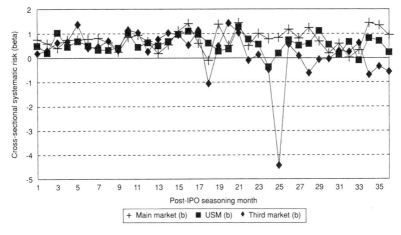

Figure 8.11 Cross-sectional abnormal performance by market on which the introduction took place (UK)

NOTES

1 In the US, IPO markets have been tracked for years by *Going Public: The IPO Reporter* journal and the joint efforts of a few academics, most notable among them Jay Ritter, Roger Ibbotson, and Randolph Beatty.
2 It is clear that assembling a sample of 8,668 IPOs over a 30-year span, as Ibbotson, Sindelar, and Ritter (1988) did, or the 5,221 firms of Loughran and Ritter (1992), is unfeasible in any other country, if only for the lack of an adequate equivalent to the CRSP tapes.
3 See e.g. Balvers *et al.* (1988), Clarkson and Thompson (1990), or Chan and Lakonishok (1992).
4 RATS is the now standard acronym in finance literature for 'Returns Across Time and Securities', a cross-sectional regression methodology introduced by Ibbotson (1975) and later improved by authors such as Ball and Kothari (1989) or Chan and Lakonishok (1992). For a complete presentation of the method, refer to Appendix A.
5 See, for example, the article in the *Financial Times* on 30 November 1992 entitled 'The Lingering Death of a Whizzkid's Haven' for more details on the evolution of the USM.
6 Under the 'placement method', shares are initially 'placed' by the sponsor to institutional or private clients. The sponsor then purchases the shares from the issuer at the issue price and resells them at the same or slightly higher price to the clients. Alternatives to this method include the traditional 'offer for sale' method or the 'introduction' where no new shares are actually issued.
7 As mentioned above, the introduction does not involve the sale of new shares.
8 Or explicit in the case of Ritter (1991), Loughran and Ritter (1992), and many others.
9 See Chan and Lakonishok (1992) for a complete exposure of the problem.
10 See Judge *et al.* (1988) for a theoretical primer on robust estimation methods.
11 See e.g. Fama and French (1988), Poterba and Summers (1988), or Ball and Kothari (1989).
12 See Judge *et al.* (1988), Koenker and Bassett (1978), Koenker and Portnoy (1987), or Chan and Lakonishok (1992) for an introduction.

REFERENCES

Aggarwal, Reena and Rivoli, Pietra (1990) 'Fads in the Initial Public Offering Market?', *Financial Management,* 19 (4): 45–57.
Alpalhão, Rui M. (1988) 'Opertas Públicas Iniciais: O Caso Português', working paper, Univesidade Nova de Lisboa.
Ball, Ray and Kothari, S.P. (1989) 'Nonstationary Expected Returns: Implications for Tests of Market Efficiency and Serial Correlations in Returns', *Journal of Financial Economics,* 25 (1): 51–74.
Balvers, Ronald, McDonald, Bill, and Miller, Robert (1988) 'Underpricing of New Issues and the Choice of Auditor as Signal of Investment Banker Reputation', *Accounting Review,* 63 (4): 605–622.

Block, Stanley and Stanley, Marjorie (1980) 'Financial Characteristics and Price Movement Patterns of Companies Approaching the IPO Market', *Financial Management,* Winter: 30–36.

Buckland, R., Herbert, P.J., and Yeomans, K.A. (1981) 'Price Discount on New Equity Issues in the UK and their Relationship to Investor Subscription', *Journal of Business Finance and Accounting,* 8 (1): 79–95.

Chan, Louis K.C. (1988) 'On the Contrarian Investment Strategy', *Journal of Business,* 61: 147–163.

Chan, Louis K.C. and Lakonishok, Josef (1992) 'Robust Measurement of Beta Risk', *Journal of Financial and Quantitative Analysis,* 27 (2): 265–282.

Cherubini, Umberto and Ratti, Marco (1992) 'Underpricing of Initial Public Offerings in the Milan Stock Exchange, 1985–1991', Banco Commerciale Italiana, Economic Research Unit, Rome, Italy.

Clarkson, W. and Thompson, Rex (1990) 'Measurement of Beta Risk Within the Differential Information Model', *Journal of Finance,* 45: 431–453.

Cotter, James F. (1992) 'The Long-run Efficiency of IPO Pricing', working paper, University of California at Chapel Hill.

Davis, W. and Yeomans, K.A. (1976) 'Market Discount on New Issues of Equity: Firm Size, Method of Issue, and Market Volatility', *Journal of Business Finance and Accounting,* 86 (343): 27–42.

Dawson, Steven M. and Reiner, Norbert (1988) 'Raising Capital with Initial Public Share Issues in Germany, 1977–1985', *Management International Review,* 28 (1): 64–72.

De Ridder, Adri (1986) 'Access to the Stock Market: An Empirical Study of the Efficiency of the British and Swedish Primary Markets', working paper, Federation of Swedish Industries.

Fama, Eugene F. and French, Kenneth R. (1988) 'Permanent and Temporary Price Components of Stock Prices', *Journal of Political Economy,* 96, 246–73.

Freixas, Xavier and Inurrieta, Alejandro (1992) 'Infravaloracion en las Salidas a Bolsa', preliminary working paper, FEDEA, Spain.

Hansson, B. and Ljungqvist, A. (1992) *Mispricing of Initial Public Offerings: Evidence from Germany,* Oxford: Oxford University Press.

Husson, Jacques and Jacquillat, Bertrand (1989) 'French New Issues, Underpricing, and Alternative Methods of Distribution', in Guimaraes *et al.,* (eds), *A Reappraisal of the Efficiency of Financial Markets,* Berlin; Heidelberg: Springer-Verlag.

Ibbotson, Roger G. (1975) 'Price Performance of Common Stock New Issues', *Journal of Financial Economics,* 2 (3): 235–272.

Ibbotson, Roger G. and Jaffe, Jeffrey F. (1975) 'Hot Issue Markets', *Journal of Finance,* 30 (4): 1027–1042.

Ibbotson, Roger G., Sindelar, J., and Ritter, Jay. (1988) 'Initial Public Offerings', *Journal of Applied Corporate Finance,* 1: 37–45.

Jacquillat, Bertrand, McDonald, J.G., and Rolfo, J. (1978) 'French Auctions of Common Stock: New Issues, 1966–1974', *Journal of Business Finance,* 2: 305–322.

Jacquillat, Bertrand (1989) *'L'Introduction en Bourse',* Paris: Presses Universitaires de France.

Jenkinson, Tim and Mayer, Colin (1988) 'The Privatization Process in France and the United Kingdom', *European Economic Review,* 32: 482–490.

Judge, G., Hill, C., Griffiths, W., Lutkepohl, H., and Lee, T.C. (1988) *Introduction to the Theory and Practice of Econometrics*, New York, NY: John Wiley and Sons, Inc.

Keasey, K., Short, Helen, and Watson, Robert (1991) 'Capital Market Efficiency and the Underpricing of New Issues on the UK Unlisted Securities Markets', in Juan Roure and Sue Birley (eds), *Growth Capital and Entrepreneurship*, Barcelona: IESE.

Keloharju, Matti (1992) 'Legal Liability, Winner's Curse and the Long-Run Price Performance of Initial Public Offerings in Finland', working paper, Helsinki School of Economics and Business Administration.

Koenker, Roger and Portnoy, S. (1987) 'L-Estimation for Linear Models', *Journal of the American Statistical Association*, 82: 851–857.

Koenker, Roger and Bassett, G. (1978) 'Regression Quantiles', *Econometrica*, 46: 33–50.

Kunz, Roger and Aggarwal, Reena (1991) 'Explaining the Underpricing of Initial Public Offerings: Evidence from Switzerland', working paper, Georgetown University School of Business Administration.

Levis, Mario (1990) 'The Winner's Curse Problem, Interest Costs and the Underpricing of Initial Public Ifferings', *Economic Journal*, 100 (399): 76–89.

Levis, Mario (1993) 'The Long-Run Performance of Initial Public Offerings: The UK Experience 1980–1988', *Financial Management*, Spring, 28–41.

Loughran, Tim and Ritter, Jay R. (1992) 'The Long-Run Performance of IPOs: II', working paper, University of Illinois.

McDonald, John G. and Jacquillat, Bertrand, (1974) 'Pricing of Initial Equity Issues: The French Sealed Bid Auction', *Journal of Business*, 33 (January): 37–47.

McStay, K.P. (1987) 'The Efficiency of New Issue Markets', Ph.D. thesis, Department of Economics, University of California.

Merrett, A.J., Howe, M., and Newbould, G.D. (1967) *Equity Issues and the London Capital Market*, London: Macmillan.

Muscarella, Chris and Vetsuypens, Michael (1989) 'A Simple Test of Baron's Model of IPO Underpricing', *Journal of Financial Economics*, 24 (1): 123–135.

Poterba, James M. and Summers, Lawrence H. (1988) 'Mean Reversion in Stock Returns: Evidence and Implications', *Journal of Financial Economics*, 22, 22–59.

Rahnema, Ahmad, Fernandez, P., and Martinez-Abascal, E. (1992) *Initial Public Offerings: The Spanish Experience*, Barcelona: IESE.

Rees, William (1992) *Initial Public Offerings in the UK: 1984–1991*, University of Strathclyde, Glasgow.

Ritter, Jay R. (1991) 'The Long-run Performance of Initial Public Offerings', *Journal of Finance*, 46 (1): 3–28.

Rogiers, Bart and Manigart, Sophie (1992) *Empirical Examination of the Underpricing of Initial Public Offerings on the Brussels Stock Exchange*, Vlerick School for Management, Ghent, Belgium.

Ruud, J.S. (1991) 'Another View of the Underpricing of Initial Public Offerings', *Federal Reserve Bank of NY Quarterly Review*, 16 (1): 83–85.

Topsacalian, Patrick (1984) 'Second marché: Sous evaluation des titres à l'introduction', *Analyse Financière*, 4: 52–61.

Uhlir, Helmut (1989) 'Going Public in the F.R.G', in Guimaraes *et al.* (eds), *A Reappraisal of the Efficiency of Financial Markets*, Berlin; Heidelberg: Springer-Verlag.
Wessels, Robert (1989) 'The Market for IPOs: An Analysis of the Amsterdam Stock Exchange (1982–1987)', in Guimaraes *et al.* (eds), *A Reappraisal of the Efficiency of Financial Markets*, Berlin; Heidelberg: Springer-Verlag.

9 Are prestigious underwriters and auditors of any value for entrepreneurs in the going-public process ?

Evidence from the French second market

Rémy Paliard

INTRODUCTION

This paper analyses the relationship between the large underpricing quoted on the French second market and the use of highly ranked underwriters and auditors. It also provides general information on the IPO market in France.

Information was gathered on a sample of 165 IPOs, representing 55 per cent of the firms which went public on the French second market from 1983 to 1991. A strong link between 'hot' markets and underpricing is noticeable, but no clear evidence of the influence of underwriters and auditors is available.

Going public is for entrepreneurs a longstanding dream and a sign of public recognition (Belletante and Desroches 1993). It can also be a way to realize part of the value created by working hard for years, and in this respect the price at which they sell their shares matters a great deal.

Research has been conducted on various aspects of the initial public offering process. Among other topics, it has focused recently on the underpricing phenomenon and on post-market performance. Of various existing theories, those based on information asymmetry and agency theory seem to offer explanations of available evidence.

This paper focuses on the certification effect documented by Megginson and Weiss (1991) and on the insiders' holdings effect proposed by McBain and Krause (1989). Three hypotheses are tested on the level of underpricing: the impact of financial investors in the firm before the IPO, the impact of the reduction of insiders' holdings, and the impact of rankings of underwriters and auditors.

Based on the second market, where most of IPOs were implemented during the last ten years, this paper also gives information on the French market's peculiarities, and on the large underpricing quoted in this country.

It is organized into three parts. The first deals with the theoretical developments, the hypothesis to be tested and the methodology used. The second part includes general results on a sample of 165 IPOs, and the third describes the test of the proposed hypotheses.

THEORETICAL DEVELOPMENTS AND TESTABLE HYPOTHESES

Empirical evidence of underpricing in Europe

Many empirical studies have been conducted on IPO underpricing in the United States and Canada. There are fewer on European markets. We give the main results in Table 9.1.

Table 9.1 IPO underpricing in European markets

Authors	Year	Country	Period	Size of sample	Underpricing
Alphao	1989	Portugal	86–87	62	54.4%
De Ridder	1986	UK (2)	83–85	240	17.7%
De Ridder	1986	UK (1)	83–85	54	6.9%
De Ridder	1986	Sweden(1)	83–85	74	61.6%
De Ridder	1986	Sweden(3)	83–85	55	40.5%
Dubois	1986	France(2)	83–86	99	19.3%
Husson *et al.*	1989	France(2)	83–86	131	10.0%
Jacquillat *et al.*	1978	France(3)	66–74	60	5.0%
Ulhir	1989	Germany	77–87	97	21.5%
Wessels	1989	Holland(1)	82–87	30	28.9%
Wessels	1989	Holland(3)	82–87	16	22.4%

Notes: (1) principal market, (2) second market, (3) third market (OTC)

From the figures in Table 9.1, one can see that large differences in underpricing exist from one country to another, and from one market to another in the same country. But in all cases significant underpricing is observed, even more on the second or third markets than on the principal ones.

Why are IPOs so widely underpriced? Many theoretical explanations have been proposed. We have organized the main ones according to five themes.

Proposed theories

1. The influence of market organization

Each national market has its peculiarities, which limit or increase the underpricing phenomenon. In the United States, for example, the 'firm commitment' procedure generates greater underpricing than the 'best effort' contract (Ritter 1984). In France four different listing procedures are available, giving contrasting underpricing levels, as already explained by Husson and Jacquillat (1989), and confirmed below. Dubois and Dumontier (1988) also suggest that in France, the freezing of funds imposed on the investors in most cases may explain part of the underpricing: the investors need a compensation for the interest lost on their frozen funds.

2. The influence of timing: the 'hot market' issue

In every country, there are periods when the number of IPOs grows dramatically. This phenomenon, known as 'hot market', occurred, for example, in the United States in 1981, 1983, and 1986, according to data used by Barry and Alii (1990), and Ritter (1991). We will discuss the same phenomenon in France in a later section.

How timing influences underpricing is not clearly established. Ibbotson and Jaffe (1975) concluded that 'issuers may obtain a higher offering price relative to the efficient price when they issued in cold issue markets.' Ritter observed higher abnormal returns during 'hot' periods, from 1977 to 1982, but only in one industry. One explanation proposed for higher underpricing in 'hot markets' is the higher perceived risk due to incomplete information on firms, when many of them are issuing IPOs at the same time. But Ritter (1984) does not confirm this higher risk.

McBain and Krause (1989) begin with a different hypothesis: 'One may speculate that during "hot" markets, investors are eager to obtain new equity issues because they observe the abnormally large short-run return performance of recent issues'. But they found no difference in the P/E ratio on the offer day according to the 'temperature' of the market. 'Owners taking their firm public cannot expect to negotiate offering P/E ratios based on the degree to which the market is "hot" or "cold".'

3. The influence of the firm's characteristics

The age of the firm and its size have been presented as influencing the level of underpricing, with the largest perceived risk for younger and smaller firms. Stoll and Curley (1970) found no significant difference in underpricing based on firm size, but Ritter (1984) finds that underwriters can underprice smaller issues, especially in 'hot' markets. Young and Zaima (1986,1988) tested for age and industry influence. They found no industry effect, but confirmed that younger firms were more underpriced.

Following agency theory, McBain and Krause (1989) expect that the higher the reduction of insiders' holdings because of the IPO, the higher the agency costs estimated by investors and the higher the underpricing. This hypothesis is confirmed by their empirical work, and they conclude that 'larger relative valuations are obtained by firms whose insiders maintain relatively large ownership positions following the public offering of securities'.

4. Information asymmetry

Information on the IPO market and on the quality of the firms going public is not equally distributed between the different actors in the process.

- The underwriters have IPO market information that the firms preparing to go public do not have. Baron (1982) suggests that underpricing could be the price to be paid to the underwriters in exchange for this information.
- Investors are not equally informed of the firm's value. Non-informed investors would not keep on investing in initial public offerings if the stocks offered were not underpriced, on an average. Beatty and Ritter (1986) showed that there is a link between underpricing and the lack of information, and that the underwriters increase the underpricing voluntarily so as to keep the non-informed investors in the market.
- Insiders have information that investors do not have on the firm's projects and its actual value. High-quality firms use the IPO underpricing as a signal to the market, and accept its cost as the price for obtaining high proceeds on their eventual secondary issues. Low-quality firms, on the other hand, will perhaps obtain higher relative proceeds from the IPO, but may be unmasked before any secondary issue (Welch 1989; Grinblatt and Hwang 1989).

5. The insurance hypothesis

Underwriters take a risk when taking a firm public. First, their reputation is at stake, and underpricing the offer is a good way to insure that all the stocks will be sold. This is particularly the case for firm commitments procedures: in this case, they are also at risk financially. Underpricing is also a way for underwriters to insure against their legal responsibility for the quality of the information they give to investors: the lower the offered price, the lower the risk of being sued later by discontented investors. Tinic (1988) demonstrated the link between the increase in underpricing and the Securities Act of 1933 which defined more precisely the underwriter's responsibility.

6. The certification effect

The presence of well-known operators on the IPO firm's side can reduce the risk perceived by investors, and so allow smaller under-pricing. This has been recently documented by Barry and Alii (1990) and Megginson and Weiss (1991). For them, venture capitalists' presence in the firm's equity has positive consequences for the firm during the IPO process. The venture capitalists can help in obtaining better underwriters and better auditors. Added to the diminution of perceived risk and linked to their efficient monitoring of the firm, this leads to lower underpricing, lower underwriter and auditor compensation, and so significantly higher net proceeds for the firm.

Among the numerous theories and hypotheses quickly summarized above, we chose to build on the certification effect proposed by Megginson and Weiss (1991),and on the influence of insider holdings, as developped by McBain and Krause (1989).

Accordingly, the hypotheses to be tested will be:

H1: Underpricing is lower for venture capital backed firms than for non-venture capital backed ones.
H2: The use of prestigious underwriters and auditors increases the certification effect, and allows lower underpricing.
H3: The smaller the reduction of insiders' holdings, the lower the underpricing.

Before detailing the methodology used to test these hypothesis, and the results obtained, we need to present in some detail the peculiarities on the French second market.

Peculiarities on the French second market

The listing conditions and procedures

One of the reasons the second market proved quite successful in bringing medium-sized firms to the market was the fact that its regulation was much looser than that of the principal market.

The mimimum percentage of equity which must be put on sale has been lowered from 25 per cent to 10 per cent. To ensure a minimum liquidity to the market, although such a small proportion of the capital becomes public, market authorities strongly recommended that the newly listed firms sign liquidity contracts with their underwriters and brokers. Two underwriting contracts, firm commitment and best effort, are available instead of the single one before 1983. In practice most IPOs are made on a best effort basis.

Three different offering methods are available:

The 'procédure ordinaire' (PO)   This procedure is quite close to a competitive auction. The shares must be sold to the underwriters before the IPO. The underwriters manage the IPO themselves, under the control of the Société des Bourses Françaises (the market authority). In this procedure, subscribers are allowed to buy shares only at the market price. If there is too large an imbalance between the number of shares put on sale and the demand for them, the underwriters can raise the offer price, and ask for new bids until an equilibrium is reached. But they can also switch at any time to the procedure 'offre publique de vente'.

The 'mise en vente' procedure (MV)   Prior to the IPO, the firm and its consulting investment banker determine a minimum acceptable price ('le prix d'offre'). This price is announced to the potential investors some days before the offering. The investors are not allowed to buy at market price. Their bids are gathered by the banks and brokers, and processed centrally by the Société des Bourses Françaises (SBF). A committee composed of the company managers, their bankers, and members of the SBF meets on the morning of the offering day. After eliminating the highest bids, considered as 'disguised market orders', the committee sets the offer price, and allocates the shares on a pro rata basis. The price is set under what the committee feels to be the equilibrium, according to the ranked list of bids they have under review.

The 'offre publique de vente' (OPV)   This is a tender offer, made by the firm's shareholders to the public, on the basis of a fixed price and a fixed quantity of stocks to be sold. In case of imbalance between supply and demand, the committee in charge of the IPO can either make a proportional reduction or, if the imbalance is too large, decide to declare the flotation impossible and ask the shareholders to propose another OPV, with a higher price. The OPV procedure is often used when the other two have failed because of the imbalance between supply and demand. It is then called indirect OPV.

2. Motivations for going public

In contrast to other countries where the main objective of an IPO is the acquisition of new funds to finance growth, on the French second market, financing is not the only nor the main motivation (Belletante and Desroches 1993). Table 9.2 from Jaffeux and Le Guen (1990), makes this quite clear.

Table 9.2 Motivation on the French second market

Motivation	Intensity					
	None	Poor	Medium	Fair	Strong	No opinion
Succession	41	9	13	9	14	13
Public image	2	5	13	32	43	5
Financing	7	8	15	24	39	7
Liquidity of property	12	13	13	31	18	12
Realizing value	22	26	15	18	7	10

Very few firms raised capital at the time of the IPO (6 cases are listed by Jaffeux and Le Guen, out of 209 firms studied). And few of them raised capital after the IPO, according to Belletante (1992), as seen from Table 9.3.

Table 9.3 Firms raising capital after the IPO

Lyon and Paris markets	85	86	87	88	89	90
Number of firms listed	102	149	217	235	247	249
Firms raising equity	9	17	28	7	19	17
Per cent	9	11	13	3	8	7

Given the small number of firms which increased their equity through the second market after their IPO, the signalling explanation discussed above (see section on information asymmetry), would not be easy to test in the French context.

The chosen variables

1. Measure of underpricing

Since we are interested in observing the impact of changes in equity structure on underpricing, we choose to select two measures of underpricing instead of using only post-market abnormal returns, so as to get a broader view. *The potential underpricing* is defined as the difference between the equilibrium price[1] and the first offered – or minimum – price, divided by the first offered or minimum price. It represents the maximum potential loss, measured a posteriori, that the sellers may have suffered, if their stocks had actually been sold at the offered or minimum price. *The actual underpricing* is defined as the difference between the equilibrium price and the first listed price, divided by the first listed price. It represents the actual 'loss' of those stockholders whose stocks were sold on the first listed price basis.

To describe more precisely how the equilibrium is reached, we will use three more variables:

1 the ratio of demand over supply, for the last offer;
2 the number of days after the first listing day, necessary to reach the equilibrium;
3 the total number of stocks exchanged during the period between the first listing day and the equilibrium, divided by the number of stocks offered. This variable shows to what extent the price increase is merely due to pure speculation, or investors selling back most of the stocks offered, during the first few days after flotation.

The presence of venture capital and investment banks

The certification effect can be obtained through the presence of venture capital firms or of investment banks, whose roles and knowledge of the firm are nearly the same. We use three variables to measure their role.

1 the per cent of equity owned by the venture capital firms before the IPO;
2 the per cent of equity owned by investment banks before the IPO;
3 the per cent of equity owned by both.

Insiders' holdings

Insiders' holdings before the IPO are measured by the per cent of equity owned by the entrepreneurs and their family or by the parent company if the venture is a subsidiary. Their evolution is measured by the variation of this percentage between before and after the IPO, as announced in the listing prospectus.

Ranking underwriters, brokers, and auditors

The banks involved in the IPO process can be either investment banks or commercial ones. There is no official ranking of banks for the IPO market. So we simply counted the number of IPOs in which each of them was involved in our sample, and ranked them according to this number (range from 1 to 68). We used the same procedure for the brokers, (range from 1 to 15). But for auditors we only separated the French representatives of the 'big six' auditing companies (33 cases) from local auditors (119 cases).

The control variables

We use the following control variables, when possible, given the size of the sample:

The *size of the firm*, estimated through its market value at the first listing price.
The *size of the offer*, in millions of francs
The *age of the firm*, on the flotation date
The *place of flotation* (Paris, Lyon, and others)
The *industry* in which the firm operates
The *'hot market'* phenomenon

To round out this theoretical and methodological first section, we hope to add some additional empirical evidence on the IPO underpricing phenomenon in the next section. We also intend to give more precise insight into this market, which remains one of the most successful junior markets in Europe.

EMPIRICAL RESULTS

The sample consists of 165 firms which went public between 1983 and 1991 on the second market. As there is no available database in France on IPOs, we had to gather the information ourselves. We obtained the prospectuses either from the firms themselves, from the Société des Bourses Françaises, from the stock brokers, or from the underwriters.

To what extent is the sample representative?

We made no actual choice of the firms: all those for which the information was available were included in the sample. Whether the sample is representative or not can be appreciated from Table 9.4.

Table 9.4 The study sample

Year of issue:	83	84	85	86	87	88	89	90	91	Total
Our sample	7	14	24	23	40	18	23	10	6	165
Total number of IPOs on the market[2]	18	29	55	51	70	26	30	13	8	292
Per cent	39	48	44	45	58	69	77	77	75	57

Because of the difficulties encountered in gathering information on the oldest issues, our sample over-represents the most recent years. This will have to be kept in mind when we analyse the 'hot market' issue.

Table 9.5 Firm values

Value of the firm (FFm.)	83	84	85	86	87	88	89	90	91	Mean
Our sample:	107	150	188	264	320	380	552	549	170	298
All IPOs[3]:	225	270	487	481	671	495	591	756	279	473

Except for 1989, our sample is composed of smaller firms. This can be explained by our decision not to deal with financial firms, and by the fact that we could obtain practically no information from those larger firms listed on the second market which eventually got listed on the principal one. In this respect, there is no significant difference between our sample and the entire population for the period for which we have the information.

Table 9.6 Listing procedures

	Listing procedure*				
	MV	PO	OPV	OPVD	Total
Our sample	40	28	46	51	165
Per cent	24	17	28	31	100
All issues 1983–1988:**	73	46	63	75	257
Per cent	28	18	25	29	100

Notes: *MV = 'Mise en vente', PO = 'Procédure ordinaire', POV = 'Offre publique de vente', OPVD = 'Offre publique de vente indirecte'. ** From Jaffeux (1990), p. 952.

Structure of equity

Table 9.7 details the composition of equity before the firms went public, and the percentage of total equity each category put on sale, according to the available information included in the prospectus. We could not get more precise information than 'family and managers' in most of the cases. So we decided to keep this quite vague group, considering that the investors were no better informed at the time of the IPO than we are now.

Table 9.7 Composition of firm equity

Whole sample	Structure before		Put on sale	
	Mean	*Std D.*	*Mean*	*Std D.*
Family and managers	66.5%	34.6%	5.7%	5.2%
Employees	2.3%	5.8%	0.1%	0.7%
Parent company	15.0%	29.9%	1.5%	3.7%
Investment banks	5.1%	13.7%	0.9%	2.6%
Underwriters	2.1%	4.7%	1.6%	3.4%
Venture capitalists	4.7%	9.2%	0.8%	2.1%
Others	4.3%	10.2%	0.4%	2.2%

According to who the main sellers are, six types can be defined, and the sample is divided into these types, as shown in Table 9.8.

Table 9.8 Types and market value of firms in sample

Types of firms	Number of firms	Market value at listing price (FFm.)	
		Mean	*Std D.*
Type 1: Family alone	56	309	596
Type 2: Family, with banks or VC	29	270	399
Type 3: Parent company	20	405	327
Type 4: Banks or VC	23	267	195
Type 5: Underwriters	27	246	797
Type 6: Others	10	355	349

There is in fact no significant difference in size between the types. Knowing that the average proportion of stocks sold during the IPO is 10.9 per cent, Table 9.9 shows that there are significant differences between the sellers, according to the defined type, so that they prove to be quite consistent.

Global underpricing

As explained in the first section, we defined two measures of underpricing: potential and actual. For the sample these two measures take values shown in Table 9.10.

Table 9.9 Mode of selling stocks, by firm

	Percentage of stocks sold by:		
	Family	Parent company	Banks or VC
Type of firm			
Type 1:	10.67%	0.13%	0.00%
Type 2:	8.87%	0.13%	1.83%
Type 3:	0.24%	9.79%	0.37%
Type 4:	1.91%	0.79%	8.40%
Type 5:	0.97%	0.33%	0.46%
Type 6:	1.65%	0.74%	1.77%

Table 9.10 Measures for underpricing

Whole sample	Mean	Std D.	Min.	Max.
Potential underpricing	40.1%	39.7%	−3%	244%
Actual underpricing	20.7%	28.8%	−7%	244%

These results can be compared to those obtained by Jaffeux (1990), on the complete population of IPOs from 1983 to 1988, i.e. 239 cases:[4] potential underpricing: 44.2 per cent; actual underpricing: 14.54 per cent. The differences can be explained by the differences in time covered and listing procedures used. Let us first analyse these two measures according to the listing procedures (Table 9.11).

Table 9.11 Analysis by listing procedure

	Underpricing			
	Potential		Actual	
Listing procedure	Mean	Std D.	Mean	Std D.
Mise en vente	45.6%	41.3%	16.4%	25.3%
Offre publique de vente	31.8%	42.9%	28.0%	41.3%
Offre publique indirecte	59.3%	34.5%	26.4%	20.4%
Procédure ordinaire	10.8%	10.2%	4.3%	6.1%

There are large differences in underpricing, both potential and actual, between the 'procédure ordinaire' and the 'offres publiques'. The 'mise en vente' stands in between, with less actual underpricing but a larger potential one than the 'offres publiques'. So, the 'procédure ordinaire', and to a lesser extent the 'mise en vente', allow lower actual underpricing, and should be preferred by the sellers. The question then is, why do sellers accept the other methods?

The effect of time

There has been a significant evolution in underpricing with time, as shown in Table 9.12.

Table 9.12 Underpricing over time

Year	Number of firms	Underpricing Potential Mean	Std D.	Actual Mean	Std D.
1983	7	52.8%	31.3%	35.6%	36.7%
1984	14	62.6%	41.7%	35.0%	30.3%
1985	24	57.2%	54.9%	28.8%	49.8%
1986	23	65.8%	38.4%	35.4%	27.9%
1987	40	33.4%	38.6%	15.3%	21.0%
1988	18	10.6%	7.7%	4.7%	5.3%
1989	23	28.9%	19.1%	13.6%	11.8%
1990	10	14.0%	8.7%	8.2%	3.5%
1991	6	25.3%	21.4%	13.6%	15.6%

Quite evidently, there was a break in 1987 when the major stock market crash occurred. This can be illustrated more precisely by separating the sample between the firms listed prior to October 1987 and those listed after this date.

Table 9.13 Effect of 1987 crash on sample

Crash	Number of firms	Underpricing Potential Mean	Std D.	Actual Mean	Std D.
Before	93	57.8%	43.4%	30.4%	34.5%
After	72	17.2%	16.5%	8.2%	9.7%

Both measures are significantly different (at 0.000%). This has been associated with a modification in the use of listing procedures, influencing at least the actual underpricing.

Table 9.14 Crash effect and modified listing procedures

Crash	Number of firms	Listing procedures MV	OPV	OPVD	PO
Before	93	31	24	35	3
Per cent		33	26	38	3
After	72	9	22	16	25
Per cent		12	31	22	35

There may have been a link between the crash and the number of firms getting listed, the crash generating a long 'cold' market. We examined the number of firms listed every month and discovered that 'hot markets' also occurred after the crash. So we focused then on the 'hot market' issue, to control for its influence on underpricing.

The 'hot market' issue

First we tested whether the demand for IPO shares is higher or lower during 'hot markets'. We defined two ways to isolate 'hot' and 'cold' markets:

1 'Hot' and 'cold' markets are defined by the number of IPOs during the three preceding months. The first quartile of the number of IPOs is considered part of the 'cold' market: four IPOs on an average during the three previous months. The fourth quartile is considered the 'hot' market: 22 IPOs on an average for the three preceding months. There are marked differences, but only the second one, on the number of stocks exchanged, is significant (at the 2 per cent level). See Table 9.15.
2 'Hot' and 'cold' markets set as fixed periods of time. The whole sample is included in this analysis, and the difference between the average number of IPOs is smaller: 19 on average for 'hot' periods, against 8 for 'cold' ones. With this definition of 'hot' and 'cold' markets, the differences are stressed, as shown in Table 9.16. In both cases, the differences are significant (at the 2% level). *We can assume that the demand is lower for each IPO when the number of IPOs increases.* Then we checked if the offering procedures were used differently, according to the state of the market.

Table 9.15 'Hot' and 'cold' markets as the number of IPOs during the three preceding months

Market	Number of firms	Demand / Supply Mean	Std D.	Number of stocks exchanged until equilibrium Mean	Std D.
'Hot'	47	53.1	50.8	39.1%	35.7%
'Cold'	40	61.5	43.2	62.8%	56.0%

Table 9.16 'Hot' and 'cold' markets as fixed periods of time

Market	Number of firms	Demand Supply		Number of stocks exchanged until equilibrium	
		Mean	Std D.	Mean	Std D.
'Hot'	62	45.2	44.6	39.8%	35.2%
'Cold'	103	66.6	40.2	61.8%	44.3%

There are more 'price-driven' procedures used in 'hot' markets, and more 'offres publiques', with fixed prices, in 'cold' markets, as can be seen in Table 9.17. The difference is significant at the 2 per cent level.

Table 9.17 'Hot' and 'cold' markets and procedures used

Market	Number of firms	Listing procedures			
		MV	OPV	OPVD	PO
'Hot'	62	19	13	14	16
Expected		15	17	19	10
'Cold'	103	21	33	37	12
Expected		25	29	32	17

'Hot' and 'cold' markets and underpricing

According to both the definitions of 'hot' markets we used, there is a significant difference in underpricing between 'hot' and 'cold' markets, as can be seen in Tables 9.18 and 9.19.

Table 9.18 'Hot' and 'cold' markets defined by the first and fourth quartiles of the number of IPOs during the three previous months

Market	Number of firms	Underpricing Potential		Actual	
		Mean	Std D.	Mean	Std D.
'Hot'	47	27.9%	29.9%	11.7%	16.3%
'Cold'	40	47.3%	47.4%	26.4%	26.7%

Table 9.19 'Hot' and 'cold' markets set as fixed periods of time

	Number of firms	*Underpricing*			
		Potential		*Actual*	
Market		*Mean*	*Std D.*	*Mean*	*Std D.*
'Hot'	62	27.8%	30.8%	11.8%	18.8%
'Cold'	103	47.5%	42.7%	26.7%	32.3%

The results are very similar, and somewhat different from those found in other studies (Ritter 1984; Ibbotson and Jaffe 1975). An explanation could be found in the fact that the demand for IPOs is not limitless.

When too many IPOs occur in the same period of time, investors have a broader choice, the demand for each IPO is lower, price-driven procedures are easier to implement, and the underpricing results lower. Given the significant differences in underpricing according to this variable, we will have to integrate it into our subsequent analysis. As many investors are regionally based, another explanation of the underpricing magnitude and variation could be found in the place where the firms went public.

Analysis by listing place

We distinguished three 'places': Paris, Lyon, and others (see Table 9.20). The reason for isolating Lyon and grouping the five other regional places comes from the number of IPOs. From 1983 to 1991, there have been 178 IPOs in Paris, 63 in Lyon, and 52 in all five other places.[5]

Table 9.20 Analysis of sample by listing place

Listing place	*Paris*	*Lyon*	*Others*
Number of firms in the sample	94	45	26
Market value at listing price	449	167	99
Potential underpricing	37.4%	49.0%	34.4%
Actual underpricing	17.9%	30.0%	14.7%

Of course, due to our special relationships with local firms we could obtain more information from them, and therefore Lyon is over-represented. But, nevertheless, the above figures indicate a special behaviour in this place, when compared to both Paris and all the other local centres.

Given the disparity in sizes and underpricing, one may wonder whether the French financial market is actually homogeneous.

Analysis by industry

The sample covers 25 different industries, according to the classification of the Société des Bourses Françaises. Few groups are significant enough to be analysed. We give the results for five of them, those including more than 10 firms (see Table 9.21).

Table 9.21 Analysis of sample by industry

| Industry | Number of firms | Underpricing | | | |
| | | Potential | | Actual | |
		Mean	Std D.	Mean	Std D.
Mechanical	13	32.8%	39.6%	22.3%	27.1%
Textiles	13	36.3%	41.5%	16.6%	20.2%
Plastics	12	38.0%	39.2%	14.8%	20.2%
Distribution	17	48.6%	41.0%	24.7%	23.1%
Computers	37	43.0%	50.2%	27.1%	45.3%

Although the figures in Table 9.21 are apparently quite different from one industry to another, none of these differences are statistically significant at the 5 per cent level.

Other control variables

We have looked for size effect, and used the market value at the first listing price as a proxy for the size. We also included the firms' age, and the amount offered, but the correlations with underpricing are rather weak, especially for the age, as can be seen in Table 9.22.

Table 9.22 Other control variables

| | Number of firms | Underpricing | | | |
| | | Potential | | Actual | |
		Correl.	Sig.	Correl.	Sig.
Market value	165	−0.120	0.063	−0.093	0.118
Volume of the offer	165	−0.156	0.023	−0.108	0.083
Age	165	0.057	0.234	0.071	0.181

In concluding this section dealing with global results one must keep in mind some important evidence:

1 the impact of the Crash, which was stronger on the second market than on the principal one. After the crash, underpricing proved to be significantly lower;
2 the very large potential as well as actual underpricing;
3 the strong imbalance between demand and supply, especially in 'cold' markets;
4 the impact of the offering procedures which modify the level of underpricing;
5 the relatively low impact of the other control variables, industry, volume of the offer, size, and age of the firm.

TEST OF THE PROPOSED HYPOTHESES

Equity structure, certification effect, and agency costs

We first test the existence of relations between underpricing, potential and actual, and the variables chosen to test the first two hypotheses, on the entire sample. The correlations with the two measures of underpricing are shown in Table 9.23.

Table 9.23 Correlations with two measures of underpricing

165 Cases	Potential underpricing	Actual underpricing
% owned by VC firms	−.0561	−.0346
p	.237	.329
% owned by Invest. Banks	−.0895	−.0762
p	.126	.165
% owned by both (VC+IB)	−.1065	−.0833
p	.087	.144
% owned by insiders	.0852	.0567
p	.138	.235
variation of insiders %	.0472	.1018
p	.274	.097

Note: As shown by this table, if the relations are bearing the expected sign, they are not significant at the .05 level

As we have already stressed the major role played by the type of market, we split the sample in two, according to 'hot' and 'cold' markets, looking for any difference between the two sub–samples. The results can be seen in Tables 9.24 and 9.25.

Table 9.24 'Cold' market segment of sample: underpricing

'Cold' market (103 Cases)	Potential underpricing	Actual underpricing
% owned by VC firms	–.1796	–.1383
p	.035	.082
% owned by investment banks	–.1061	–.0579
p	.143	.281
% owned by both (VC+IB)	–.1947	–.1313
p	.024	.093
% owned by insiders	.1493	.0815
p	.066	.207
variation of insiders %	–.0006	.0735
p	.497	.230

According to these figures, during 'cold' markets, there is a significant negative relation between the per cent of equity owned by venture capital or investment banks and the potential underpricing: when controlling for the status of the market, the first hypothesis is verified. But the second one is not: there seems to be no relation at all between the reduction in 'insiders' holding and the level of underpricing.

Table 9.25 'Hot' market segment of sample: underpricing

'Hot' Markets (62 cases)	Potential underpricing	Actual underpricing
% owned by VC firms	.1518	–.1761
p	.119	.085
% owned by investment banks	–.0895	–.0762
p	.126	.165
% owned by both (VC+IB)	.0342	.0059
p	.396	.482
% owned by insiders	–.0300	–.0079
p	.138	.476
variation of insiders %	.0943	.1299
p	.233	.157

It is obvious from table 9.25 that during 'hot' markets the relations are much looser, (none is even significant, at the .05 level).

We could summarize these results by saying that when too many IPOs occur at the same time, investors pay less attention to the certification effect provided by the presence of financial investors in the equity, or to the agency costs that the reduction of insiders' holdings may generate.

The certification effect through underwriters and auditors

Contrary to Megginson and Weiss (1991), we found absolutely no relation between underpricing and the 'prestige' or experience of underwriters or auditors used by the firm, and this was so even when splitting the sample between 'cold' and 'hot' markets.

Table 9.26 Underpricing and underwriters

152 Cases	Potential underpricing	Actual underpricing
Ranking of the Société de Bourse	.0750	.1113
p	.171	.079
Ranking of the Bank in charge of the IPO	−.0865	−.0475
p	.143	.279
Ranking of the auditor	−.0232	−.0504
p	.389	.269

Table 9.27 'Cold' markets

95 Cases	Potential underpricing	Actual underpricing
Ranking of the Société de Bourse	.0654	.0918
p	.258	.181
Ranking of the bank in charge of the IPO	−.0962	−.0402
p	.177	.349
Ranking of the auditor	−.0560	−.0863
p	.294	.202

Table 9.28 'Hot' markets

56 Cases	Potential underpricing	Actual underpricing
Ranking of the Société de Bourse	.0607	.1358
p	.320	.146
Ranking of the bank in charge of the IPO	−.0502	−.0897
p	.353	.250
Ranking of the auditor	.0722	.0645
p	.298	.318

We can conclude that the use of experienced and well-known underwriters or auditors does not allow any lower underpricing on the whole. On the contrary, using an experienced Société de Bourse leads to higher underpricing. That would be paradoxical, if it proved statistically significant!

In conclusion, we find:

1 poor evidence of a certification effect due to the presence of venture capital firms or investment banks in the firm's equity, prior to the IPO. The Megginson and Weiss hypothesis is only supported in 'cold' markets.
2 no evidence supporting the hypothesis proposed by McBain and Krause of a relation between the insiders' holdings reduction and underpricing: the investors do not seem to anticipate higher agency costs when insiders sell a larger part of their shares. But this could also be the result of the relatively similar percentage of shares sold in all the IPOs: most of the time only 10 per cent of the shares are put on sale, i.e. the minimum required only.
3 absolutely no evidence of any reduction of underpricing obtained through using high-ranked underwriters or prestigious auditors. Although these results may seem surprising and will need to be checked on a larger sample, they indicate that entrepreneurs thinking of flotation do not need to look for the more expensive underwriters in order to reduce underpricing.

CONCLUSION

The answer to the title question of this paper is, according to these early results, and quite surprisingly: Not in France, on the second market. Nevertheless, a lot of work remains to be done before obtaining really significant results:

• A possible industry effect must be looked for more carefully, and that will entail an increase in sample's size.
• Although the total number of IPOs may make it difficult, we will try to use matched samples to get a more precise insight into the certification effect.
• We also intend to test the signalling approach by analysing for differences in underpricing according to the existence or not of secondary offers in the months following the IPO.

NOTES

1 In the economic meaning, i.e. when supply equals demand, without any reduction in the asked number of stocks.
2 Non-financial firms. According to the COB report (1992): 'Le second marche', p. 16
3 According to the COB report (1992), p. 16
4 Our figures for the period 1983–1988 are, respectively, potential underpricing: 44.9%; actual underpricing: 23.3%. Although we do not have the standard deviation of Jaffeux, it seems that a significant difference exists on actual underpricing.
5 According to the COB report (1992), p. 10.

REFERENCES

Allen, A.R. and Faulhaber, G.R. (1989) 'Signaling by Underpricing in the IPO Market', *Journal of Financial Economics*, 23: 303–323.
Alphao, R.M. (1989) 'Initial Public Offering in the Lisbon Stock Exchange', Universidade de Lisboa, Faculdade de Economia, avril.
Balvers, R.J, McDonald, B. and Miller, R.E. (1988) 'Underpricing of New Issues and the Choice of Auditor as a Signal of Investment Banker Reputation', *The Accounting Review*, (Oct.) 4.
Baron, D.P. (1982) 'A Model of the Demand for Investment Banking Advising and Distribution Services for New Issues', *Journal of Finance,* 37 (September): 955–976.
Barry, C., Muscarella, C., Peavy, J., and Vetsuypens, M. 'The Role of Venture Capital in the Creation of Public Companies', *Journal of Financial Economics*, 27: 447–471.
Beatty, R. and Ritter, J.R. (1986) 'Investment Banking, Reputation and the Underpricing of Initial Public Offerings', *Journal of Financial Economics*, 15: 213–232
Belletante, B. (1992) 'Territoire financier des PME et présence en Bourse', *Cahiers Lyonnais de Recherche en Gestion*, 13 (avril): 59–85.
Belletante B. and Desroches J. (1993) 'Atouts et contraintes de la cotation des entreprises moyennes, bilan de 10 ans du second marché', Etude SBF/SEGESPAR, Groupe ESC Lyon, Lyon.
Brealey, R. and Myers, S. (1984) *Principles of Corporate Finance*, 1st edn, New York: McGraw Hill.
Chalk, A.J. and Peavy, J.W. (1987) 'Initial Public Offerings: Daily Returns, Offering Types and the Price Effect', *Financial Analysts Journal*, 43.
Commission des Opérations de Bourse – COB – (1992) *Rapport sur le Second Marché*, Paris.
Dawson, S.M. and Robbins, E.H. (1989) 'Anatomy of IPOs of Common Stock: A Comment', *College of Business Administration of Hawai*, (July).
De Ridder, A. (1986) *Access to the Stock Market*, Federation of Swedish Industries.
Grinblatt M. and Hwang, C.Y. (1989) 'Signaling and the Pricing of New Issues', *Journal of Finance*, 44 (2) (June) 383–420.
Husson, B. and Jacquillat, B. (1989) 'French New Issues, Underpricing and Alternative Methods of Distribution', NATO Series, vol. F54, *A*

Reappraisal of the Efficiency of Financial Markets, ed. by Rui M.C. Guimaraes *et al.*, pp. 349–368.

Husson, B. and Jacquillat, B. (1990) 'Sous-évaluation des titres et méthodes d'introduction au second Marché, 1983–86', *Finance*, 11 (1): 123–134.

Ibbotson, R.G. (1975) 'Price Performance of Common Stock New Issues', *Journal of Financial Economics*, 3: 235–272.

Ibbotson, R.G. and Jaffe, J.K. (1975) 'Hot Issue Markets', *Journal of Finance*, 30: 1027–1042.

Ibbotson, R.G., Sindelar, J.L. and Ritter, J.R. (1988) 'Initial Public Offerings', *Journal of Applied Corporate Finance*, 1: 37–45.

Jacquillat, B., McDonald, J.G., and Rolfo, J. (1979) 'L'introduction en bourse des sociétés, 1966–1974,' *La Revue Banque*, 385 (juin).

Jaffeux, C. (1990) 'Essai d'explication de la sous-évaluation des titres à leur introduction sur le Second Marché', *La Revue Banque*, 509 (octobre): 952–958.

Jaffeux, C. and Le Guen, M. (1990) 'La partition des sociétés sur des critères psycho-financiers est-elle rationnelle? L'exemple des introductions sur le Second Marché', *Analyse Financière*, 1er trimestre: 64–81.

Jensen, M. and Meckling, W. (1976) 'Theory of the Firm: Managerial Behavior, Agency Costs and Ownership Structure', *Journal of Financial Economics*, 3 (4): 305–360.

Logue, D.E. (1973) 'On the Pricing of Unseasoned Equity Issues: 1965–1969', *Journal of Financial and Quantitative Analysis*, 8: 91–103.

McBain, M.L. and Krause, D.S. (1989) 'Going Public: the Impact of Insider's Holdings on the Price of IPOs', *Journal of Business Venturing*, 4: 419–428.

Megginson, W. and Weiss, K.A. (1991) 'Venture Capitalist Certification in IPOs', *Journal of Finance*, 45 (1): 3–28.

Neuberger, N.M. and LaChapelle, C.A. (1983) 'Unseasoned New Issue, 1975–80', *Financial Management*, Autumn: 23–28.

Paliard, R. and Belletante, B. (1992) 'Does Knowing Who Sells Matter in IPO Pricing?', Efer conference on 'Realising Enterprise Value', London, 13–15 Dec.

Ritter, J.R. (1984) 'The 'Hot Issue' Markets', *Journal of Business*, 32: 215–240.

Ritter, J.R. (1987) 'The Costs of Going Public', *Journal of Financial Economics*, 19: 269–281.

Rock, K. (1986) 'Why New Issues are Underpriced', *Journal of Financial Economics*, 15: 187–212.

Stoll, H.R. and Curley, J.A. (1970) 'Small Business and the New Issues Markets for Equities', *Journal of Financial and Quantitative Analysis*, 5: 309–322.

Tinic, S.M. (1988) 'Anatomy of Initial Public Offerings of Common Stock', *Journal of Finance*, 43 (Sept): 789–822.

Welch, I. (1989) 'Seasoned Offerings, Imitation Costs, and the Underpricing of IPOs', *Journal of Finance*, 44 (June): 421–449.

Wessels, R.E. (1982/87) *The Market for Initial Public Offering: An Analysis of the Amsterdam Stock Exchange*, Taylor, Nato, ASI Series, vol. F54.

Wessels, R.E. (1989) *The Reappraisal of the Efficiency of Financial Market*, Berlin; Heidelberg: Springer Verlag.

Young, J.E. and Zaima, J.K. (1986) 'Does it "Pay" to Invest in Small Business IPOs?', *Journal of Small Business Management,* 24: 39–50.
Young, J.E. and Zaima, J.K. (1988) 'The Aftermarket Performance of Small Firm Initial Public Offerings', *Journal of Business Venturing,* 3: 77–87.
Uhlir, H., *Going Public in the Federal Republic of Germany,* Taylor, Nato, ASI Series, vol. F54.

Section III

Life-style issues

10 Entrepreneurial behaviour of French engineers

An exploratory study

Alain Fayolle and Yves-Frédéric Livian

INTRODUCTION

This paper tries to identify the circumstances under which the two main categories of French professionals, the entrepreneur and the engineer, merge into one.[1] Our study details how we identified the characteristics of the entrepreneurial engineer. The identification was based on a sample of twenty engineers who decided to start their own companies.

The first part of our paper describes the typical training for French engineers and the effects of this on their career development. The second part gives the results of our exploratory study. Finally we try to draw conclusions and offer suggestions for the future development of this study.

According to economic literature, the entrepreneur has played successively the role of capitalist (Smith 1991; Knight 1971), organizer (Say 1972, Marshall 1964), innovator (Schumpeter 1935), and coordinator of resources (Casson 1982). Overall, they come across as atypical persons, who are unlikely to fit into any predefined schema of personality.

The emergence of an entrepreneur from the engineer is certainly an important occurrence. Economic history has shown us the innovating and entrepreneurial tendencies of many engineers both in France and other countries. Eiffel, Bouygoues, and Schlumberger are some of the French entrepreneur–engineers; in other countries, Watt, Trevithick, Fulton, Siemens, Daimler, Diesel, and Fleming fall into the same category.

The international literature on the subject, surprisingly enough, has little on the entrepreneurial behaviour of engineers. The interest of such a study seems, however, obvious. Entrepreneurial engineers seem to be innovators and creators of economic wealth: they contribute heavily to the renewal of social and industrial structure. A study carried out by 'l'Usine Nouvelle' in France, on the 'champions of innovation', gives us an overview of innovating, young start-up companies. It shows that, very often, engineers originated the innovating companies selected for the study.

The engineer is a key element in technological innovation. The economic future of an industrialized country lies essentially in its ability to innovate in the technological field. Kent (1982) points out that a close link often exists between, on the one hand, the level of technological growth of a country and, on the other hand, the number and the skills of its entrepreneurs. Engineers have always played an essential role in the economy. But the increase in the varieties of specialities and the diversity of career development has led to many questions concerning their entrepreneurial behaviour. This issue is the starting point of the second reason for our study.

Young people who succeed in winning competitive scientific exams in France are those who have been educated by a secondary educational system that is far removed from everyday economic reality. The French educational system rewards those who can adapt best to its abstract content. The student will always be influenced more by his years at preparatory school than by his years of training at engineering school. This, in spite of the fact that his engineering degree will be his ticket to professional success. We believe that such loyalty is not very favourable to entrepreneurial behaviour. The last point of interest concerns policymaking. Our findings will give us information which would allow us to establish policies to encourage the development of start-up companies. The starting point of our work was an analysis of a study recently carried out by a research team at HEC Montreal, Canada. This study, by Toulouse and Vallee (1991), was carried out on a group of Quebec engineers.[2] It seems to demonstrate that:

- the entrepreneurial behaviour of Quebec engineers is not, or only slightly, related to opportunities presented by the environmental context;
- their behaviour is influenced by the number of years since graduation.

We think this study is interesting for two reasons. First, it concerns the entrepreneurial behaviour of a well-defined target group, but one which has not been studied as a group *per se* in the field of entrepreneurship. Secondly, it calls into question the classical schema of a company being pushed by political or environmental circumstances to set up business. Such a schema contrasts with the more linear model postulated by the study, where the target sample seems to be relatively independent of the environment. This study led us to investigate the French context and consider testing this hypothesis there. As a result we have oriented our study toward the entrepreneurial behaviour of French engineers, with a view to comparing them with their Quebec counterparts.[3]

Certain authors have pointed out the importance of cultural differences (see Gunther McGrath and MacMillan 1992) in studies of this kind. So, our approach was to start by identifying national characteristics and looking for an appropriate methodology.

THE SPECIFICITIES OF THE FRENCH ENGINEER

A cultural and historical dimension

The historical evolution of the engineer's status

As Lasserre (1989) highlights, the notion of engineer in France is ambiguous and unclear. It designates a diploma, a function, and a professional status. These three aspects do not always coincide. Not every graduate of an engineering school carries out the functions of an engineer. The common denominator of the engineer is the training, which is principally scientific and technological. The social status of the engineer has evolved through time, and this evolution has led to a transformation of the place and the role of the engineer within companies and within the social and economic system.

During the second half of the eighteenth century and the first half of the nineteenth century, engineers were civil servants, working for the state. According to Shinn (1978), around 1850, a new type of civil engineer came into being whose function was to apply theoretical and empirical knowledge to the concrete problems of industrial production. The industrial revolution and other factors, such as the intellectual climate which affirmed the prevalence of industry amidst human activity as a whole, favoured the rise of civil engineers as a professional group. The creation of the Ecole Centrale in 1829 and of the Society of Civil Engineers in 1848 were important steps in this process.

At the beginning of the twentieth century, the engineer was at the forefront of industrial leadership. He fulfilled an essential role particularly linked to his ability to innovate techniques and organize work scientifically, to improve industrial output, and to reduce costs. These organizational qualities allowed engineers to envisage a historical alliance with businessmen which could transform them into social agents of production and, from there, to partners of heads of companies. The social power of engineers remained strong until the crisis in the 1930s when engineers realized that they were merely executives. They also became conscious that they belonged to the middle class, and were in an intermediary situation between the working and the ruling classes.

In the 1960s, the traditional concept of the engineer as one who combined and associated the technical and executive roles evolved and these roles became disassociated. More and more, the engineer was defined by his techno-scientific function. Emphasis was placed on the purely intellectual aspect of his profession: he was someone who applied scientific knowledge to production. His managerial function disappeared. This change was seen in the curriculum of the 'Grandes Ecoles', where the necessity for scientific and theoretical studies became more evident and opened the way to the creation of more theoretical courses, and allowed the addition of research projects.

During the same period, new links between science and industry were established, revealed in a dependence of technological and industrial progress on the development of basic technical knowledge. Thus we saw the arrival of applied science, or research and development, which acquired the status of a productive factor in economic activity. This gave innovation great importance as a factor in the maintenance of steady growth in the productivity of work. An even greater division of these factors contributed to the reduction of the engineers' autonomy and to the delimitation of their work. During the same period there was an exceptional growth in the number of engineers and technicians.[4]

The collective result of this evolution was to bring about an erosion in the traditional allegiance of executives, as highlighted by Crozier (1975). Considerable uneasiness within the executive population set in. This can explain on one hand the appearance of the first great social conflicts in which many engineers and managers actively participated, and on the other hand, and in certain sectors, the adherence of managers to workers' unions. The traditional attitude towards managers as the sole reference of authority, along with faithfulness and loyalty to them, was eroded and replaced progressively by a very different attitude: that of 'professionalism'. 'Professionalism' is an attitude which constitutes the possession of authority and the judgement of one's peers. Thus, the authority of a manager is only accepted if it is based upon manifest competence and not merely on the principles of hierarchy. This phenomenon first appeared in the United States at the beginning of the 1960s and was elucidated by Kornhauser (1972), Dvorak (1963), and Goldstein (1955). In France this was observed in the studies of the aeronautic industry by Maurice, Guillon, and Gaulon (1967) and Durand (1972), and shows that the notion of professionalism applies mainly to engineers in technically advanced industries. It seems to be favoured in situations where work autonomy and immobility prevail in the career paths.

For Lasserre (1989) there are two main models of professional identity for engineers. One of them is based upon the ability to command, the other upon expertise. There are two types of ideological attitudes, one favourable and the other hostile, to collective action. The 'expert' has a favourable attitude towards collective action; the 'generalist' is more characterized by his hostile attitude.

What will the future status of the engineer in France be? Will it follow a technocratic evolution along the path of professionalism and expertise to the engineer whose social status and power is based upon the growing technical complexity of production processes? Or will it be a proletarian-style evolution in a movement which brings together all the actors in the production process – from manual workers to engineers – and who have in common the fact of being excluded from production responsibilities ?

Beyond these principal paths, many other evolutions are possible. In particular, that of the partial evolution within an entrepreneurial-type model is persuasive. This places the engineer in a position of unsalaried actor with more autonomy and freedom as far as his own destiny is concerned. The orientation which he then gives to his professional direction could lead him either to play an individual expert role, or adopt entrepreneurial behaviour which goes beyond the level of individual effort.

Cultural elements

The family of French engineers is not homogenous. There are those engineers who come from the classical model of Grandes Ecoles, and others who are more oriented towards technical aspects, application, and production and are trained in different systems. The appearance of Grandes Ecoles in the French higher education system goes back to the sixteenth and seventeenth centuries, coinciding with a great and lasting decline of universities. In the eighteenth century the Grandes Ecoles saw a truly significant expansion. The Ecole de Ponts et Chaussées was created in 1715, the Ecole de l'Artillerie in 1720, the Ecole des Mines in 1783. From then on engineering 'Grandes Ecoles' multiplied and the system was consolidated. The apotheosis of engineering 'Grandes Ecoles', the Ecole Polytechnique, came into being in 1794. Before 1816 there were 6 schools. After a pause during the first half of the nineteenth century, this figure rose to 56 in 1914, then to 82 in 1945, 151 in 1978, and 178 in 1989.

Even if 'Grandes Ecoles' have characteristics in common (selectivity, a small number of students, close links with professional circles, high quality of training programmes and teachers), it is nevertheless clear that some are more important than others. The system is very hierarchical and is based on the reputation of the school. A particularity of the French system is that engineering 'Grandes Ecoles' fulfil a social function. Thus, for the most important schools, the academic title carries a double function of social reproduction. On the one hand, it legitimizes the transmission of economic capital among families from the 'owner' section of the ruling class. On the other hand it constitutes a substitute for economic capital absent in other sections of the ruling class. The 'Grandes Ecoles' undeniably allow the ruling class to reproduce itself, firstly by allowing the transmission of privileges, and, secondly, by organizing a whole series of barriers into the social group. The dominating class, the 'Noblesse d'Etat', as the sociologist Bourdieu (1989) refers to it, legitimizes its reproduction through an academic meritocracy. And, to further ensure the reproduction of its privileges, the ruling class has conferred upon 'Grandes Ecoles' a very efficient function: the creation and development for its graduates, of a social capital in the form of networks of relations and protection. The aim is to give value to the academic capital which each student possesses by creating and developing a group spirit, and a feeling of belonging to a social elite.

One of the most remarkable elements of the training of French engineers is the extraordinary diversity of paths of access to the title of engineer and the many possibilities of specialization, which contribute to the reinforcement of the engineers' heterogeneity.

It is possible to obtain the diploma after an initial training period. The selection of students is then made either from preparatory classes (one or two years of study after the baccalauréat), after a first university degree, after the baccalauréat, or after having obtained another university degree. It is also possible to obtain the engineer's diploma through continuing adult training. Here many possiblilities exist. This path is, however, in its developmental stage, started by recent decisions taken by the French government.

In this abundance of paths of access, the title of qualified engineer is protected by the Commission of Engineering. Title constitutes a discriminatory element. The fact that the engineers, and therefore the engineering profession, is not regulated in France, gives the title of engineer an extreme importance. Although the use of the title 'Qualified Engineer' is regulated, the use of the description 'Engineer' is completely free. The carrying out of engineering activities in France cannot be strictly defined. This creates a strange situation in a European Community where most of the member states regulate the professional activity of the engineer.

A career path linked to the educational system

A quick analysis of the social origins of French engineers clearly shows that social background has an important influence on their training and career path. A study carried out by the CEFI (1987)[5] shows that more than half the number of engineers (55.6 per cent) come from families of executives, company owners, and professionals. This corresponds with the more general view of Maurice, Sellier, and Silvestre (1982), who highlight the importance of the rate of social reproduction of French senior executives. According to these authors, more than half of French senior executives come from the same socio-professional category. The study of the CEFI shows, moreover, that the proportion of engineers whose fathers are also engineers is far from negligible.

Laurens (1988) shows that the choice of a particular engineering school is very directly linked to the status and reputation of the school. Those schools that use the large traditional competitive entrance examinations (Ecole Polytechnique, Ecole Centrale de Paris, Ecole Nationale Supérieure des Mines de Paris, etc.) select their students from well-off categories. Schools which select from preparatory classes, either with their own or common entrance examinations, have an intermediary position. Selection after the baccalauréat (INSA, ENI, etc.) and other possibilities probably reach the least well-off.

In terms of functions carried out, according to the CEFI study, engineers are split evenly into those who have executive functions, and those who have little or none at all. The favoured functions of the engineer are theoretical studies, research and development, production, and functions connected to production. Commercial functions and functions linked to management seem to interest engineers very little. The engineer tends to work in large industrial companies, which constitutes the classic opening for the profession.

If we attempt to characterize the typical engineer's work today, we find great heterogeneity and difficulty in defining it correctly. This is highlighted by Benguigul and Monjardet (1984), who establish a distinction between the nineteenth century, when the engineer could define himself by a profession, and the present situation in which the engineer is considered to be just another executive in the hierarchical chain.

The notion of engineer has changed into the notion of manager primarily defined by a position in a hierarchical network. Engineers have become a subset within a much larger group: managers. What is common to these engineers, this subset, is not their type of activity. Rather it is their education, their title of qualified engineer which is protected by the law. What brings them together is a scientific and technical training which leads to a status, but which in no way indicates the type of function the engineers will carry out in a company.

It is certainly possible to find engineers in a company performing, in addition to technical functions, administrative, commercial, and financial functions. The range of tasks carried out by engineers is very wide and calls for very diverse skills. These are not necessarily acquired during the engineer's initial training. However, more recently what seems to be a certain deviation has appeared: the tendency for young engineers without experience to move to consulting or management activities which they are then only able to tackle from a theoretical perspective.[6]

Many authorities underline the need to train engineers in economics and management as quickly as possible in order to prepare them to carry out the executive functions that they will face sooner or later, and to acquire a certain professionalism in their area of activity. Management training and the openings which it offers allow engineers to move out of their profession and head towards other careers. This reinforces the phenomenon of engineers leaving their original function, as seen above. Management training is, from this viewpoint, a 'career accelerator' for engineers.

The training for engineers, based on mathematics and physical science, is conceived as if the technical and managerial branches were fundamentally different. The overriding importance given to logico-deductive sciences compared with experimental science and the technical emphasis of the training give the qualified engineer a strong technical culture. This creates specific behaviour patterns and ways of conceptualization which make it difficult for engineers to take into account that which is not measurable.

Thus the role of the company and of continuing education is essential. It can make up for the effects of the initial training and allow the engineer to go into new fields. In this way he can change the direction of his professional path, influenced initially by the school he attended and his specialization, and later by his accumulated experiences and complementary training, particularly in management and social sciences. From this point, access to managerial functions is possible for an engineer along three prevailing paths:

1 the first is linked with the school, the 'Grande Ecole'; status being connected with its prestige, its reputation, and its interconnections with the ruling class.
2 the second is linked with complementary training in management acquired either on leaving the engineering school or after several years of professional experience in a prestigious management training establishment.
3 finally, there is entrepreneurship which allows the engineer to leave his employee status by creating or taking over a company.

The French educational system plays an important role in influencing the actors' predilection towards entrepreneurship. In effect, this very stratified system (Silvestre 1990) guarantees superior positions to graduates: exclusive and high-status functions in large companies and administrations. This particular way of functioning does not encourage graduates of French 'Grandes Ecoles' to follow an entrepreneurial path which is, by definition, less prestigious and presents more risks. For the French engineer, entrepreneurial tendencies occur in inverse proportion to the rank of the school attended.

This is even more marked in that the entrepreneur is a nomadic figure who is not easy to classify within the social hierarchy. The immediate social profits of the diploma are worth more than the real aptitudes that it sanctions. A higher diploma can satisfy the search for a social identity whereas the lack of a diploma or a lower diploma leads one to search for this identity.

ENTREPRENEURIAL BEHAVIOUR OF FRENCH ENGINEERS: A FIELD STUDY

Methodological approach

Due to the specific characteristics of French engineers, we thought it important to validate a number of hypotheses concerning their entrepreneurial behaviour, before starting an international study.

The first set of hypotheses which we have formulated deal with the role of the school of origin in the entrepreneurial process.

Hypothesis 1:   Engineer-entrepreneurs come more often from second-rank engineering schools, with a lower reputation, than from first-rank schools.

Hypothesis 2:   The continuing education path tends to favour, by definition, entrepreneurial behaviour.

The second set of hypotheses concerns the technical or professional specializations acquired.

Hypothesis 3:   Engineer–entrepreneurs start businesses in fields close to their original specialization.

Hypothesis 4:   The degree of entrepreneurial behaviour of engineer–entrepreneurs is strongly determined by whether or not they received a general or specialized training.

Hypothesis 5:   There is a strong link between the career path and the type of company created or taken over.

The third set of hypotheses concerns the motivation factors in the entrepreneurial process.

Hypothesis 6:   The essential entrepreneurial motivation of the engineer is technical, combined with a will to develop externally a know-how or a product with technical origins.

Hypothesis 7:   Financial motivation is not dominant in the development of engineers' entrepreneurial behaviour.

The fourth set of hypotheses concerns the goals sought by engineers in adopting entrepreneurial behaviour.

Hypothesis 8:   Engineers have a professional model of achievement based on expertise. Their entrepreneurial behaviour is coherent with this model.

Hypothesis 9:   The status of entrepreneur is not dominant among the goals sought by engineer-entrepreneurs.

Our methodological approach is based on a qualitative field study using semi-directive interviews lasting, on average, three hours. The sample was made up of twenty engineers who have either set up or are setting up their own companies.[7] It was constituted in such a way as to cover the different modes of engineering training in France, give a sufficiently wide sample in terms of age of entrepreneuring, and present a large diversity of sectors of activity.[8] An interview guide was prepared. This interview guide was constructed around the following themes:

- personal and family data
- initial and complementary training
- social origin
- career path
- personal and entrepreneurial process
- characteristics of the company created or taken over.

It was used in semi-directive interviews which served as a basis for a thematic content analysis.

Results

The results are presented below around four main themes.

The career path of engineer-entrepreneurs

The career path of the engineer-entrepreneur is very much influenced by a number of factors. We propose to examine here those which seem to us the most determinant.

The role of the school of origin

The role of the school plays an important part at two levels: the status of the school and the structure of the studies. The status of the school was often mentioned during our interviews. The engineer–entrepreneurs interviewed all emphasized the opportunities represented by entrepreneurship, as a privileged path leading to the position of managing director. Here, there seems to be a clear opposition between engineering 'Grandes Ecoles', which prepare future managers of public and private companies, and other engineering schools. In fact, engineering 'Grandes Ecoles' train a ready-made group which permanently supply the system. For engineers who are unable to follow this model, access to a managerial function is considerably reduced. In this case entrepreneurial behaviour, even if it includes difficulties and risks which cannot be neglected, remains a preferred, if not unique means to the managerial goal. Here, our findings support the literature.

Some engineer–entrepreneurs (in all, 10 out of 20) highlighted the importance of the structure of their studies. The structure of the curriculum in certain schools may predispose students to future entrepreneurial behaviour by encouraging them very early to develop behaviour close to that which will later allow them to set up or take over a company. Thus all courses of action, which allow the student engineer to interact with his training and to set up his own programme by choosing options, electives, and other similar possibilities, were seen by the engineers as an element contributing to the development of entrepreneurial behaviour. Naturally, such courses of action should allow the student to make a personal investment, make choices adapted to his project and his own situation, and above all be capable of execution. For this last point, the role of the institution is of utmost importance.

The status of the school and the structure of the studies divided schools into those more or less favourable to entrepreneurial attitudes and behaviour. Establishments which train their engineers through continuing education appeared to us to be the best positioned in this respect.

The role of initial training and specialization

Ten of the twenty engineers interviewed had aquired high levels of specialization in various fields. Eight of these ten engineers had created or taken over a company related strongly to their original specialization. The question of specialization is not very easy to deal with. Engineering schools offer specialities and majors, but students also have the opportunity to specialize, independantly of these majors, by taking options and other electives. To understand this situation, it is thus necessary to look beyond what is indicated on the diploma. A few examples describing the career paths of engineer–entrepreneurs will illustrate the importance of specialization.

The first concerns an engineer from a school generally considered to be generalist. This person specialized in electronics and then obtained a doctorate in his speciality. After working for fifteen years in this field he created a company for which the accumulated expertise in his specialization proved crucial.

The second example concerns a computer engineer who set up a service company in seven years after leaving school, a service company in the field of computer engineering.

A generalist training can open up greater opportunities and can lead to executive and managerial functions. A specialist training can endow the engineer with technical expertise which can be extremely useful in the creation or acquisition of a company.

The role of previous experience

All the start-ups in our study show a link with the previous activity of the engineer–entrepreneur. This finding corresponds with the conclusions of Vesper (1980), Hoad and Rosko (1964), and Ronstadt (1984). Certainly, the technical expertise of the engineer is acquired during specialized training. But, more important, it is nourished by knowledge developed throughout professional history. The accumulation of experience differentiates engineers from each other. Thus the creation of a company must necessarily be seen within the context of a professional trajectory.

Thus:

- the former head of innovation of a French multinational envisages the creation of a service company aimed at industrial companies to help them manage their technological resources and promote innovation.
- the former head of component and programmes testing for real-time computers in a diversified company sets up a service company dealing with the architecture of real-time computer systems.
- seven engineers in our sample, all project leaders in data processing, created a service company in data processing.

The consultant created a consultancy company, the mechanical engineer created or took over a mechanical company, the computer engineer created a computer service company. The engineer does not abandon the know-how and technical skills that he masters and which he has developed throughout his professional experience. Our interviews show therefore that the engineer does not move too far away from the activities and professions that he is familiar with. Moreover, his professional history has allowed him to build up a dense network of relations. The close links between pre- and post-creation activities will allow him to take advantage of this network, particularly during the launching phase of this new activity. The importance of this point was very often highlighted by the engineer–entrepreneurs we met. The influence of networks has also been noted in the literature (e.g. Birley 1985).

To sum up, previous professional experience seems to bring to the engineer technical knowledge, skills, relation networks, and the necessary access to his environment which can allow him to spot the best opportunities for creating or taking over a company. So, it can strongly influence his initial behaviour and attitudes as an entrepreneur.

The factors which influence entrepreneurial behaviour

Having benefited from favourable conditions in education and initial training, having more or less consciously prepared and endowed oneself with entrepreneurial potential, and having taken advantage of opportunities, the engineer–entrepreneur finds himself with indispensable elements for the activation and smooth running of the entrepreneurial process. However, these elements are not sufficient for entrepreneurial behaviour. Other conditions must occur to accelerate the project. Those which appear the most important from our study coincide with, in most cases, notions and concepts already explored in the literature on entrepreneurship.

A rupture in the career path

The concept of displacement referred to in the literature by Shapero (1975 and 1982) was verified in more than one out of two cases. Displacement can be analysed as a rupture situation brought on by elements beyond the control of the individual and which he can only influence to some extent. Displacement can result in a wish to do, in one's own company, what one could not do elsewhere because of strategic reasons, lack of means, or unadapted structures. The most characteristic situation is a pet technical project which could not be undertaken by the original company. This was the reason behind the start of one-third of the companies in our sample. Displacement can also be something which has been forced on the engineer. This occurs in situations where the engineer, often over 40 years old, loses his job.

When there is no displacement, other types of motivations more connected with the individual personality clearly appear. We can thus mention the need for independence, the need for a sense of accomplishment, or the search for autonomy. Our results here are coherent with the literature (McClelland 1965; Timmons 1971; and Hornaday 1982). In conclusion, as far as sources of motivation are concerned, money and power seem far from constituting the main foundation of the decision. On the other hand, the intellectual, social, even affective dimensions are often mentioned and are seen in expressions such as 'to do it for you', 'to create a company in your own image', 'for personal enrichment'.

Social origin and family environment

An important point which we would like to deal with is that of social origins and family environment. Modest social origins can explain some entrepreneurial behaviours which are seen by the actors themselves as steps towards obtaining social value.

The engineers from Grandes Ecoles who we interviewed and who came from modest social origins explained that they were unable to totally benefit from the 'caste effect'. They found access to managerial functions difficult. In these conditions, their career path found itself quickly assimilated with those of engineers from schools with a lower reputation. Unable to become company managers by way of the 'royal path', their only alternative was to create their own company, and for some, their own job.

Family background can have other kinds of influence. This can be seen when engineers have been in close contact, for many years, with immediate family (father, uncle, grandfather) who were entrepreneurs or who had independent professions. Nearly half of the engineers in our sample fell into this category. The role of the wife, her agreement, even her participation in the project was equally highlighted, and presented as being important by several engineers.

Representations of the engineer–entrepreneur

The majority of engineers interviewed strongly wished to create 'human-sized' companies. This is probably as opposition to the very large companies with very structured organizations they worked for. This point was frequently reiterated. They seemed very attached to human management, and anxious to build their employer–employee relationships on a different basis from the one they experienced. The majority of engineers interviewed spoke of the 'social dimension' or the 'social project', of 'human participation', even 'company citizen', without, however, elaborating these notions.

The entrepreneur is seen by the engineers in our sample as, first and foremost, an actor who is able to elaborate and realize a project. This is to say, he is able to fix goals and to obtain them through proper coordination of all the resources at hand. The entrepreneur commits himself and is capable of taking and insuring risks.

The engineers in our sample claimed to have a sense of rigour, of method, of organization, of professional work, and they try to spread these values throughout the companies they have created or taken over. What comes out of our interviews is that the engineer uses levers such as innovation or creativity, putting the maximum of chance on his side. The project which he expands constitutes a powerful engine to reach his goals. It is of such great importance that he will not hesitate to question his own ability if this can contribute to the project's continuation, to comfort himself or to put himself back on the right track. What guides him is the will to concretize. For this he is ready to 'give up some of the capital' or 'all of it' or even 'to take important decisions – to transfer the activity to the United States for example. He can also 'separate from his best friend', who he carelessly promoted to the position of wage-earning partner.

The functions carried out by the engineer–entrepreneurs in our sample are linked to the application of acquired technical skills: design, research and development, production. Very quickly, at the same time, the engineer takes on functions linked to management which become more and more important as the company develops. At the same time, the engineer displays a cultural opposition to the commercial function which he usually delegates and which he carries out only when he has to. This he does with much reticence, prudence, and clumsiness.

These types of behaviour and attitudes towards the commercial function create strong psychological impediments for engineer–entrepreneurs. Yet it also appears that the engineers interviewed meet no major difficulties in the setting up of accounting and financial functions. The last element which we would like to highlight is the tendency of engineers to work by building teams. This occurs when the sharing of essential common values and the search for complementary characteristics are unifying and fundamental elements.

To sum up, it is clear from our interviews that the French engineer who starts his own company or takes over an existing one appears to try to model this company in his own image. This seems to us to highlight a model of professional identity, focused on expertise and favourable toward collective action. The social legitimacy and power of this model are based solely on the technical skills of the engineer.

Toward the elaboration of a set of hypotheses

To carry out our field study of the entrepreneurial behaviour of engineer–entrepreneurs we formulated four series of hypotheses concerning the role of the original school, the specialization acquired, the factors which indicate the entrepreneurial process, and the goals sought by engineers when they adopt entrepreneurial behaviour.

Using, as a basis, our first results, and including the literature already dealing with this field, we would like to propose:

1　a model explaining the entrepreneurial path of engineers.
2　on the other hand, a model which leads to the understanding of the entrepreneurial process as far as French engineers are concerned.

The path which leads to the setting up of a company

The engineer appears to seek security in his behaviour, and to permanently put into practice mechanisms which reduce risk, whether this concerns a situation, a problem, or a project. From this perspective, the entrepreneurial behaviour of the engineer seems to present interesting characteristics. The notion of project is central, it is familiar to him, and it corresponds perfectly with the intellectual approach which he has assimilated.

Everything leads him to consider the creation or acquisition of a company as a project, with its different stages, with each condition to be fulfilled before passing from one stage to another, the diverse and varied means which must be put into practice. Simply, this project can be seen from the viewpoint of a manager or a technician. This depends heavily, on the one hand, on the type of path followed within engineering, and on the other hand, on the state and combination of the main factors regulating the entrepreneurial process.

Toward a distinction between the two paths

Looking at studies which we carried out throughout this research, it appears to us that, at the beginning of his experience, the scientific and technical training of the engineer leads him to concentrate on technical aspects. During this stage, in fact, the approach is that of the apprentice who diversifies his knowledge and skills. Following on from this, the engineer can, with more or less rapidity, look to concentrating on other aspects and develop other dimensions in accordance with promotions and changes.

Progressively he has the choice of:

- moving towards activities and functions where the technical aspect becomes relatively less important as compared to other aspects: for example, management.
- following his path in order to aquire a real technical expertise in his preferred branch(es).

The absence of certain dimensions in the engineer's initial background, and the scientific approaches which are instilled into him lead him to have certain characteristic attitudes which can explain the preceding point.

We find here two main models which can characterize the engineer:

1 the engineer seen as an architect of large technical works, with a strong concentration on the technical dimension and a weak economic role.

| The engineer leaves his technical context before setting up a business |

Engineer ⟶ Manager ⟶ Entrepreneur manager

or

| The engineer leaves his technical context before setting up a business |

Engineer ⟶ Technician ⟶ Entrepreneur technician

Figure 10.1 The taking over of a company by an engineer

2 the engineer who plays the role of an economic development agent.

The creation or the taking over of a company by an engineer can, from a professional perspective, be schematized under these conditions in two different ways (see Figure 10.1). We will now develop each of the paths shown in the figure, and illustrate with examples.[9]

The path of the engineer 'entrepreneur–manager'

This path takes the engineer, focused on the technical dimension at the beginning, to a growing involvement with wider functions, allowing him to acquire new non-technical skills. Pushed by diverse motivations and having identified a good opportunity, the engineer takes the entrepreneurial path. The main functions for this type of engineer are as innovator and as resource coordinator. In this schema are included engineer entrepreneurs who, from the beginning of their career paths, have chosen non-technical professions. The most telling example of this is offered by the history of a 38-year-old engineer who graduated in 1975. The main stages in the development of his career are given below. During the first period (year 1) of his career, he finished the first part of his training with a period of applied research in a scientific and technical centre in the branch of a construction company. Then, he joined a national company working in water planning. There, he worked as public works engineer in charge of design and compilation of technical dossiers (plans, descriptions, etc.). In this company he was offered the opportunity of partially giving up his 'concentration on the technical aspect' by taking on a project concerning the creation of a technical data-processing department. For the first time, having just turned 30, this engineer was allotted a mission which concerned the general management of a project.

With this experience as a basis, and with new acquired skills, this engineer continued his career and joined a computer consultancy company where he stayed for five years as head of project. During this period, his own perception was that he managed to move out of his 'technical bubble', where only the technical dimension was taken into consideration, towards managerial functions, helped by the acquisition of new skills. This change was accompanied by short training periods intended to help him put his ideas into practice.

Following this, he joined another computer service consultancy which was larger than the first and where he was appointed head of department. He spent three successful years in this company but had many dissatisfactions, and spotting a unique opportunity, he decided to take the big step and create his own company.

The path of the engineer 'entrepreneur–technician'

This is the path of the engineer who goes into business pushed by a technical project which he can no longer develop within his present company, although he is still concentrated on the technical dimension. This type of engineer conceives his entrepreneurial role as technician. At the beginning of this activity he has a tendency to see himself as an inventor. Following on from this he can either continue this behaviour, in which case he must delegate managerial functions to others, or he can progressively evolve towards combining several dimensions, both technical and non-technical.

The most representative example is offered by an engineer, 44 years old, who graduated in 1970 and who was interested very early in technical matters. This was shown (which is quite rare) at a young age by an evident willingness in this direction within the engineering profession. Very quickly, this engineer specialized in electronics and sucessfully prepared a doctorate at the Ecole Centrale de Lyon where he successively climbed all the levels within the electronics laboratory between 1970 and 1980. While following his pedagogical and scientific activities in 1988, this engineer, pushed by 'the desire to carry out technical projects which I am unable to do at the CNRS', created a company.[10]

The opportunity for creating depends on the discovery of a product which does not exist and which can be made concrete in an industrial context. This engineer has the skills to design and produce it. Furthermore, a quick analysis of the situation led him to think that any attempt to transfer this product towards industry would certainly lead to failure. During the first years of this young company, this engineer immersed himself firmly in the technical functions where the research and development and production aspects dominated. At present, because of external pressure, he seems to have accepted other tasks even though there has been no significant evolution towards a different status.

Factors which influence the entrepreneurial profile of the engineer

In our opinion, the fact that different profiles of engineer–entrepreneurs exist is linked to several factors:

1   The willingness, or lack of it, of the engineer to leave the technical aspect. This depends on the vision he has of his profession and its components.
2   The professional experience which offers, to a greater or lesser extent, the chance to diversify, to enrich oneself, to find openings, which the engineer may or may not take. In this vein it is clear that the younger an engineer is in the entrepreneurial process, the more likely he is to adopt behaviour patterns resembling the engineer–technician. In our sample, six engineers out of the nine who are younger than 35 show such behaviour. On the other hand, an advanced age does not necessarily mean that the engineer has evolved towards the status of entrepreneur–manager. In our sample one entrepreneur is 48 years old, another is 44. In our opinion, neither of these two really wants to change function in order to become more managerial.
3   The project itself and the nature of the key factors for the success of the project (technical, commercial, financial, etc.) can, starting from an interactive process between the actor and the project, progressively motivate the engineer to change his entrepreneurial status or to maintain it and reinforce himself in his present status.

The scientific and technical training of the engineer as well as his professional experience automatically gives the project, and therefore the company, a technical dimension, particularly if the technical function is generally given importance. This point is confirmed by an examination of all the projects in our sample,where, at the beginning, the key factors for success come mainly from specific technical skills. The technical aspect, so important to the engineer, can be seen in a psychological light. It is often a refuge, a need to reassure himself, a way of staying within the scientific and rational approach which has been instilled in him and which is the basis of his training.

    To sum up, the path which leads to setting up a business is strongly influenced by the engineer's intial training, by the professional experience which he has acquired, by the technical skills which he has developed, and by his visions and ideologies. This path leads to two very contrasting entrepreneurial profiles. The first gives a significant place to the managerial dimension. The second does not recognize this aspect, or only slightly so, and emphasizes the technical dimension.

The entrepreneurial process of the engineer

Starting with the analysis of the situations observed, and taking into account the literature, it appeared to us that a study concerning a model for understanding the entrepreneurial process would be useful.

A model for the understanding of the entrepreneurial process

The model which we propose for the creation of companies by engineers is dynamic and interactive. Dynamic, because it seems to us that time plays an essential role. Its importance lies in what must be presented and analysed as a process. It is also dynamic because this process leads to a construct highly influenced by the initial training and the focus taken there (specialist or generalist), by previous experience, and as much by the functions carried out as by the diverse skills accumulated. Time appears to be necessary for the engineer to perfect and complete a first training which is deficient in at least two aspects:

- specialization and technical expertise,
- resource management in a project or sub-group of the organization.

Time appears to be equally necessary to enable the engineer to step back from the uniquely technical dimension, to change some of his views, particularly his vision of the company, which is a vision too attached to the technical side. This view can then evolve normally towards a more complex object, less rational, more multi-dimensional.

The model is interactive because the entrepreneurial decision (create or take over a company) finds its foundations in the various exchanges and flows between the engineer and his personal and above all professional environment.

The process by which an engineer adopts entrepreneurial behaviour includes, in our opinion, a phase of entrepreneurial awakening, a phase of development of the entrepreneurial potential, and a phase of the entrepreneurial decision.

The entrepreneurial awakening phase

The entrepreneurial awakening can be defined as a particular moment in the life of an individual when, for various reasons, a first interest (in the form of sensitization) in entrepreneurship appears. The entrepreneurial awakening is linked to social influences in that the individual can be placed very early in a favourable context. In particular, certain social conditions are brought together and play a part in the awakening. It can equally be brought about much later. The entrepreneurial awakening depends very much on the family, the institutional and professional environment, the social origins, and the personality of the engineer. The dominant culture and values propagated within the society and social group to which engineers belong also play an important role.

In our sample, the components of entrepreneurial awakening raise two distinct questions: Which sources of interest originate in personality traits, cultural, social, or family characteristics? What form does the interest take? (This leads back to the sections dealing with entrepreneurial motivation. Why set up a business? Money, power, personal accomplishment, independence, autonomy, a will to promote ideas and practices, or a new social vision?)

These two questions interact to create a favourable scene which can be used later. We have highlighted the role, as it was deserved, of the school, of professional institutions, of the family, and of social origins. The creation of a company can be, for the engineer, a means of obtaining recognition and increasing his social value which his modest origins did not allow him.

The degree of the entrepreneurial awakening appears to us to be a vital element. If this model is correct, it should allow the development of measures of early awakening. An engineer with a high degree of awakening will be more sensitive to the triggers which can lead him to launch his own company. He faces a better chance of becoming an entrepreneur. Concerning this point, we totally agree with the conclusions of Aurifeille and Hernandez (1991).

Engineering schools are at present considering the issue of entrepreneurship and are thinking about ways to nurture an entrepreneurial spirit in engineers (CEFI 1989). However, the solutions sketched out and tentatively put into practice show a misunderstanding of the problems of identifying future entrepreneurs.

The entrepreneurial potential

The creation of entrepreneurial potential is only possible within a process which is to a greater or lesser extent conscious. That is to say, the necessary steps can be consciously thought out and programmed. Or it can be the complete opposite. The acquisition and development of this particular potential can be the result of unconscious mechanisms. Whatever it may be, and this seems to be a remarkable point about engineers, the existence of this incubation period very often seems to be a given in the entrepreneurial behaviour of this group of creators. It helps to satisfy needs, to fill gaps. The main gaps originate in the engineers' training and means of access to training institutions. These elements help to create a non-correspondance (felt by the engineer) between the future profession and the content of his studies. This non-correspondance can be explained both by the maladjustment to the training and by a certain spirit on entering the school which is revealed by a clear consciousness of belonging to a scientific elite: 'you manage to enter into this type of study because you are good at science'.

The probation period is thus, first and foremost, a period which completes the engineer's training through experience in adapted functions and services in a company. It allows the engineer to aquire the skills, knowledge, and know-how which he considers indispensable to entrepreneurship and management. The process can be carried out in one or several companies. It can also mobilize resources from outside these companies, mainly complimentary training either as sandwich courses or sabbatical leave. The engineer, before demonstrating entrepreneurial behaviour, will thus accumulate diverse experience as a designer and producer in charge of projects and businesses.

Maital (1991) and Mraz (1989) highlight this point very clearly. In particular they give the estimation of the length of experience in technical fields (at least 5 years, more frequently 10 years). The literature in this field and our empirical study indicate similar results. Engineer–entrepreneurs seem to be older than other groups of entrepreneurs. The average age at which the engineer decides to adopt entrepreneurial behaviour (35 years old) is consistent with the figures proposed.

Moreover, by trying to qualify this experience, it seems that, from an entrepreneurial perspective, engineers who manage projects or businesses or who develop products (diversified experience) are 'better' entrepreneurs than those who only work on very specialized research operations and theoretical or applied studies (Maital 1991). Here we can make a link with the two models of engineer–entrepreneurs presented above. The first family of engineers (engineers who manage projects) appear to be consistent with the model.

Engineer–technician → manager → entrepreneur–manager

The second family (engineers who work on specialized tasks) belong more to the second model.

Engineer → technician → entrepreneur–technician

The process of encouraging entrepreneurial potential can be affected by many factors which interact with each other. We have grouped them into four families of elements:

1 accelerator elements which allow a shortening of the process while still guaranteeing the quality of the path.
2 amplifier elements which help to significantly enlarge the entrepreneurial potential. The two first families of elements find their source in professional experience (quality, length, functions carried out).
3 inhibitor elements (brakes) which delay or stop the process during a certain period or even indefinitely. In these conditions the entrepreneurial potential already constituted can be displaced and invested in other activities. Certain factors can be noted here, such as the attitude towards commercial functions, the quest for too much security, the fear of failure, or the inability to make a project concrete.
4 trigger elements which lead the engineer progressively or sharply to the entrepreneurial decision.

Here we can make a link with the concept of displacement mentioned above. In effect, certain trigger elements can originate in a family or professional problem (the threat of unemployment, a conflict with a superior, the abandoning of a project, a non-correspondence between a social vision and the reality offered, some sort of dissatisfaction). Moreover, our study has highlighted the importance of this point. The identification of these elements, and the definition of their respective roles seems to us to be a key to the understanding of the entrepreneurial behaviour of engineers.

The entrepreneurial decision

The entrepreneurial decision represents a particular moment in the career of an engineer when he engages in an intense thought process around the issue of whether or not to adopt entrepreneurial behaviour. This moment accompanies the precise definition of a project. The decision can concern precisely the opportunity to study in detail a new project-venture or the taking over of a company. In the spirit of the cultural and behavioural framework of the engineer, the study of this project represents a significant investment in terms of time and money. Furthermore, the decision to offer these resources constitutes an important, even decisive act.

The phase of the entrepreneurial decision has two possible conclusions:

1 the decision to continue at least provisionally a career as a wage-earning engineer, and therefore to focus resources upon this objective.
2 the decision to start a company which consequently involves a large investment of resources in an entrepreneurial project.

The process of the entrepreneurial decision seems to us to be both the final result of the previous phase and an element essential to the process of maturation. It appears that once the engineer has detected an opportunity, he will have to, on the one hand, complete his potential, should there be a need; and on the other hand, take a decision.

DISCUSSION AND RESEARCH PERSPECTIVES

In this paper we have attempted to contribute to the knowledge and understanding of the entrepreneurial behaviour of French engineers. While remaining conscious that the work presented here has clear weaknesses linked mainly to our sample, we believe that our initial results have practical implications.

Our work, by increasing the knowledge of the factors which influence the entrepreneurial awakening of French engineers, demonstrates the need to stimulate the entrepreneurial spirit in engineering schools and identify students who exhibit the development of entrepreneurial behaviour very early. This highlights the importance of developing courses in entrepreneurship in engineering schools, providing tools as early as possible, and, in the long term, strengthening the chances of success of entrepreneurial approaches.

However, and this is a major point, immediate results cannot be expected. This is because the entrepreneurial process must be placed in the context of a professional path where time plays an essential role. It is time which allows the engineer to develop an entrepreneurial potential through the accumulation of experience and continuing education. The second phase of our research will be based on a collaboration with a team of researchers from HEC in Montreal (Quebec). This collaboration will consist of perfecting a questionnaire in order to conduct a quantitative study based on a sample of engineers in the two countries.

The main methodological stages we are thinking of for this second phase are: (1) the definition of the sample (we envisage limiting the study to the Rhône-Alpes region); (2) the sending out of questionnaires (we are considering using the infrastructure of the Comité National des Ingénieurs et Scientifiques Français to administer these): (3) the collection and quantitative analysis of data;[11] (4) a complementary qualitative analysis, based on in-depth case studies; (5) the production of a definitive research document.

We strongly believe that the study of entrepreneurial behaviour of engineers can lead to a better understanding and fostering of business venturing in industrialized countries.

NOTES

1 This paper comes from a working paper which was given at the Doctorate Programme ESC-University Jean Moulin in Lyon on 20 October 1992. The working paper was in completion of the 'Diplôme d'Etudes Approfondies ès Sciences de gestion'. Its title is: 'Engineer and Entrepreneur: An Exploratory Study of Entrepreneurial Behaviour of French engineers'.

2 A working paper concerning this study was presented at the 'First Global Conference on Entrepreneurship Research' which set up in London, 18–20 February 1991.

3 We define entrepreneurial behaviour as the whole of variables which describe an orientation, a decision, or an action in a specific context. This context is characterized by a particular way an economic actor engages himself in order to start up or buy or expand a company, by taking individual risks.

4 The number of graduate engineers on the labour market each year rose from 5,000 in 1960 to a little more than 15,000 in 1990. The manager categories rose from 159,000 in 1954 to 290,000 in 1968. In 1982 there were about 500,000 managers in France.

5 'Comité D'Etudes Sur Les Formations D'Ingénieurs'. The CEFI has a global mission which consists of managing information on the main topic: the adaptation of the training of French engineers to the economical and technological context.

6 The initial conclusions of a study carried out by the conference of Grandes Ecoles show that about one-third of those engineers who have a degree are working in the areas for which they were trained. L'APEC has shown that about 15 % of all engineers are working in parallel areas of activity.

7 The selection of interviews was made from lists of engineer–entrepreneurs aided by the Entrepreneurship Centre in the Groupe ESC Lyon, the Ecole Centrale de Lyon, and the association Saint-Etienne Technopolis.

8 The main characteristics of the sample are the following:
   • average age: 35 (variation 6.8)
   • 20% of engineer–entrepreneurs come from French engineering 'Grandes Ecoles'

- 50% of engineers are very highly specialized:
  - chemistry: 1 person
  - computing–electronic–electricity: 6 people
  - mechanics: 3 people.

  In all, the 20 engineer–entrepreneurs interviewed have created 17 companies (3 companies were created by teams composed of 2 engineers who we met separately). These companies are in different businesses:
  - 3 consulting companies
  - 9 dealing with services and the development of computer products
  - 5 industrial companies
9 In our sample 12 engineers belong to the first schema. The remaining 8 belong to the second schema.
10 The CNRS is the large state institution research labroratory.
11 Our objective is to receive 1,000 usable questionnaires.

REFERENCES

Aurifeille, J.M. and Hernandez, E.M. (1991) 'Détection du potentiel entrepreneurial d'une population étudiante', *Economies et Sociétés*, 4: 39–55.

Benguigul, G. and Monjardet, D. (1984) 'Le Travail des ingénieurs', *Culture technique*, 12: 103–112.

Birley, S. (1985) 'The Role of Networks in the Entrepreneurial Process', *Journal of Business Venturing*, 1 (1): 107–117.

Bourdieu, P. (1989) *La Noblesse d'état: Grandes écoles et esprit de corps*, Paris: Les Editions de Minuit.

Bunel, J. and Saglio, J. (1979) *L'Action patronale*, Paris: P.U.F.

Casson, M. (1982) *The Entrepreneur*, Oxford: Basil Blackwell.

Comité D'Etudes Sur Les Formations D'Ingénieurs, CEFI (1987) 'Les ingénieurs: Quel(s) profil(s)?', *Les Dossiers des cahiers du CEFI*, 17.

Comité D'Etudes Sur Les Formations D'Ingénieurs, CEFI (1989) 'Inciter les jeunes ingénieurs à créer leur entreprise', *La Gazette du CEFI*, 1: 6–7.

Cooper, A. and Komives, W. (1972) *Technical Entrepreneurship: A Symposium,* Milwaukee: The Center for Venture Management.

Crozier, M. (1975) *Les Cadres et l'organization*, Paris: A.D.S.H.A.

Durand, M. (1972) 'Professionnalisation et allégeance chez les cadres et techniciens', *Sociologie du travail*, 2.

Dvorak, N. (1963) 'Will engineers unionize?', *Industrial Relations*, 2 (3), 45–65.

Goldstein, B. (1955) 'Unionism among Salaried Professionals in Industry', *American Sociology review*, April.

Gunther McGrath, R. and MacMillan, I.C. (1992) 'More Like Each Other Than Anyone Else? A Cross-cultural Study of Entrepreneurial Perceptions', *Journal of Business Venturing*, 7 (5): 419–429.

Hoad, W.M. and Rosko, P. (1964) 'Management Factors Contributing to the Success and Failure of New Small Manufacturers', Ann Arbor, MI: Bureau of Business Research, University of Michigan.

Hornaday, J.A. (1982) 'Research about Living Entrepreneurs', *Encyclopedia of Entrepreneurship*, Englewood Cliffs: Prentice Hall.

Kent, C.A. (1982) 'Entrepreneurship in Economic Development', *Encyclopedia of Entrepreneurship*, Englewood Cliffs: Prentice-Hall.

Knight, F. (1971) *Risk, Uncertainty and Profit*, Chicago: University of Chicago Press.
Kornhauser, W. (1972) *Scientists in Industry*, Berkeley: University of California Press.
Lamont, L. (1972) 'What Entrepreneurs Learn from Experience', *Journal of Small Business*, Summer: 36–41.
Lasserre, H. (1984) 'Systèmes de représentations et idéologies des ingénieurs français', *Culture et technique*, 12: 239–246.
Lasserre, H. (1989) *Le Pouvoir de l'ingénieur*, Paris: Editions l'Harmattan.
Laurens, J.-P. (1988) 'Le Recrutement social des écoles d'ingénieurs', *Les cahiers du CEFI*, 21: 14–19.
McClelland, D.C. (1965) 'Achievement and Entrepreneurship: A Longitudinal Study', *Journal of Personality and Social Psychology*, 1: 389–392.
Maital, S. (1991) 'High-tech Start Ups: Which Make It?', *Across the Board*, September: 7–9.
Marshall, A. (1964) *Principles of Economics*, London: Macmillan.
Maurice, M., Guillon, R., and Gaulon, J. (1967) *Les Cadres et l'entreprise*, Paris: I.S.S.T.
Maurice, M., Sellier, F., and Silvestre, J.-J. (1982) *Politique d'éducation et organisation industrielle en France et en Allemagne*, Paris: P.U.F.
Mraz, S.J. (1989) 'Engineers Turned Entrepreneurs', *Machine Design*, 61 (10): 123–128.
Ronstadt, R. (1984) *Entrepreneurship: Text, Cases and Notes*, Dover, MA: Lord.
Say, J.-B. (1972) *Traité d'économie politique*, Paris: Calmann-Lévy. (First pub. 1802.)
Schumpeter, J. (1935) *Théorie de l'évolution économique*, Paris: Dalloz.
Shapero, A.A. (1975) 'The Displaced Unconfortable Entrepreneur', *Psychology Today*, 7 (11): 83–89.
Shapero, A.A. (1982) 'The Social Dimensions of Entrepreneurship', *Encyclopedia of Entrepreneurship*, Englewood Cliffs: Prentice-Hall.
Shinn, T. (1978) 'Des Corps de l'Etat au secteur industriel: génèse de la profession d'ingénieur, 1750–1920', *Revue française de sociologie*, 19 (1), 39–71.
Silvestre, J.-J. (1990) 'Systèmes hiérarchiques et analyse sociétale', *Revue française de gestion*, 77: 107–115.
Smith, A. (1991) *Recherches sur la nature et les causes de la richesse des nations*, Paris: Flammarion. First pub. 1776.
Timmons, J.A. (1971) 'Black is Beautiful – Is it Beautiful?', *Harvard Business Review*, Nov.–Dec.
Vallee, L. and Toulouse, J.-M. (1991) 'Business Creations by Quebec's Engineers: Stability of Entry from 1970 to 1987', Montréal: HEC Montréal, working paper.
Vesper, K. (1980) *New Venture Strategies*, Englewood Cliffs, N.J.: Prentice-Hall.

11 New businesses in the UK brewing industry
Entrepreneurial ventures or life-style enterprises?

Kevin McNally and Colin Mason

> Britain is fast rediscovering a taste for real ale. Around the country
> traditional brews with such thirst-satisfying names as Hop Back,
> Summer Lightning, Malton Old Bob, Oakhill Black Magic and
> Felinfoel Double Dragon, roll off the tongue in increasing numbers.
> (Rawstorne 1993a: 10)

INTRODUCTION

The United Kingdom, in common with much of the rest of Western
Europe and North America, has experienced a substantial increase in
the rate of new business formation since at least 1980 and possibly
since the mid–1970s. The annual number of businesses registering
for Value-Added Tax (VAT), which is widely regarded as a useful
surrogate measure of business start-ups, increased steadily during the
1980s from 158,000 in 1980 to 256,000 in 1989, a 62 per cent increase.
With the onset of recession at the end of the decade, the number of
business start-ups declined (in marked contrast to the 1980–82 recession), with only 189,000 VAT registrations in 1992 (although because
of an increase in the VAT registration threshold this figure is not
strictly comparable with previous years). However, recent figures
from Barclays Bank indicate that the upward trend in business start-
ups resumed in 1993: indeed, the number of start-ups in the first three
quarters of 1993 have been the highest quarterly totals since 1990
(Barclays Bank plc 1993).

The forces underlying this rising trend in new business formations
remain a matter for debate (Keeble 1990). However, there is a broad
consensus that several processes have been at work and that the
significance of any single factor varies considerably between sectors,
regions, and time-periods. Keeble (1990) identifies five factors as
being of particular importance in stimulating new business start-ups
(also see Keeble, Walker, and Robson 1993):

1 Recession-push mechanisms such as redundancies which have pushed individuals into business formation (Mason 1989), recession-induced closures which have created a supply of low-cost second-hand plant and machinery to reduce start-up costs (Binks and Jennings 1986), and retrenchment of peripheral activities by large firms which has created market niches that small firms can profitably fill by capitalizing on their lower overheads (Economists Advisory Group 1981).

2 Large firm fragmentation strategies, involving the subcontracting of manufacturing processes and, in particular, the outsourcing of specialized business services (Shutt and Whittington 1987; Keeble, Bryson, and Wood 1992).

3 Technological change, which has created commercial opportunities for technical entrepreneurs (Rothwell and Zegveld 1982; Keeble and Kelly 1986).

4 Government assistance to the small firm sector (Mason and Harrison 1986), the promotion of an 'enterprise culture' (Bannock 1987), and policies of deregulation and privatization.

5 Changing market demand, associated with rising real incomes and growing consumer sophistication, resulting in the appearance of numerous market niches for customized and specialized products and services (Brusco 1982; Bollard 1983a).

Mason and Harrison (1990) provide a slightly different perspective on the factors behind the growth in business start-ups in Western Europe. They distinguish between causal and facilitating factors. Causal factors include the following: recession-related influences such as rising unemployment and corporate restructuring; technological change, which both created opportunities for new innovative enterprises in emergent industries, and exerted 'downstream' effects of lower minimum efficient scales of production on established industries to reduce barriers to entry for new businesses (Carlsson 1989); and structural changes, of which the emergence of the information economy, and the growing consumer demand for a greater variety of customized goods and services which necessitate short production runs, are the most significant. Facilitating factors include the availability of resources (e.g. finance, premises, advice) and changing societal attitudes towards enterprise.

Our focus in this paper is on business formation that is associated with the changing nature of consumer market demand. The importance of this factor is stressed by Keeble (1990): he argues that 'customization and specialization of market demand is a major contemporary stimulus to small business development' (p. 238).

Rising real incomes and increasing affluence have contributed to the break-up of the mass market. Consumers have increasingly rejected mass-produced, often synthetic, items and instead sought better quality, more varied, customized, and sophisticated products and services (Brusco 1982). The result has been the appearance of numerous market niches for higher quality products produced in small quantities and requiring flexible production technologies which small firms have been better able to exploit than large enterprises (Brusco 1982; Bollard 1983b). Market niches of this type are found in a number of industries, including furniture, ceramics, textiles, clothing and knitwear, and publishing. However, many of the best examples are in the food and beverage industries where the stabilizers, suppressants, colourants, flavourings, preservatives, and packaging used to facilitate large-scale factory production have inevitably changed the character of the product. This has led to growing consumer resistance, opening up market opportunities for small enterprises (Bollard 1983b).

The brewing industry exhibits these trends. Indeed, this industry is claimed to provide 'the most striking case of consumer resistance encouraging industrial change' (Bollard 1983a: 34). As we discuss in more detail below, there has been a significant increase in the formation of new breweries (referred to as 'microbreweries' in the UK and 'boutique' or 'designer' breweries in North America), particularly in the UK but also in North America and Australasia. The formation of such businesses is a result of the emergence of market niches that have arisen for precisely the reasons discussed in the preceding paragraph. Our concern in this paper is to consider the growth potential of such businesses. Specifically, to what extent are such businesses able to break out of these market niches, and to what extent are the owner–managers motivated to do so, in order to become sizeable enterprises? The example of the Boston Beer Company, best known for its *Sam Adams* brand, illustrates that rapid growth is certainly possible: established in the early 1980s as a 'boutique brewery' producing European-style beer – a very different kind of beer from that which Americans are used to drinking – it is now the thirteenth largest brewer in the United States. Its beer is distributed extensively in the US and is now exported to Europe (*Financial Times*, 31 December 1992).

STRUCTURAL CHANGE IN THE UK BREWING INDUSTRY: THE EMERGENCE OF MICROBREWERIES

The brewing industry in the UK experienced a rapid growth of concentration in the 1960s through a process of merger and takeover of smaller local and regional brewery companies by a handful of large national brewing companies (Watts 1977; 1981). In the subsequent rationalizations many of the acquired breweries were declared uneconomic, and closed down (Bollard 1983a) and replaced by a smaller number of large, highly automated new plants built to exploit economies of scale. The dominant market position of these major firms was further consolidated during the 1970s and 1980s by another round of acquisitions of smaller, regionally-based brewers. Thus, by the late 1980s just six corporate groups accounted for over three-quarters of UK beer production and controlled, through their own tied outlets such as pubs and restaurants, the majority of retail outlets (Watts 1991).

One of the consequences of these trends has been that the number and variety of beers has fallen drastically as the production of milds, speciality ales, stouts and cask conditioned bitters that used to be produced by local and regional brewers have ceased. In their place have emerged a small number of heavily promoted homogeneous national brands of 'keg' beer and lager produced in large, automated breweries to common quality standards. The brewing methods used allow beers to be produced more quickly than traditional cask-conditioned beer and have a much longer shelf-life.

Consumer dissatisfaction with the reduction in the choice of beer and the loss of distinctive brews was articulated by the Campaign for Real Ale (CAMRA). Started in 1971 as a consumer movement by a group of beer lovers, its objective was to lobby for the revival of 'real ale' – i.e. cask-conditioned beers, brewed by traditional methods, containing no chemical preservatives, and served without the use of gas-infusing hand pumps. The most important effect of CAMRA's activities was to make the drinking public aware that there is an alternative to the mass-produced, bland, chilled and over-gassed keg beers and lagers produced by the national brewers. Membership of the movement grew rapidly, confirming the emergence of a more discerning marketplace. As the editor of CAMRA's *Good Beer Guide* comments, 'British drinkers are undoubtedly undergoing a conversion . . . [they are] trading up to beers full of flavour and character. Keg beer is fading fast and lager is past its peak' (quoted in Rawstorne 1993a: 10).

The formation of a considerable number of craft breweries producing real ale since the mid–1970s is a direct response to this growing demand for traditional beers. Bollard (1983a) suggests that more than 70 microbreweries were formed in the 1970s. The Small Independent Breweries Association (SIBA) was formed in 1980 to represent the interests of these new brewers, who were denied voting rights in the Brewers' Society which is dominated by the large firms (Bollard 1983a). The numbers of microbreweries increased even faster in the 1980s. By 1987 there were nearly 150 real ale breweries in existence, with a further 143 which had started and subsequently closed (Glover 1988). Recent evidence suggests that the high formation rate of microbreweries has continued during the 1990s, with more than 50 start-ups in 1991 and 1992 (Rawstorne 1993a). As a result, commercial brewing has returned to many localities where it had long been abandoned.

Some of the founders of the first wave of these new breweries were experienced brewers who had previously worked for national or regional companies. Other founders had previously worked in related industries such as off-licences, restaurants, beer wholesalers and soft drinks distributors or had been pub landlords. However, many new brewers – particularly those following the first wave – came from a variety of backgrounds that were unconnected with the brewery industry (Glover 1988).

These 'new wave' breweries are typically small and owner-managed. They rely on selling their beer to the free trade. The high cost of buying pubs prevents them from acquiring their own tied house network. The effect of the licensing laws of England and Wales is to severely restrict the conversion of retail sites into public houses. Licensing justices have considerable discretion when deciding whether to grant new on-licences and applicants must try to convince licensing committees that a need exists for a new pub. There has also been a revival of the once dominant publican–brewer. Brew-pubs are based upon traditional methods but incorporate many technical and biochemical advances to create a scaled-down system which takes up little space, can brew a small output sufficient for a public house's own requirements and requires little attention from the publican. Output that is surplus to the pub's own requirements is sold on the free trade.

Some microbreweries and brew-pubs have installed new custom-built equipment which draws upon engineering advances in brewing technology while still relying upon traditional chemical principles. Indeed, the growth of the microbrewery sector has stimulated the formation of specialist equipment manufacturers. However, because of the size of investment required to purchase new equipment, most microbrewers have relied largely or exclusively on second-hand equipment.

The emergence of microbreweries in the UK is paralleled in a number of other countries. For example, in both the USA and Canada 'boutique' breweries have been established in recent years to produce real ale to fill the taste gap left by the bland, iced lagers of the mega-brewers such as Miller and Anheuser Busch in the USA and Labatts and Molson in Canada (Fleming 1986; *New York Times*, 10 April, 1988; Masters 1986; Milne and Tufts 1993). In both countries the growing demand for imported premium beers highlighted the market opportunities created by consumer dissatisfaction with the limited choice of domestic beers available. One recent estimate suggests that there are some 400 microbreweries scattered across the USA (Griffith 1993) while in Canada there were 33 microbreweries in 1990 compared with just four in 1983 (Milne and Tufts 1993). The founders of British real ale breweries have been employed by a number of US and Canadian breweries as consultants. Some have also utilized equipment that has been supplied by British manufacturers (Glover 1988). Peter Austin, founder of Ringwood Brewery in Hampshire and widely regarded as 'the father of the new brewery revolution' (Glover 1988: 13) has acted as consultant and sold his equipment to breweries in a number of countries.

METHODOLOGY

New breweries were identified from *The New Beer Guide* (Glover 1988) – a CAMRA publication – which lists all new breweries and brew-pubs which have been established since 1971 (i.e. since the formation of CAMRA), including those which subsequently closed. More recent start-ups were identified through *What's Brewing*, the official CAMRA magazine. From these sources a total of 58 new breweries were identified in the south of England (i.e. south of a line running from Norfolk to Devon), of which 32 participated in the study (Figure 11.1). Of the non-respondents, 14 had ceased operations and 12 refused to participate in the survey. Information was collected in face-to-face interviews using a semi-structured questionnaire. Interviews were undertaken during the summer of 1991.

The sample comprised 20 specialist breweries and 12 brew-pubs. None had been founded prior to 1978. Over half had been established in the period 1978 to 1982 and only 4 were less than five years old. A number were no longer owned by their original founders. Although new breweries are found throughout the south of England, there is nevertheless a clear concentration in the south-west, notably Somerset (6), Wiltshire (4), and Devon (3), which together accounted for 41 per cent of all respondents. The majority of breweries are

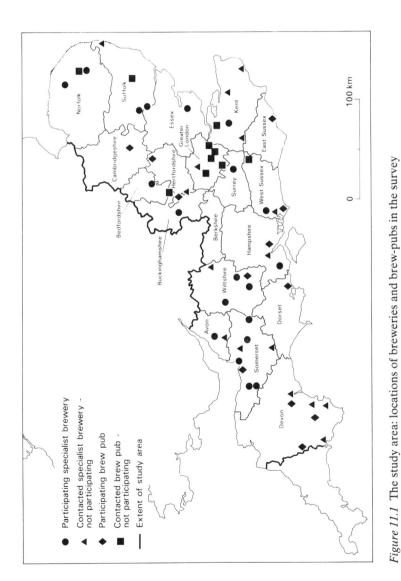

Legend:

● Participating specialist brewery
◀ Contacted specialist brewery - not participating
◆ Participating brew pub
■ Contacted brew pub - not participating
— Extent of study area

Figure 11.1 The study area: locations of breweries and brew-pubs in the survey

located in rural areas (17) and small towns (6), with relatively few in cities (4) or large towns (5). However, brew-pubs exhibit a greater affinity for larger urban areas, with 42 per cent located in cities and large towns compared with only 20 per cent for specialist breweries.

THE BUSINESS FORMATION DECISION

The 32 breweries had a total of 52 founders: 44 per cent of firms were started by one individual, 40 per cent by two founders, and the remainder by three or more founders. The majority of founders (62 per cent) were in the 30–45 year age group when they started their brewery, while just over one-quarter were over 45 years old. The majority had received high school education and 44 per cent had degrees.

In most cases, the decision to start or buy a brewery has been a positive one, associated with the nature of the product or the conditions of employment. Half of all respondents cited the love of the product as their main motive, while over one-quarter emphasized the opportunity to involve the entire family as a major attraction. Other commonly cited motives included the desire to work for oneself and the ability to work near home. Conversely, only 12.5 per cent gave redundancy as a reason why they decided to go into business on their own account.

Most founders had held more than one job prior to setting up their business. A majority had managerial backgrounds (54 per cent) and a few had been employed in skilled manual occupations. However, unlike most founders of manufacturing firms (e.g. Johnson and Cathcart 1979; Fothergill and Gudgin 1982; Keeble and Gould 1985; Mason 1989) a majority of brewery founders were previously employed in large firms (52 per cent worked in firms with 500 or more employees compared with 27 per cent who were employed in firms with less than 50 employees). Nevertheless, almost one-third of respondents had been self-employed at some time prior to establishing their brewery, of whom four had previously owned breweries. Half the respondents also had self-employed parents.

A further contrast with conventional routes to new business formation – in which the founders generally start their business in the same industry in which they had previously been employed (Gudgin 1978; Johnson and Cathcart 1979) – is that only 10 founders of micro-breweries had a background in the brewing industry. Thus, the majority – some 73 per cent – of the founders of new breweries had no prior experience in the brewing industry before starting their business.

Most of the new brewing entrepreneurs were therefore venturing into a business sector which was unfamiliar territory. It is therefore not surprising that nearly one-quarter of founders expressed a lack of confidence in their ability to handle production matters (although an equal proportion indicated that this was the aspect that they were most confident about).

Another difference from general patterns in new firm formation is the geographical mobility of the founder. Most studies have found that the vast majority of new firm founders set up their business in the locality in which they are already living (e.g. Gudgin 1978; Lloyd and Mason 1984; Mason 1989). However, 41 per cent of brewery founders had chosen to establish their business in an area different from that in which they were living and working. Most of these breweries were established in rural and semi-rural areas. In this respect new firm formation in the brewery industry is a microcosm of general new firm location patterns in rural areas: Keeble, Tyler, Broom, and Lewis (1992) note that a significant minority of new enterprises in rural areas have been established by people who moved to such locations specifically to set up their business.

RESOURCES FOR START-UP

Finance

The amount of start-up finance used by new-wave breweries varied quite considerably (Table 11.1). Taking the sample as a whole, at one extreme, one-quarter of firms began with between £1,000 and £5,000 while at the other extreme 37 per cent of firms invested over £25,000 at start-up. Brew-pubs have required considerably less start-up finance than specialist brewers: half of the brew-pubs started with less than £5,000 and only two used more than £25,000, whereas half the breweries invested over £25,000 at start-up. The majority of firms attempted to reduce start-up costs by using second-hand equipment; indeed, for 69 per cent of firms more than half of their equipment was second-hand. However, because of the scarcity of second-hand equipment (Bollard 1983a) this is not a particularly low-cost strategy, in contrast to many other industries where cheap second-hand plant and machinery is often widely available.

The main sources of start-up finance used by brewery founders were personal savings and 'love money' from family and friends, supplemented by bank loans and bank overdrafts. Five firms benefited from government schemes to assist small businesses (Loan Guarantee

Table 11.1 Financial requirements at start-up

Amount invested	Breweries	Brew-pubs	Total
< £1,000	0	0	0
£1,000 – £5,000	2	6	8
£5,001 – £10,000	2	1	3
£10,001 – £25,000	6	3	9
> £25,000	10	2	12

Source: Survey

Table 11.2 Sources of start-up finance

Source	Breweries	Brew-pubs	Total	% of firms
Personal savings	12	4	16	50.0
Bank loan	9	4	13	40.1
Bank overdraft	4	3	7	21.9
Redundancy pay	4	1	5	15.6
Family/friends	4	0	4	12.5
Loan Guarantee Scheme	3	1	4	12.5
Mortgage	1	1	2	6.3
Stock market flotation	1	0	1	3.1
Venture capital	0	1	1	3.1
Enterprise Allowance Scheme	1	0	1	3.1

Source: Survey
Note: respondents could give more than one source

Scheme and Enterprise Allowance Scheme). One firm raised finance from a venture capital fund and another raised finance from the Stock Market (Table 11.2). The overwhelming majority of firms (84 per cent) reported no problems in raising start-up finance.

Most firms have invested heavily since start-up. An average of £28,000 has been spent on premises and £42,000 on equipment, largely to cope with expansion of production. Most of this expenditure has been financed by a combination of retained profits (39 per cent of firms) and bank loans (29 per cent). Here again there have been few difficulties in raising finance. Just two firms reported that they had abandoned projects because of the inability to raise finance.

Premises

Including eight breweries that had relocated from their original premises, the firms in the survey occupy small premises (average size of 2,055 sq ft). Over three-quarters have freehold premises. However, a number of firms, predominantly in urban areas, which would have preferred to rent had been forced to purchase freehold premises because of difficulties in obtaining suitable rented premises. Just under half (44 per cent) of the firms occupy pre–1914 premises. As Rawstorne (1993a: 10) observes, 'casks of beer are rolling out of the most unlikely places: former cowsheds . . ., an old foundry . . ., a disused sawmill'. A similar proportion are in new industrial units constructed since 1970. Firms encountered few problems in finding premises.

Labour

Although the brewing of real ale is a relatively labour-intensive process, microbreweries nevertheless tend to be small. The largest firm in the survey had 15 employees, the smallest just 1 employee, while the average was 4.9 employees. Nevertheless, this represents a doubling of employment since start-up, when the average firm had just 2.2 employees.

Information

Two-thirds of founders sought advice before starting their business. The major sources of general information were other business owners, particularly in the microbrewing industry (43 per cent), professional advisors (23 per cent), and family and friends (20 per cent). In contrast, business organizations and government agencies were rarely utilized for advice. The main sources of specialist information were trade journals (31 per cent), other microbrewers (18 per cent), CAMRA and SIBA (16 per cent), and large brewing companies (10 per cent).

NEW BREWERIES: OPERATIONAL CONSIDERATIONS

Products and processes

Most microbreweries in the survey produce beer using traditional methods and materials. Their average annual output is 1,942 barrels, while the extremes of the range are 100 and 10,000 barrels. A majority of breweries (63 per cent) concentrate solely on beer production, with only 9 per cent producing other drinks as well as beer. The remainder of the firms derive some income from providing services such as consultancy and local wholesaling.

All of the microbreweries in the survey produce at least two types of beer, with one-quarter of breweries producing five or more beers. Some 40 per cent of breweries reported that they were planning to expand their product range in the short-term. Less than one-third of breweries produced bottled and canned beers. With just one exception, the brewers considered their products unique, or at least distinctive in character.

Sales

The main market for the output of microbreweries in the survey is the free trade, where their beers compete for custom with those of the much larger national and regional brewers. Many microbrewers would like to establish their own tied estate for their brewery. However, only 35 per cent of respondents have been able to do so (mainly brew-pubs) for the reasons discussed earlier, namely the limited availability and high cost of pubs for sale and the legal restrictions on the creation of new licensed premises. The number of outlets served ranged from 2 to 200. Pubs are the dominant type of customer but some breweries sell their output to hotels, clubs, and retailers.

Most small breweries serve local markets. Indeed, 44 per cent of breweries derive half or more of their sales from within a 10-mile radius of the brewery. A further 31 per cent derive half or more of their sales from within 100 miles of the brewery. Most breweries (90 per cent) have expanded their sales area since start-up by using wholesalers, although reliance on wholesalers for sales varies quite considerably. The proportion of the output of firms in the survey that was distributed via wholesalers ranged from under 1 per cent to 60 per cent.

The highly localized nature of the markets of most breweries reflects their limited marketing effort. Most customers have been obtained though informal methods of marketing. Word-of-mouth is relied upon by 40 per cent of brewers. Only 21 per cent undertake any advertising and just 18 per cent employ sales representatives.

CONSTRAINTS ON THE GROWTH OF NEW BREWERIES

It is clear from these findings that those microbreweries established in the UK during the past 10 to 15 years to take advantage of consumer dissatisfaction with limited choice of beers are very small and rely upon local markets. Industry reports indicate that most breweries struggle to survive and face a high failure rate (Glover 1988). There is no British success story among the new-wave breweries to match that of the Boston Beer Company.[1] The reasons are largely a function of two factors, namely the background and motivations of the founders of microbreweries and the restricted distribution channels available to new breweries.

As noted earlier, the opportunities to set up new breweries to meet the demand for real ale have attracted many individuals who want to achieve a change of life-style. Indeed, a high proportion of respondents regarded their business more as a hobby than a business. The following comments from respondents in the survey are by no means atypical:

> 'It's an expensive hobby, not so much a business.'
> 'It's both a job and a hobby and therefore with financial and enjoyment sides'.

For these respondents, motivation and satisfaction came from the quality of the product rather than from the financial returns of the business. This is reflected in the following response:

> 'We're not really motivated by an end goal, not a financial goal anyway. We just want to survive from day to day and produce quality beer.'

Thus, as Table 11.3 shows, the majority of respondents in the survey have limited growth ambitions. Survival was the primary objective for nearly one-third of microbreweries in the survey. As one respondent stated: 'our goal is to stay alive. Growth is possible but it's not a priority.'

A similar proportion of respondents anticipated modest, often gradual, expansion. The following comments are typical of this group of firms:

> 'We want to be a successful microbrewery with a few more staff.'
> 'We don't want to expand too much.'

Table 11.3 Future objectives of microbrewery owners

Objective	Number	%
Survival; little or no expansion likely	10	31.2
To supply good beers/choice of beers	3	9.4
Modest/gradual expansion	8	25.0
To be a successful small business	3	9.4
Expansion	7	21.9
To get a tied estate	1	3.1

Source: Survey

No more than one-quarter of microbreweries in the survey had ambitions to achieve significant expansion.

However, a minority of microbrewery owners who do have growth aspirations encounter major constraints in achieving market penetration because of the peculiar structure of the industry's retail end. Prior to recent government-induced changes in the structure of brewery retailing (which we discuss below) the majority of Britain's pubs were either 'managed houses', owned by the brewing companies and staffed by their employees, or 'tied houses', owned by the brewers but managed by tenants. Both managed houses and tied houses can only sell the beers that are supplied by their parent brewery. Thus, as few microbreweries own pubs they must compete by selling to 'free houses' – which are able to sell any beer that they wish – if they are to survive and grow. However, free houses comprise a minority of the total public house market. Moreover, small breweries complain that their ability to compete in the free trade is constrained by the 'cheque book marketing' practices of the national brewers who provide cheap loans to licencees who take their beer (Glover 1988). For these reasons, most of the respondents with growth ambitions emphasized that obtaining a tied estate of public houses was 'vital' to their expansion plans.

The incidence of free trade varies across the country, hence there are spatial variations in the nature and extent of competition encountered by small breweries. Specialist brewers encounter more competition than brew pubs which are primarily producing for the needs of the pub itself. Amongst the respondents to the survey, the specialist breweries in the south-east and East Anglia experienced more competition than those in the south and south-west. Small brewers in the south-east and East Anglia identified larger regional brewers as providing the greatest competition. In contrast, there were more than twice as many small breweries in the south and west that identified their main source of competition as coming from other small brewery companies than those whose main competition was from regional and national brewers (47 per cent compared to 21 per cent). These differences in the nature of competition reflect the relative lack of regional and national brewers in the south and south-west and the consequent greater number of small breweries which have filled the market gap. A further factor is that half of the small breweries in the south and south-west have their own tied estate, compared with only 17 per cent in East Anglia and the south-east, and so have a captive market for their beer.

Paradoxically, the effect of recent government attempts to encourage competition in the brewing industry, following a report by the Monopolies and Mergers Commission (MMC) in 1989, has been to increase rather than reduce this constraint on the growth of micro-breweries. The report concluded that a complex monopoly existed in the brewing industry largely as a result of its vertical integration. The control exerted by brewers over the retailing of beer through direct ownership or loan-tying of licensed premises discouraged new entrants into the brewing industry at all levels. The MMC therefore recommended radical changes to the industry's structure to remedy this situation. Among its key recommendations were that no brewer could own, lease or have any other interest in more than 2,000 pubs, that tenants should be permitted to purchase at least one brand of draught beer (termed a 'guest beer') from a supplier other than the landlord or nominated supplier and that loan-tying should be abolished (Monopolies and Mergers Commission 1989).

Following a period of consultation, the government decided to implement the MMC's recommendations in modified form. In partic-ular, the government announced that national brewers would only have to dispose of half of their pubs in excess of the 2,000 threshold. The disposals had to be completed by November 1992. It also decided that the guest beer provision would only apply to tenants of national brewers (i.e. those brewers retaining more than 2,000 outlets) and the guest beer would have to be a cask-conditioned ale. Contrary to MMC recommendations, the government decided not to abolish loan-ties (House of Commons 1993).

The restructuring that has followed implementation of the MMC report has had the opposite effect to that intended, with fewer brewers, fewer breweries, fewer beer brands, and more expensive beer (Rawstorne 1992a). However, while very critical of government intervention in the brewing industry, an all-party committee of MPs nevertheless conceded that the effect of the government's changes has been to accelerate structural changes within the industry which were already in prospect (House of Commons 1993).

The decline in the number of brewers has arisen because one national and four regional brewers decided to withdraw from brewing in order to become pub-retailers. As a result, they have no restriction on the number of pubs that they can own. In a breweries-for-pubs swap among two of the six national brewers, Grand Metropolitan withdrew from brewing in the UK by selling its four breweries and their associated brands to Courage, owned by Elders IXL of Australia, who in turn combined its pubs with those of Grand Metropolitan to create a jointly-owned estate of 6,500 pubs managed by Grand Metropolitan. These pubs are supplied by Courage (House of Commons 1993). Allied-Lyons and Carlsberg have merged their UK brewing operations, despite the MMC initially judging that the deal was against the public interest. Brewery closures have occurred as the national brewers have sought further production economies (Rawstorne 1992a): twelve breweries closed between 1989 and 1992 (House of Commons 1993). The five remaining national brewers now control 82 per cent of the country's beer production compared with 77 per cent held by the six national brewers in 1989 (House of Commons 1993).

The objective of substantially increasing the number of free houses by forcing the national brewers to sell or lease a significant number of their pubs, and thereby increase market opportunities for smaller breweries, has also not had the intended result. Some 11,000 pubs have been freed from ties with national brewers (although this figure would have been 22,000 had the MMC's recommendation been implemented). However, this has had little impact on opening up markets for small brewers. First, the large brewers tended to dispose of their low barrelage pubs which had benefited from cross-subsidization but which were only marginally viable as independent operations. About 2,000 pubs are estimated to have closed. Second, at least 8,000 of the pubs disposed of or freed from the tie are now owned by new multiple pub operating companies, some of which are national chains owning several hundred pubs while others are smaller local and regional operators. Other pubs have been purchased by regional brewers who have been eager to expand their existing tied estate. Thus, relatively few of the pubs that the brewers have released from the tie have been purchased either by small breweries or by the sitting tenants of the big brewers (House of Commons 1993). Moreover, industry observers have predicted that some independent pub companies and stand-alone pubs may close under the pressures of high borrowings and a decline in the pub-going population (Rawstorne 1992a).

The increase in the proportion of on-trade beer sales accounted for by the independent pub sector (from 37 per cent in 1989 to 49 per cent in 1992) that has resulted from these developments has also had little, if any, benefit to small brewing firms. Most multiple pub operating companies have supply agreements with major brewers – often the same brewers from whom the outlets were acquired – which prevents their tenants from obtaining beer from other companies. National brewers also have minority equity stakes in a number of pub operating companies. In effect, therefore, these developments have re-tied a large section of the on-trade.

The sole success of the government's intervention has been the 'guest beers' provision (House of Commons 1993). This required the national brewers to allow tenants in the remaining pubs that they own to buy spirits, cider, soft drinks, and one brand of cask-conditioned ale from any supplier. This guest ale provision was intended to benefit regional and smaller brewers by giving their products access to the pubs owned by the big brewers. However, even this has had a less favourable impact than anticipated as a result of associated changes in the structure of the industry. First, the forced divestment of pubs owned by the national brewers has reduced the market for guest beers. Second, as noted above, two-thirds of the pubs disposed of by the brewers have been bought or leased by the multiple pub operating companies which are not covered by the guest beer provision. Third, as a result of pressures exerted by the large brewers, fewer than one-third of the tenants of the big brewers have taken advantage of the guest ale provision. Fourth, the guest ale provision does not apply to smaller regional breweries who have fewer than 2,000 pubs. Furthermore, many of these regional brewers have local monopolies, owning a high proportion of the pubs in par-ticular localities. As a result, there are various parts of the country where the market for guest beers is extremely limited. Finally, the major beneficiary has been regional brewers with well-known brands who have been able to dominate the guest beer market.

A further constraint on the growth of small breweries arises from their need to use wholesalers to supply non-local outlets. Many of the small breweries in the survey complained that wholesalers demanded high discounts and were often slow to pay. There were also problems in getting their casks returned. Some small breweries were also concerned with the deterioration in the quality of beer caused by improper handling by the wholesalers. These problems are, in part, a reflection of the unequal power relations that are involved (Taylor and Thrift 1982). However, they also stem, more mundanely, from the fact that wholesaling of real ale is new to the brewing industry. Most of the wholesalers used by small breweries specialize in distributing soft drinks (which are not as perishable as real ale) and are therefore less sensitive to the different handling and distribution requirements of real ale.

CONCLUSIONS AND IMPLICATIONS

The formation of more than 300 new breweries in the UK since the early 1970s – of which about half are still trading – largely reflects the creation of life-style businesses rather than entrepreneurial ventures. Most founders have been attracted to the industry for non-financial reasons – notably their interest in both product and process – and have limited growth ambitions for their businesses. This is a characteristic of businesses in many 'craft industries' (Bollard 1983a; Rosa *et al.* 1988). Moreover, the ownership structure of pub retailing represents a formidable barrier to market penetration and is a major impediment for the minority of microbrewery entrepreneurs who have growth aspirations. The effects of government measures introduced after the MMC report have not made the competitive position of microbreweries any better. The clear implication is therefore that new brewing firms with growth ambitions must identify strategies that circumvent market constraints arising from the ownership structure of the UK brewing industry.

Brew-pubs and specialist brewers face different growth constraints and growth opportunities and so different strategies are appropriate for each. The obvious approach for brew-pubs is to expand by opening additional brew-pubs, thereby developing a chain. There have been some attempts to pursue this approach, notably by David Bruce with his 'Firkin' brew-pubs and pubs (supplied by the chain's own brewery) and by some other companies that imitated the style. However, these chains have remained fairly small and a number have failed. Indeed, Bruce was unsuccessful in his attempt to expand outside his London base: his brew-pub in Bristol proved unprofitable. He concluded from this experience that it was not possible to operate a chain of this type of brew-pub across a large geographical area (Dickson 1984). The difficulties in developing a large chain of brew-pubs revolve around the drawbacks of decentralization: it involves operating a large number of fairly small, dispersed outlets remote from head office, undertaking people-centred transactions which, in turn, creates difficulties in quality control, personnel motivation, and supervision. This is confirmed by an early study of David Bruce's company which found that its biggest challenge was 'how to expand while retaining the personal touch' (Dickson 1984). The response in other sectors which have encountered a similar situation has been to introduce franchising (Curran and Stanworth 1983). Use of business format franchising may therefore be the most appropriate way in which to develop a large chain of brew-pubs. Indeed, franchised brew-pubs have been established in France.

The most appropriate strategy for specialist brewers seeking expansion would appear to lie in selling bottled beers through distribution channels other than pubs – notably grocery supermarkets and specialist off-licence chains (and also wine bars and restaurants). This strategy has been successfully pursued by Granville Island Brewery on Vancouver, one of Canada's most successful boutique breweries (Masters 1986). Indeed, for a variety of reasons, an increasing amount of alcohol is being drunk at home rather than in pubs and restaurants. The take-home trade is the fastest growing sector of the UK drinks market, accounting for 19 per cent of beer sales in 1989 but predicted to increase to 28 per cent by 2001 (House of Commons 1993; Rawstorne 1993b; 1993c). Supermarkets and off-licence chains are stocking increasing numbers of bottle-conditioned real ales – that is, brews which enjoy secondary fermentation in the bottle on a sediment of living yeast. At present this comprises almost entirely imported brews (Rawstorne 1992b), although one of the UK's leading chain of specialist off-licences has recently launched its own-label bottle-conditioned ale. US supermarkets are already stocked with dozens of brands of distinctive beers, many of them produced by small, local breweries (Griffith 1993). UK supermarkets and off-licence chains may also be receptive to approaches from microbreweries to stock their products.

However, this marketing strategy has three potential drawbacks. First, at present, the output of most of the new breweries in the UK is largely or exclusively in the form of barrels. In order to penetrate the take-home market, microbreweries will therefore have to devote an increasing proportion of their output to bottled beers. But small packaging of beer is both a difficult and highly specialized branch of engineering: quality control is more difficult and cost is highly sensitive to the scale of production. It would, however, be possible to utilize the services of other brewers who specialize in contract bottling. The second drawback is that the high level of concentration in UK retailing enables the major grocery supermarket chains to exert considerable power over suppliers, for example in terms of price and delivery schedules. Finally, microbreweries must be aware of the potential threat from large breweries who might be attracted to the real ale market. Although the market is still very small it is growing fast, as consumers tend to be affluent and the products enjoy a price premium. Indeed, in both the US and Canada, the large brewers have started to produce their own specialist beers for this market (Griffith 1993; Milne and Tufts 1993). In order to gain a competitive edge, microbreweries must therefore market their beers in an imaginative way – for example, by appealing to local pride – and capitalize on their flexibility – for example, by offering variety in the form of seasonal beers (Griffith 1993).

ACKNOWLEDGEMENTS

We are grateful to Iain Loe and Iain Dobson of CAMRA for their advice and information and to Richard Gascoigne for his thoughts on retailing issues. We also thank Daniel Muzyka, Benôit Leleux, and Jonathan Virdon for their comments on an earlier version of this paper. Most of all we are grateful to the 32 microbrewers who participated in the study for the time that they gave to answering our many questions.

NOTE

1 Just one British real ale brewery has acheived significant growth. However, this company – Hoskins – is based in Leicester (and so was outside the study area) and dates back to 1890. Its present owners took it over in 1983 and raised £1.8m under the Business Expansion Scheme. Its shares are now traded on the Unlisted Securities Market. It had 60 employees in 1988 (Glover 1988).

REFERENCES

Bannock, G. (1987) *Britain in the 1980s: Enterprise Reborn?* London: 3i Company.

Barclays Bank plc (1993) *Small Firms Research Conference Special: Figures for Third Quarter 1993*, London: Paragon Communications.

Binks, M. and Jennings, A. (1986) 'Small Firms as a Source of Economic Rejuvenation', in J. Curran, J. Stanworth, and D. Watkins (eds), *The Survival of the Small Firm. Volume 1: The Economics of Survival and Entrepreneurship*, Aldershot, Hants: Gower, 19–38.

Bollard, A. (1983a) *Small Beginnings: New Roles for British Businesses*, London: Intermediate Technology Publications.

Bollard, A. (1983b) 'Technology, Economic Change and Small Firms', *Lloyds Bank Review*, 147: 42–56.

Brusco, S. (1982) 'The Emilian Model: Productive Decentralization and Social Integration', *Cambridge Journal of Economics*, 6: 167–184.

Carlsson, B. (1989) 'The Evolution of Manufacturing Technology and its Impact on Industrial Structure: an International Study', *Small Business Economics*, 1: 21–37.

Curran, J. and Stanworth, J. (1983) 'Franchising and the Modern Economy – Towards a Theoretical Understanding', *International Small Business Journal*, 2 (1): 8–26.

Dickson, T. (1984) 'When Rising Sales May Mean that Trouble is Brewing', *Financial Times*, 20 March.

Economists Advisory Group (1981) *Enterprise West: A Study of Small Business in the West of England*, London: Shell UK Ltd.

Fleming, S. (1986) 'How Mr Wrigley Aims to Fill the Taste Gap', *Financial Times*, 21 June.

Fothergill, S. and Gudgin, G. (1982) *Unequal Growth: Urban and Regional Employment Change in Britain*, London: Heinemann.

Glover, B. (1988) *New Beer Guide*, Newton Abbott: David and Charles.

Griffith, V. (1993) 'More than Just Beer', *Financial Times*, 23 September.

Gudgin, G. (1978) *Industrial Location Processes and Regional Employment Growth*, Farnborough, Hants: Saxon House.

House of Commons (1993) 'Agriculture Committee, Fourth report. *Effects of the Beer Orders on the Brewing Industry and Consumers*, London: HMSO.

Johnson, P.S. and Cathcart, D.G. (1979) 'New Manufacturing Firms and Regional Development: Some Evidence from the Northern Region', *Regional Studies*, 13: 269–280.

Keeble, D. (1990) 'Small Firms, New Firms and Uneven Development in the United Kingdom', *Area*, 22: 234–245.

Keeble, D., Bryson, J., and Wood, P. (1992) 'Entrepreneurship and Flexibility in Business Services: The Rise of Small Management Consultancy and Market Research Firms', in K. Caley, E. Chell, F. Chittenden, and C. Mason (eds), *Small Enterprise Development: Policy and Practice in Action*, London: Paul Chapman Publishing, 43–58.

Keeble, D. and Gould, A. (1985) 'Entrepreneurship and Manufacturing Firm Formation in Rural Regions: The East Anglia Case', in M. Healey and B. Ilbery (eds), *The Industrialization of the Countryside*, Norwich: Geo Books, 197–219.

Keeble, D. and Kelly, T. (1986) 'New Firms and High Technology Industry in the United Kingdom', in D. Keeble and E. Wever (eds), *New Firms and Regional Development in Europe*, Beckenham, Kent: Croom Helm, 75–104.

Keeble, D., Tyler, P., Broom, G., and Lewis, J. (1992) *Business Success in the Countryside: The Performance of Rural Enterprise*, London: HMSO.

Keeble, D., Walker, S., and Robson, M. (1993) *New Firm Formation and Small Business Growth in the United Kingdom: Spatial and Temporal Variations and Determinants*, Sheffield: Employment Department.

Lloyd, P.E. and Mason, C.M. (1984) 'Spatial Variations in New Firm Formation in the United Kingdom: Comparative Evidence from Merseyside, Greater Manchester, and South Hampshire', *Regional Studies*, 18: 207–220.

Mason, C.M. (1989) 'Explaining Recent Trends in UK New Firm Formation Rates: Evidence from Two Surveys in South Hampshire', *Regional Studies*, 23: 331–346.

Mason, C.M. and Harrison, R.T. (1986) 'The Regional Impact of Public Policy Towards Small Firms in the United Kingdom', in D. Keeble and E. Wever (eds), *New Firms and Regional Development in Europe*, Beckenham, Kent: Croom Helm, 224–255.

Mason, C.M. and Harrison, R.T. (1990) 'Small Firms – Phoenix from the Ashes?', In D.A. Pinder (ed.), *Challenge and Change in Western Europe*, London: Bellhaven, 72–90.

Masters, J. (1986) 'Brave New Breweries', *Canadian Business*, April: 56–63, 105–107.

Milne, S. and Tufts, S. (1993) 'Industrial Restructuring and the Future of the Small Firm: The Case of Canadian Microbreweries', *Environment and Planning A*, 25: 847–861.

Monopolies and Mergers Commission (1989) *The Supply of Beer*, London: HMSO.

Rawstorne, P. (1992a) 'Morning After in the Pub', *Financial Times*, 19 August.

Rawstorne, P. (1992b) 'Fashion Beers: Pulling Ahead Before the Bubble Bursts', *Financial Times*, 2 January.

Rawstorne, P. (1993a) 'Strange Brews Prompt a Real Ale Renaissance', *Financial Times*, 18 October.

Rawstorne, P. (1993b) 'New Drink Tastes Force Take-home Changes', *Financial Times*, 3 August.

Rawstorne, P. (1993c) 'Brewers' Heads Down for Prolonged In-fighting', *Financial Times*, 21 May.

Rosa, P., Hale, R., McAuley, A., McKay, J., and Wilkinson, R. (1988) *The Crafts Industry: The Problem of Small Business Expansion and the Constraints Faced by Such Businesses*, Stirling: Scottish Enterprise Foundation.

Rothwell, R. and Zegveld, W. (1982) *Innovation and the Small and Medium-Sized Firm*, London: Frances Pinter.

Shutt, J. and Whittington, R. (1987) 'Fragmentation Strategies and the Rise of Small Units: Cases from the North West', *Regional Studies*, 21: 13–23.

Taylor, M.J. and Thrift, N.J. (1982) 'Industrial Linkage and the Segmented Economy: Some Theoretical Considerations', *Environment and Planning A*, 14: 1601–1613.

Watts, H.D. (1977) 'Market Areas and Spatial Rationalization: The British Brewing Industry after 1945', *Tijdschrift voor Economische en Sociale Geografie*, 68: 224–240.

Watts, H.D. (1981) *The Branch Plant Economy: A Study of External Control*, London: Longman.

Watts, H.D. (1991) 'Understanding Plant Closures: The UK Brewing Industry', *Geography*, 76: 315–330.

Section IV
General

12 Analysing foreign direct investment in research and development

An entrepreneurial perspective

Walter Kümmerle

INTRODUCTION

Foreign direct investment (FDI)[1] has become an important issue for private enterprises and governments. Particularly, FDI among industrialized countries has risen strongly during the last decade. In 1989, FDI inflows in the Group of Five industrialized countries were nearly triple the 1980 value (Graham and Krugman 1991). This development creates new issues involving private enterprises and public bodies.

On the one hand, private enterprises, facing the challenge of maintaining and expanding their world market share in an increasingly competitive global environment, are forced to make cross-border investment decisions.

On the other hand, the greater interweaving of national economies and the upsurge of the multinational corporation (MNC) force governments to analyse more than ever before the consequences of FDI for the long-term welfare of their country's citizens and take appropriate measures (Reich 1990; Reich 1991).

Because FDI has been of interest to economists and administrative scientists for a long period of time, a considerable body of literature has evolved on the subject.[2] Theory was mainly advanced in line with empirical observations about firm behaviour. This meant that most advancements in theory during the 1970s and 1980s focused on FDI in production facilities. (Buckley and Casson 1976; Caves 1971; Caves 1982; Kindleberger 1970; Knickerbocker 1973; Rugman 1981). Some researchers did examine the location of R&D within large US corporations (Behrman and Fischer 1980; Ronstadt 1977), but no global analysis of R&D locations was undertaken. Only recently have some conceptual and exploratory studies focused on understanding R&D investment flows at a global level (DeMeyer 1993; Gomes-Casseres 1992; Howells 1990).

There is some evidence that among industrialized countries during the late 1980s FDI in R&D grew faster than FDI in other assets. While R&D activities can be described through classic production functions and underlying theory constructs, it seems that a different set of analytic tools can help to reveal more about the whole complexity of cross-border investment in R&D.

The purpose of this paper is to develop an explanatory framework for FDI in R&D and analyse some of the entrepreneurial aspects of the resource allocation process. The framework evolves from a functional analysis of R&D within an industrial organization. The paper then takes a closer look at how the explanatory framework can be used in analysing the R&D investment moves of Japanese firms, who have been prominent investors in R&D assets abroad since the late 1980s. Japan was selected for this paper because Japanese investments accentuate the influence of entrepreneurial elements on decisions about FDI in R&D in large corporations.

Section 1 of the paper provides some empirical evidence of FDI in general and FDI in R&D in particular, section 2 examines the nature of FDI in R&D, section 3 develops the analytical framework. Section 4 applies the framework to Japanese investments. Section 5 concludes the paper.

1 SOME EMPIRICAL EVIDENCE

FDI in general

Official statistics cover foreign direct investment by industry and country. Data about FDI by function (production, sales, R&D) is available only from large-scale surveys and industry studies. Industry studies have shown that FDI in R&D is a rather recent and costly form of investment which is (so far) carried out mainly by the largest firms in technology-oriented industries such as pharmaceuticals and semiconductors.[3] While estimates are difficult, it appears that in these two industries, foreign direct investments by the largest five to ten Japanese and German firms account for at least 50 per cent of total FDI in R&D by Japan and Germany.[4]

FDI inflows among the Group of Five have risen considerably since the mid-1980s. Since 1986, FDI inflows have strongly exceeded the growth rate of GDP of the Group of Five, in 1989 they reached three times their 1980 value, while GDP of the Group of Five reached only 1.2 times the 1980 value (Graham and Krugman 1991). Surveys suggest, that at least for the US and the UK, the growth rate of FDI inflows in R&D has risen more strongly than the growth rate of FDI inflows in general. These inflows originated from other industrialized countries, mainly from Japan. While Japanese companies invested mainly in R&D in the US and in the UK, companies of the European community invested mainly in R&D in the US and Japan. US companies, to a more limited extent, invested in R&D in Japan (MITI 1992; Mitsubishi Research Institute 1991).

Japanese FDI

More detailed surveys are available for Japanese FDI in R&D than for other countries. The survey by Mitsubishi Research Institute of 607 Japanese companies revealed that the rise of FDI in R&D facilities has started later than the rise of FDI in production facilities, but the growth rate of the former has been stronger. While there were 147 cases of FDI in factories from 1981 to 1984 and 312 from 1985 to 1990, the respective figures for R&D facilities are 27 and 94. Furthermore, from 1985 to 1990, about 30 per cent more R&D facilities were constructed in the US than in Europe.

Unfortunately, detailed figures on the amount invested in each laboratory are not available. A field study (Kümmerle 1993a) revealed that initial investments in laboratories that carry out sophisticated information search or support production activities, ranged from $1 to $10 million, while initial investment for laboratories that carry out mainly original research ranged from $10 to $50 million; in some cases the figures were even higher. With support from the qualitative analysis of the survey by Mitsubishi Research Institute, it can be assumed that the first wave of FDI in laboratories in the US and Europe concerned mainly small units that collect information and carry out local adaptation of existing products, while the second wave that started in the mid-1980s concerned mid-size to large-size units that mainly carry out original R&D.

A survey by JETRO (JETRO 1992b) shows that in 1990, 368 out of 747 Japanese manufacturing units in the US also performed R&D either on the same premises or at a different location in the US, and that this percentage of 49.3 per cent has risen from 46.5 per cent in 1989. This upward trend is expected to continue. Of the factories that started in the form of capital participation, 66.7 per cent have expanded their activities into R&D. The same is true for 60.6 per cent of the factories acquired through mergers and for 43.0 per cent of the green-field investments.

Another survey of 721 European subsidiaries of Japanese manufacturing firms by JETRO (JETRO 1992a) shows that R&D laboratories owned by Japanese companies in Europe have increased significantly from 73 in 1990 to 138 in 1991 and to 203 in 1992. Of the 203 facilities, 149 were set up for production bases and 54 are dedicated exclusively to design or R&D. The number of manufacturing bases in Europe increased from 520 in 1990 to 721 in 1992. This means an increase of 278 per cent for R&D laboratories and an increase of 'only' 39 per cent for factories.

The above data show that the importance of FDI flows in general and FDI in R&D in particular has increased during the latter half of the 1980s. This is true particularly for Japan, but fragmented empirical evidence suggests that the situation is similar in the US, the UK, and Germany. For the UK and the US, inflows of FDI in R&D seem to exceed outflows, while the opposite seems true for Japan and Germany (Mitsubishi Research Institute 1991; Pearce and Singh 1992).

2 CHARACTERISTICS OF FDI IN R&D

The OECD defines R&D as 'creative work undertaken on a systematic basis in order to increase the stock of knowledge, including knowledge of man, culture, society, and the use of this stock of knowledge to devise new applications'. *Basic and applied research* are original investigations undertaken to acquire new knowledge, while *development* is systematic work undertaken to create new products or to improve existing ones (OECD 1981). Returns on research investments will generally be more volatile than returns on development investments, because in the case of research it is less certain whether the exploratory activity will actually yield the desired results. In the case of development, the individual development steps towards a new or improved product have often been carried out before, in the form of other products that have similar characteristics or that require similar manufacturing technology.

Both research and development are not only investments of uncertain returns but also of uncertain cost. At the beginning of an R&D project it is rarely clear how much effort will be needed to achieve the targeted outcome. The characteristic of uncertain cost requires decision-makers to consider probabilities of cost structures in addition to considering probabilities of payoffs. Pindyck (1992) argues that under certain circumstances it might make sense to carry out investments of uncertain cost and stop them in the course of the project because of the additional knowledge gained in the course of the project.

In addition to this basic uncertainty, large R&D agendas that often stretch over more than a decade are characterized by the following issues:

1 Successful industrial research draws increasingly from different *interdependent areas of science and technology*. A survey by MITI among 100 leading Japanese scientists revealed that each of nine areas of applied science is somehow dependent on at least three other areas (MITI 1992).
2 Industrial R&D is a *cumulative process*. Some firms seem to be (temporarily) trapped in a vicious circle that leads to decreasing R&D output, while others enjoy a virtuous circle (Pavitt 1978).
3 R&D is increasingly organized in *international networks* of laboratories and information sources (Cantwell 1989). Different cultural environments make R&D management even more difficult. This is especially true when a firm decides to build up a new R&D location in a cultural environment which is unknown to the company. A different culture not only implies a different language, but also different research structures and different rules of conduct and performance among researchers.

The reality of R&D management is 'messy'. Managers generally rely more on qualitative heuristics about R&D projects than on detailed quantitative analyses of risk–return ratios. This is especially true for the operation of a network of R&D laboratories in different countries. Investment and budgeting decisions in R&D are made under heavy constraints, which are even heavier in the case of FDI in R&D. While these difficulties limit accuracy of managerial planning, they also open up opportunities for entrepreneurial thinking even within large organizations. R&D managers with a firm vision can exploit the very nature of investments in R&D, i.e. the high level of uncertainty both on the cost side and on the benefit side, to override objections to the project by other managers. The potential for entrepreneurial R&D management within a large firm will depend on the *form of R&D* (basic research or development), on the *research discipline* (i.e. whether this discipline is known to the company or not), and on the familiarity with the *research environment*, such as the culture and the research institutions from which the company recruits and obtains advice. Figure 12.1 gives an idea of the nature of R&D investments abroad.

For the purpose of this study 'entrepreneurial' will be defined as *'being beyond rational-quantitative evaluation'*. Entrepreneurial behaviour according to this definition implies that firms apply certain

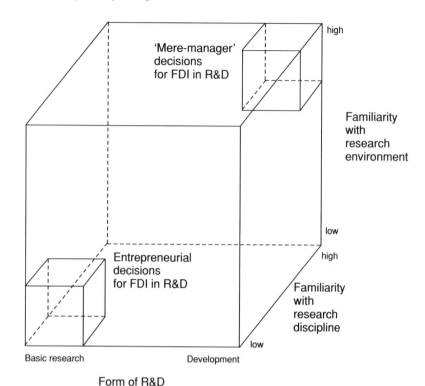

Figure 12.1 Scope of R&D decisions within the firm
Source: Kümmerle 1993

heuristics for their investment decisions because probabilities and final payoffs are too difficult to determine. A good heuristic could be to try to look forward a few moves (in the investment plan or research strategy) and to calculate intermediate payoffs for each intermediate position.

3 DEVELOPING AN ANALYTICAL FRAMEWORK FOR FDI IN R&D

Various theories search to explain FDI. One way of classification is the distinction between country-level and firm-level theories.[5] A discussion of the different hypotheses would go beyond the scope of this paper. It seems however, that while some of the theories cover some determinants of FDI in R&D, none of the theories provides a complete and operational framework of motives. This might be due to the fact that none of the theories was developed specifically for FDI in R&D, which is a relatively recent phenomenon.

As a basis for future extension of FDI theory, this paper proposes a simple analytical tool that helps to classify motives of FDI in R&D. The tool results from a matrix analysis of a firm's R&D activities and the constituencies involved in R&D.[6]

Constituencies in R&D

Three constituencies impose constraints on the R&D process: markets, environment, and organization members, particularly researchers (Freeman 1982).

1 *Markets:* Firms' short-term market focus will normally result in development activities, while long-term market focus will lead to some form of research. These development and research activities are primarily driven by evaluating the match between a firm's stock of knowledge/skills and a market's present and future potential. Furthermore, firms might monitor the evolution of science alone, independent of present market demand for finished goods, in order to profit from scientific inventions and use them for innovations at a much later point in time.

2 *Environment:* Environment shall be defined here as 'the group of constituencies relevant to the firm other than employees and markets'. The environment consists mainly of public bodies and groups represented by them. R&D activities of a firm influence the firm's environment. On the one hand these activities generate high value-added employment, on the other hand some forms of research represent considerable risks for the green environment (e.g. nuclear research) or for ethical standards (e.g. biotechnology). Environments measure these trade-offs and react accordingly, by setting investment incentives or establishing restrictive regulations. Firms react to signals from their environments and also try to influence them actively, for example through lobbying.

3 *Employees:* While contributing to the organization's goals, employees pursue individual goals, such as careers within the organization, preparation for careers in other organizations, or simply minimization of personal effort for a given remuneration. Particularly in the case of R&D, additional goals such as satisfying individual curiosity and reputation in the science community (publications, etc.) are important. Since labour is a very important input factor in R&D, an organization must strive to focus on

possible conflicts of interest between the individual's and organization's goals and try to resolve these conflicts.

The multiple constraints imposed on the organization by the three constituencies change over time and are not always fully disclosed. Simon (1976) and Nelson and Winter (1982) argue that particularly in the case of multiple, fundamentally different constituencies, management decisions are based on satisficing rather than on elaborate evaluation of constraints and subsequent maximization.

Firm capabilities in R&D

Firm capabilities in the area of R&D can be classified into three activity categories:

1 Information collection and resource allocation
2 Creative activity (discovery and development)
3 Transfer of R&D output into the firm's value chain

All three capabilities have two aspects in common. First, they require routines, and second, they require distinctive managerial action.

It is clearly in these routines that entrepreneurial elements of R&D management reside.[7] 'Routines' means that all of the three activities mentioned above will generally require feedback and input from several sources. Many of the routines are documented (*explicit routines*), others are tacitly understood because prior experience has helped establish mutual trust (*tacit routines*). At an even higher level of routine sophistication, the routine might be valuable not 'in spite of' the fact that it is not spelled out, but 'just because' it is *not* spelled out. The latter type of routines could be called *hidden routines*. Lawrence and Lorsch (1967) found that a research organization within a firm is generally less structured than other functional organizations within the same firm. This characteristic makes R&D departments particularly likely candidates for tacit and hidden routines. While these latter routines are elusive and thus difficult to understand or to change, they play a key role in successful R&D management (Allen 1971).

Importance of localization

So far, we analysed the different constituencies influencing R&D in a firm, and identified types of capabilities necessary in the R&D process. Putting together these two pieces of analysis leads to a matrix of R&D localization. The matrix can be developed into a taxonomy of DI (direct investment) in R&D. From this taxonomy it is only a small step to the inclusion of the multinational dimension: in other words, adding F to DI.

Not all activity categories mentioned above concern all constituencies, at least not primarily. This is due to the different interests of the constituencies and the different focus of the activities. However, they are overlapping and this overlapping nature might vary among industries and companies. Therefore, the categorizing lines in the following taxonomy should be regarded as indicative rather than rigid. Figure 12.2 shows the matrix.

Figure 12.2 shows that markets play an important role at the beginning and at the end of the R&D process. Markets both provide information and absorb R&D results. Environments limit or enhance the actual creative process, while employees seek to maximize their interests across all capability-relevant activities of R&D. Other 'members' of the R&D organization were included here because key contributors to R&D activities might not be employed by the firm itself, e.g. the development engineers working for suppliers of a Japanese firm. Other 'members' include all subcontractors for R&D that work under close intellectual guidance from a firm's R&D department.

Managing the capabilities across the marked fields (✔) of the matrix efficiently is the task of an entrepreneurial general manager in

Activities in R&D (capability view)

	Information collection and resource allocation	Creative activity (discovery and development)	Transfer of R&D output into the firm's value chain
Markets	✓		✓
Environment		✓	
Employees and other 'members' of the R&D organization	✓	✓	✓

(left axis label: Constituencies in R&D)

Figure 12.2 Matrix constituencies and activities in R&D
Source: Kümmerle 1993

R&D. This implies evaluating different locations and different forms of research organization. Not all constituencies have an equally strong influence on R&D across different locations. Furthermore, the input–output ratio for the different capability-relevant activities might differ across different locations. Exploiting these differences requires management to decide about initial and future locations for R&D.

The analytical framework

By forming clusters of some adjacent fields in the capability–constituency-matrix we obtain the analytical framework. Clustering was based on the analysis of a sample of 19 laboratories of the pharmaceutical and semiconductor industry owned by Japanese and German firms. Figure 12.3 shows how the five main motives have evolved from the analytical framework. It seems that this set of motives is capable of explaining all forms of FDI in R&D that exist in the constituency–capability matrix.

<table>
<tr><th colspan="4">Activities in R&D (capability view)</th></tr>
<tr><th></th><th></th><th>Information collection and resource allocation</th><th>Creative activity (discovery and development)</th><th>Transfer of R&D output into the firm's value chain</th></tr>
<tr><td rowspan="3">Constituencies in R&D</td><td>Markets</td><td>✓
CM</td><td></td><td>✓
CP</td></tr>
<tr><td>Environment</td><td></td><td>✓
CG</td><td></td></tr>
<tr><td>Employees and other 'members' of the R&D organization</td><td>✓
LC</td><td>✓
LC   LT</td><td>✓
LT</td></tr>
</table>

Figure 12.3 Developing the analytical framework from the matrix of constituencies and activities in R&D

Source: Kümmerle 1993

Notes: Factors: CM = closer to the market; CP = closer to production; CG = closer to the government; LT = learning–transferring; LC = learning–creating

In action-oriented vocabulary the motives can be described as follows:

Closer to the Market (CM)
   Understanding customers' needs better
   Faster response to demand changes
   Tracing of potential fundamental changes in competition

Closer to Production (CP)
   Making local production more reliable and flexible through
   proximity to local laboratories

Closer to the Government (CG)
   Maintaining access to markets
   Circumventing legal and other restrictions in home country

Learning–Transferring (LT)
   Acquiring specific partial knowledge abroad and transferring
   it to another location where it is integrated with other
   knowledge

Learning–Creating (LC)
   Acquiring and mobilizing local creative potential
   Focus on building up autonomous local research capabilities

A field study (Kümmerle 1993b) showed that the analytical framework of these five factors is a viable tool for the classification of
discrete investments in laboratories and research cooperation abroad.
In the case of most of the laboratories examined, one of the motives
clearly dominated all other motives.

Clearly, the decision to invest in a new location requires a trade-off
between easy integration and exploitation of local advantage.
Furthermore, the firm has to decide whether it wants to invest at all
instead of out-sourcing R&D (Dunning 1977; Dunning 1988). The
analytical framework can provide a tool for a firm to evaluate its
capabilities against demands by the constituencies. The firm should
carry out the analysis for each desired/existing location using the
above taxonomy, i.e. the range of motives, and then match the taxonomy figures with the firm's strategy in order to determine whether
a new location makes sense and which location fits best with the
firm's internal possibilities (capabilities) and externally oriented
needs (strategy).

Entrepreneurial capabilities and FDI in R&D

FDI in R&D offers potential for entrepreneurial managerial action
among members of the firm and between the firm and third parties.

FDI in R&D is generally carried out by large firms that use formal decision routines for resource allocation. Nevertheless, there is room for entrepreneurial elements in the field of FDI in R&D because of the high levels of uncertainty involved, particularly in the case of Learning–Creating (LC) and Learning–Transferring (LT) investments. Managers who are willing to take the chance of pushing forward an investment plan for the construction of a laboratory abroad can make things happen even in a large and rigid organization. On the other hand, this managerial leeway requires responsible behaviour from the manager who proposes and supports the investment project. Furthermore, FDI in R&D requires long-term commitment because the investment in a laboratory abroad is only the first step in the management of a rather delicate asset.

The high level of uncertainty concerning R&D abroad also offers potential for the firm's behaviour versus third parties such as potential joint-venture partners, sellers of R&D assets, and public bodies. Information asymmetries concerning the firm's laboratory portfolio, its learning capabilities, or its desired scope of learning might lead to a differing evaluation of assets. The prices paid by Japanese firms for R&D assets in the US and for cooperation with professors at top US universities were considered high by some outsiders who looked only at the potential gains in terms of mid-term R&D output. Some of the Japanese firms, however, considered these investments as an expensive but necessary training period for successful R&D management in the US over the long term (Committee on Government Operations 1992; National Academy of Sciences 1992).

4 EXAMINING JAPANESE FDI IN R&D

Analysing Japanese FDI in R&D is interesting for three reasons. First, Japan has become the world's dominant investor in R&D assets abroad. Second, the investment strategy of Japanese firms accentuates some of the characteristics described by other students of the Japanese firm (Aoki 1984; Itami 1987). Finally, the case of Japan provides an example for application of the analytical framework.

The findings are based on a detailed field study of 58 laboratories abroad owned by four leading Japanese pharmaceutical companies and eight leading Japanese electronics companies with focus on semiconductors (Kümmerle 1993a). Here, only a brief summary of the results will be given.

It was found that Japanese electronics companies generally start their international R&D activities by investing in laboratories that increase proximity to markets and factories abroad (CM and CT). After a period ranging from 3 to 15 years, the companies start constructing laboratories for learning purposes with an initial focus on learning–transferring and a shift to learning–creating. Since beginning R&D activities abroad, companies in the electronics industry have accumulated a rather balanced laboratory portfolio, in the sense that the portfolio consists of a roughly equal number of laboratories focusing on either CM or CP or LT or LC. Japanese pharmaceutical companies who are much less competitive on the world market are just starting to build up LT- or LC-type laboratories with the aim of creating world-class drugs in the long run.

Most investment decisions analysed in the field study were entrepreneurial in the sense that they were beyond rational–quantitative evaluation and were thus often regarded by industry analysts as not well thought through. Four factors seem to have induced these decisions. Two concern organizational characteristics of the Japanese firm: long-range commitment to learning and the availability of funds. Two other factors were external to the firm: the belief among managers that creativity in basic R&D in Japan is still low, and the growing importance of systemic innovations. Figure 12.4 gives an idea of the process.

It seems that while the four factors lead to a seemingly risky and entrepreneurial decision-making style, there is at the same time a solid level of confidence among the investing firms that even bad investment decisions can be turned into good ones. In several field interviews conducted by the author, managers used the same words to explain their actions. '*Yatte miyou*' (= let's invest and see what happens) for the phase of investment in R&D abroad, and '*naka naka akiramenai*' (= we hardly ever give up) for the subsequent phase during which management seeks to improve the performance of the new laboratory or of the research cooperation.

Long-range commitment to learning

Freeman (1987) observes that in the late 1940s, an intense debate among Japanese bureaucrats concerning Japan's development strategy was resolved in favour of MITI, which advocated an emphasis on building high-technology industries, over the contention of Bank of Japan staff that Japan should cultivate low-technology industries and pursue comparative advantage through its low labour costs. The strategy fostered by MITI required extensive technology transfer from abroad and such transfer could not be justified from a short-

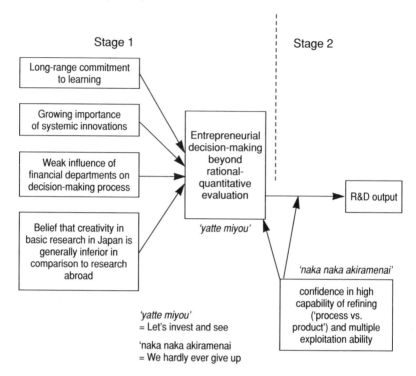

Figure 12.4 Model of foreign direct investment decisions in R&D by
Japanese companies
Source: Kümmerle 1993

term perspective. Scherer (1992) interprets MITI's behaviour in the
above case as 'distinctly Schumpeterian'.

In a country where a ministry with strong ties to industry shows
such behaviour, it is not surprising that similar behaviour can be
observed in industry itself, particularly in the area of R&D.

While different companies prefer different organizational forms
for R&D–FDI, such as mergers, joint-ventures, joint research with
universities, independent organizations, and minority stakes, all start
from a rather small scale and build up larger foreign R&D assets
gradually. Cases of divestment of laboratories are so far very rare.
Apart from its long-range nature, learning is perceived as an activity
of rather broad scope. In the case of pharmaceuticals, companies
intend to learn not only how to design and develop new drugs but
also how to conduct clinical tests, how to obtain government approval
for drugs, and how to manage foreign researchers.

Growing importance of systemic innovation

The short product cycles in Japan have trained firms on 'routinized innovation', a term coined by Schumpeter (1942) for the kind of innovations produced by routines in a highly predictable way. At present, in some industries the importance of systemic innovations is growing (Baba and Imai 1992; Imai 1990). Systemic innovations are innovations that cause a basic change in manufacturing processes or product performance and thereby change a whole array of different products. R&D on systemic innovations is not limited to learning about science and technology in the respective core area, but also concerns related areas such as electronic image-processing technology for the field of optics. Firms aspiring to be leaders in systemic innovation are forced to perform R&D on a world-wide level, since the centres of excellence in the different areas of research are often geographically dispersed. For example, in the case of drugs synthesized through biotechnology processes, while Japanese companies are strong in fermentation technology, most of the basic gene-assembling research takes place in the US and the UK.

Weak influence of financial departments on decision-making

Hoshi, Kashyap, and Scharfstein (1991) find that Keiretsu-style Japanese companies' investments are significantly less influenced by liquidity constraints than are the investments of non-Keiretsu Japanese companies. (Keiretsu: a large, integrated Japanese conglomerate.) Since most FDI in R&D is carried out by large companies that belong to a keiretsu, we assume that FDI in R&D in particular faces low liquidity constraints. This was confirmed by the field study (Kümmerle 1993a).

Belief that Japanese creativity in basic research in Japan is low

Public bodies in Japan started to shift research funding more toward basic research since the early 1980s. However, some of these measures have not had an impact yet because research pipelines are long (often 10 years and more) and also because of the fact that the Japanese education system does not foster creativity (Agency of Science and Technology 1992; MITI 1992). Japanese enterprises have lost much of their competitive advantage concerning cost leadership, and many managers are afraid that the advantages of shorter development cycles and incremental innovation (Clark and Fujimoto 1989) will not be sufficient for sustainable international competitiveness.

Confidence in high capability of refining and multiple exploitation

Mansfield (1988) found in an analysis of 100 matched Japanese and American corporations that on average, Japanese firms devoted 64 per cent of their R&D budgets to internal process development and improvement, while their US counterparts spent only 32 per cent on process development. Ferguson argues that the American high-technology venture industry has succeeded in luring away technical talent from established companies with a stronger interest in cost cutting. Ferguson concludes that this phenomenon has lowered the quality of American products (Ferguson 1988). Japanese engineers seem to have been more willing to take on the unpleasant task of learning about a product and improving it. The improvement process in Japan is by no means pure refining, but recently also includes bringing in results from basic in-house research. Japanese companies' track record of 'learning by improving' gives reason for the assumption that such learning is also valid for research and development done abroad, even if the research will be carried out mainly by local researchers and not by Japanese researchers. Furthermore, Japanese firms tend to exploit knowledge acquired for one division throughout the whole company. The intense networking within companies contributes to smooth knowledge transfer.

Only a small part of total Japanese investment abroad, but a large part of Japanese FDI in R&D, could be labelled 'entrepreneurial'. While the line between entrepreneurial and regular investments is rather fuzzy, it becomes obvious that there is a strong underlying logic for the entrepreneurial style. Five factors: proximity to markets, to manufacturing plants, and to governments, highly specific learning, and general learning, are pushing Japanese companies to invest in R&D abroad in the first stage, while one other factor, the capability for improvement, supports the return on investment in the second stage. In summary, one could say that Japanese firms are willing to pay a high tuition for their learning experiences.

The transfer of knowledge has so far taken place mainly on a one-way street towards Japan. A new wave of criticism against Japan seems certain. In accordance with 'trade friction', the new wave of criticism could be summarized as 'knowledge friction'. However, one big difference between 'knowledge friction' and 'trade friction' is that there were immediately effective measures for palliative treatment in the case of trade friction, such as forced opening of the Japanese semiconductor market.[8] This kind of palliative treatment will not be available in the case of knowledge friction. It seems important that

European and American firms invest in their own R&D networks instead of criticizing Japan for doing so.

5 CONCLUSIONS

This paper has tried to show that entrepreneurial action plays a critical role in FDI in R&D. This is true in spite of the large size of the firms who presently invest in research and development abroad. Research managers and public bodies trying to attract FDI in R&D should be aware of this leeway. It gives them the potential to influence investment decisions in their interests. Decision-makers should be aware of it too, while keeping in mind that classic investment evaluation is largely inappropriate in the case of FDI in R&D.

The paper develops an analytical framework for classification of different investment motives. The framework illustrates that particularly in the case of learning-oriented FDI in R&D, entrepreneurial action is required. The example of Japan points out that investing in research abroad is a complex process that requires more than a simple investment decision at a given point of time. Furthermore, it also shows that it is important for a firm to understand not only a competitors' global R&D strategy but also the underlying factors influencing it.

Future research should concentrate on analysing US and European firms' FDI in R&D by using the analytical framework. Eventually this research could evolve into a comprehensive study of entrepreneurial aspects influencing resource allocation in R&D; ultimately such research could lead to an extension of FDI theory.

NOTES

1 FDI is defined by the US department of commerce as the acquisition of 10 per cent or more of a foreign asset.
2 See the literature surveys by Hufbauer (1975) and Stehn (1992).
3 Costly as measured by investment per employee.
4 This estimate was given by MITI officials in an interview. It was confirmed by the field study (Kümmerle 1993b).
5 Cf. again the literature surveys by Hufbauer (1975) and Stehn (1990).
6 For an elaborate development of the analytical framework see (Kümmerle 1993c).
7 Nelson and Winter (1982) find that routines that involve a strong tacit dimension are not easy to identify.
8 Some researchers would argue that measures against Japanese trade friction have been largely ineffective.

REFERENCES

Agency of Science and Technology (1992) *White Paper on Science and Technology*, Tokyo: Agency of Science and Technology.

Allen, T. J. (1971) *Managing the Flow of Technology*, Cambridge: M.I.T. Press.

Aoki, M. (1984) *The Economic Analysis of the Japanese Firm*, Amsterdam: North Holland.

Baba, Y. and Imai, K. (1992) 'Systemic Innovation and Cross-Border Networks: The Case of the Evolution of the VCR Systems', in F. M. Scherer and M. Perlman (eds), *Entrepreneurship Technological Innovation and Economic Growth: Studies in the Schumpeterian Traditio*, Ann Arbor: University of Michigan Press.

Behrman, J.N. and Fischer, W.A. (1980) *Overseas R&D Activities of Transnational Companies*, Cambridge, MA: Oelgeschlager, Gunn & Hai.

Buckley, P.J. and Casson, M.C. (1976) *The Future of the Multinational Enterprise*, London: Macmillan.

Cantwell, J. (1989) *Technological Innovation and Multinational Corporations*, Oxford: Basil Blackwell.

Caves, R. (1971) 'International Corporations: The Economics of Foreign Direct Investment', *Economica*, 38: 1–27.

Caves, R. (1982) *Multinational Enterprises and Economic Analysis*, Cambridge: Cambridge University Press.

Clark, K.B. and Fujimoto, T. (1989) 'Lead Time in Automobile Product Development – Explaining the Japanese Advantage', *Journal of Engineering and Technology Management*, 6: 25–58.

Committee on Government Operations (1992) *Is Science on Sale? Transferring Technology from Universities to Foreign Corporations*, Washington: US Government Printing Office.

DeMeyer, A. (1993) 'Internationalizing R&D Improves a Firm's Technical Learning', *Research Technology Management*, July–Aug.: 42–49.

Dunning, J.H. (1977) 'Trade, Location of Economic Activity and the Multinational Enterprise: A Search for an Eclectic Approach', in B. Ohlin, P. O. Hesselborn, and P. M. Wijkman (eds), *The International Allocation of Economic Activity*, London: Macmillan.

Dunning, J.H. (1988) 'The Eclectic Paradigm of International Production: A Restatement and some possible Extensions', *Journal of Business Studies*, 19 (1): 1–31.

Ferguson, C. (1988) 'From the People who Brought you Voodoo Economics', *Harvard Business Review*, 88 (May–June): 55–62.

Freeman, C. (1982) *The Economics of Industrial Innovation*, Cambridge, MA: M.I.T. Press.

Freeman, C. (1987) *Technology, Policy and Economic Performance: Lessons from Japan*, London: Pinter.

Gomes-Casseres, B. (1992) 'Technology Flows and Global Competition: A Framework for Research and Management', in S.B. Prasad and R.B. Peterson, *Advances in International Comparative Management*, Greenwich, Conn: JAI Press, 3–22.

Graham, E. and Krugman, P. (1991) *Foreign Direct Investment in the United States*, 2nd edn, Washington: Institute for International Economics.

Hoshi, T., Kashyap, A., and Scharfstein, D. (1991) 'Corporate Structure, Liquidity and Investment: Evidence from Japanese Industrial Groups', *Quarterly Journal of Economics*, 106 (1): 33–60.

Howells, J. (1990) 'The Internationalization of R&D and the Development of Global Research Networks', *Regional Studies*, 24 (Dec.): 495–512.

Hufbauer, G. (1975) 'The Multinational Corporation and Direct Investment', in P. Kenen (ed.), *International Trade and Finance*, Cambridge: MIT Press.

Imai, K. (1990) 'Patterns of Innovation and Entrepreneurship in Japan', in A. Heertje and M. Perlman (eds), *Evolving Technology and Market Structure – Studies in Schumpeterian Economics*, Ann Arbor: University of Michigan Press.

Itami, H. (1987) *Managing Invisible Assets*, Cambridge, MA: Harvard University Press.

JETRO (1992a) *8th Survey of European Operations of Japanese Companies in the Manufacturing Sector*, Tokyo: JETRO.

JETRO (1992b) *White Paper on Foreign Direct Investment*, Tokyo: JETRO.

Kindleberger, C.P. (ed.) (1970) *The International Corporation*, Cambridge, MA: M.I.T. Press.

Knickerbocker, F.T. (1973) *Oligopolistic Reaction and Multinational Enterprise*, Boston: Harvard University Press.

Kümmerle, W. (1993a) *Foreign Direct Investment in R&D – Intermediate Results from Empirical Research*, Unpublished Report no. 3/93.

Kümmerle, W. (1993b) *Investing to Stay Ahead – Analyzing the Big Three German Chemical Companies' Pharmaceutical Research Networks*, Working Paper no. 0722–6748, Science Centre Berlin.

Kümmerle, W. (1993c) *Rationality, Resources and Capabilities*, Unpublished Draft no. stratus221293, Harvard University, Graduate School of Business Administration.

Lawrence, P. and Lorsch, J. (1967) *Organization & Environment*, Boston, MA: HBS Press.

Mansfield, E. (1988) 'Industrial R&D in Japan and the United States: A Comparative Study', *American Economic Review*, 78 (2): 223–228.

MITI (1992) *Issues and Trends in Industrial/Scientific Technology – Towards Techno-Globalism*, MITI Background Informations no. BI–80, Ministry of International Trade and Industry, Tokyo.

Mitsubishi Research Institute (1991) *Grobaraizeishon no shinten to sangyo ni kan suru chosahokusho*, Tokyo: Mitsubishi Research Institute.

National Academy of Sciences (1992) *Japanese Investment and Technology Transfer: An Exploration of its Impact*, Washington: National Research Council.

Nelson, R. and Winter, S. (1982) *An Evolutionary Theory of Economic Change*, Cambridge: Harvard University Press.

OECD (1981) *The Measurement of Scientific and Technical Activities: Proposed Standard Practice for Surveys of Research and Experimental Development*, Paris: OECD.

Pavitt, K. (1978) 'International Patterns of Technological Accumulation', in N. Hood and C. E. Vahne (eds), *Strategies in Global Competition*, London: Croom Helm.

Pearce, R.D. and Singh, S. (1992) *Globalizing Research and Development*, London: MacMillan.

Pindyck, R.S. (1992) 'Investments of Uncertain Cost', Cambridge: National Bureau of Economic Research.

Reich, R. (1990) 'Who is Us?', *Harvard Business Review*, Jan.–Feb.

Reich, R. (1991) 'Who is Them?', *Harvard Business Review*, March–April.

Ronstadt, R. (1977) *Research and Development Abroad by US Multinationals*, New York: Praeger.

Rugman, A.M. (1981) *Inside the Multinationals: The Economics of Internal Markets*, London: Croom-Helm.

Scherer, F.M. (1992) *International High-Technology Competition*, Cambridge, MA: Harvard University Press.

Schumpeter, J. (1942) *Capitalism, Socialism, and Democracy*, New York: Harper & Row.

Simon, H. (1976) *Administrative Behavior*, 2nd edn, New York: Free Press.

Stehn, J. (1992) *Auslaendische Direktinvestitionen in Industrielaendern*, Kiel: Institut fuer Weltwirtschaft.

13 Decoding a black box?

Evaluating marketing consultancy schemes for SMEs

David Molian and Sue Birley

INTRODUCTION

There is considerable evidence that publicly funded consultancy aimed at helping SMEs (small and medium-sized enterprises) improve their marketing capability is considered unsatisfactory by the client firms. This paper examines the data from one such scheme in the UK, the Department of Trade and Industry Enterprise Initiative. The authors review the possible reasons for marketing consultancy under-performance, and suggest ways in which empirical findings on (a) marketing and the small firm; and (b) marketing strategy and implementation can be employed to investigate this problem. A case study testing associated propositions is also included.

Over the past twenty years it has become virtually axiomatic that publicly funded support for small and medium-sized enterprises (SMEs) is 'a good thing'. In Europe, this idea transcended national boundaries when in June 1986, the Council of Ministers created a new SME Task Force responsible for setting a coherent framework for implementing European Community policies for the enterprise sector. In 1989, the Task Force metamorphosed into a new Directorate-General (XXIII) responsible for enterprise policy 'and in particular [for] the establishment of a business environment conducive to the creation and development of small and medium-sized businesses in the Community' (Report by the Commission on Administrative Simplification Work in the Community in Favour of Enterprises 1992). The motivation for this focus, job generation, can be found in the results of a study by Birch (1980) in the United States and echoed more than ten years later by the Department of Employment in the United Kingdom (1991):

> One of the most striking facts about small firms is their quite disproportionate contribution to job creation. . . . small firms

employing fewer than 20 people created more than twice as many jobs as larger firms over the period 1985–1989.

Changing priorities

Based upon the premise that *new* firms are the seed corn for the future industrial base, much of the support in the early years was aimed at encouraging potential entrepreneurs to locate, or relocate, manufacturing businesses in areas of economic deprivation. However, Mason and Harrison (1990) argue that since 1988, a regionally directed policy has given way to the regionalization of national industrial and enterprise policies: rather than encouraging enterprises to locate in selected areas, support has been targeted at increasing the competitiveness of local indigenous owner-managed firms. One of the main instruments of achieving this has been the the UK Enterprise Initiative, whereby qualifying SMEs receive up to 15 days external consultancy which is partially funded by the government's Department of Trade and Industry (DTI). Thus, for the year 1989–90, the Department's expenditure on the Initiatives was £59.6 million, and for the years 1990–91 through to 1993–94, estimated expenditure was approximately £225 million in real terms (DTI 1991). Within the overall scheme, six options are open to the client firms: business planning; design; financial and management informations systems; manufacturing and services systems; quality; and marketing. The focus of this paper is one component of the Scheme, the Marketing Consultancy Initiative.

The contribution of the SME Sector

The move away from a *dirigiste* approach which attempts to pick and predict winners as a way of channelling scarce resources (Storey *et al.* 1987; Storey and Johnson 1987) has received considerable empirical support (Hakim 1989). Arguing a position that would once have been considered quasi-heretical, even by himself, Storey (1992) suggests that UK public policy makers should seriously consider abandoning support for start-up businesses altogether. Using data collected during the 1980s, he argues that there has been no net job creation in the start-up business sector, since high rates of new firm formation are cancelled by equally high death rates. Citing his own longitudinal research, Storey goes on to observe that: 'over a decade, 4 per cent of the businesses which start will end up providing 50 per cent of the jobs'. North, Leigh, and Smallbone (1992) confirm this trend in another ten-year study, which shows 25 per cent of their original sample of 293 London manufacturing firms generating 73 per cent of all surviving jobs (see also Owen 1992). These studies also confirm that high death rates decline with a firm's longevity. Thus, UK Department of Employment figures cited by Storey show that 36 per cent of start-ups stop trading within the first three years, but that it takes a further seven years before the next 37 per cent of firms cease to trade. The clear implication, then, is that the longer a business survives, the longer it is likely to survive; and, following from this, it can be argued that the economy as a whole will benefit more from support directed at mature firms rather than at start-ups. This finds support in Joyce and Woods' (1992) study of small-firm formation in relation to the performance of the US economy from 1946 to 1986, which found their expectations were confounded by the analysis:

> But most noteworthy is the reduction of GNP around its long term trend by the growth of new businesses. Should we be diagnosing a depressive effect on real GNP because new businesses include large proportions that fail?

None of this is new. All of these conclusions were also to be found in the early job generation studies in the USA (Birch 1980; Birley 1986) and in the United Kingdom (Fothergill and Gudgin 1979). They are, however, now more acceptable.

Support for the established SME

Publicly funded support for SMEs is one element of the potential sources of advice and assistance for the owner-managed firm which also includes:

- Semi-public agencies such as the Enterprise Agencies
- Trade Associations and Chambers of Commerce
- Consultants, professional advisers, and educational institutions
- Banks, accountants, and lawyers
- Informal sources of friends and family members not directly involved in the business.

However, use of these different sources is variable. For example, in their analysis of owner–manager perception of 'new venture environments', Birley and Westhead (1993) listed eighteen potential support services but found that only six were seen as being available by more than 50 per cent of respondents, all of which were 'soft' measures of business advisory service, start-up courses, skills training courses, market information, a locally-based enterprise agency, and low cost consulting services. However, of these, only the business advisory service was seen as both available and affordable, suggesting that even the subsidy offered in the consulting initiatives was insufficient to attract many new owner–managers. However, in their sample of 306 *mature* UK manufacturing firms, Smallbone, North, and Leigh (1992) found that only 21 per cent had made use of public and semi-public agencies, whereas 25 per cent had used *paid* consultants. Moreover, closer examination of these figures reveals that such broad categorizations understate the scale of publicly funded support. Of the 75 firms who reported using paid consultants, one-third had received a subsidy (which could be as much as 67 per cent of the cost) through the DTI Enterprise Initiative.

Among the authors' conclusions from this latter study, three are of particular relevance to this paper. The first is that they consider the relatively low use of external sources of support (55 per cent of all firms surveyed) evidence of a 'support gap', given that firms had been in existence at least ten years. This contention is strengthened by the finding that 25 per cent of the sample identified problems encountered over the decade where external assistance could have been useful but was not (to the knowledge of the firm) available. Second, they argue that the use of consultants was associated with 'better performing' firms. The authors classify the sample into five groups based on measures of turnover growth, profitability, and relative size. High growth firms (Group 1) more than doubled their turnover in real terms over the decade, had by 1990 reached a size likely to ensure continuing viability (£0.5 million turnover), and had been consistently profitable in the latter part of the decade. One-third of these firms had used paid consultants, whereas the comparable figure for the other four groups was in each case approximately one-fifth. Third, they report that there is a significant discrepancy between firms' experience of subsidized and non-subsidized consultancy:

- firms were less inclined to implement subsidized consultancy, than non-subsidized;
- subsidized consultancies were in overall terms less successful than non-subsidized.

The authors also report that in a third of subsidized consultancies managers were 'clearly dissatisfied with what they had received'.

The reasons given by firms for their lack of satisfaction cite the quality both of the consultants and of their recommendations. Regarding the consultants, it was reported 'that [their] expertise was either inadequate or that the consultant simply did not understand the business'. As for the recommendations: 'Other reasons given for partial implementation were that the consultants' recommendations were judged too expensive to introduce completely or were impractical in some way.'

Reports of dissatisfaction with publicly funded support schemes aimed at SMEs are not confined to the United Kingdom. In their longitudinal tracking of the US micro-electronics industry, Schwartz, Southern, Teach, and Tarpley (1992) record very poor levels of satisfaction among SMEs with only technical or professional advisers providing assistance of perceived value. Indeed, their findings lead the authors to echo Storey's (1992) already cited questioning of received wisdom:

> are the public programmes merely perpetuating themselves with mediocre, poorly focused, unwanted, perhaps unneeded services, thus obviating the need for understanding how to market services to entrepreneurs? If this is true, perhaps the programmes should be curtailed.
>
> (Schwartz *et al.* 1992: 255)

They conclude that SMEs – at least in the micro-electronics sector – will solve their problems of acquiring additional expertise as they grow on their own, by hiring suitably qualified staff. Public support schemes, if unchanged, will remain an irrelevance.

THE ENTERPRISE INITIATIVE

Mixed success, the implication of a support gap, yet some evidence that the use of outside consultants is linked with growth, all provide a suitable context in which to look in detail at the UK DTI Enterprise Initiative – the keystone of British state-funded support to the mature SME. This basic policy of pump-priming using public funds and private sector resources is characteristic of the Thatcher administration of the 1980s. It has two main aims: to increase competitiveness and to achieve quantifiable results within a reasonable timescale (usually two years), as part of the firm's business plan.

Established in 1988, the scheme had received over 85,000 applications for consultancy assistance by the end of 1991, leading to more than 75,000 business reviews and to the approval of some 60,000 projects. Under the scheme, a qualifying firm receives between 5 and 15 days of consultancy, with a subsidy of 50 per cent or 67 per cent for firms in assisted regions. Eligible firms are, broadly speaking, independently-owned SMEs in manufacturing or services employing fewer than 500 staff.

The Marketing Initiative

There are three reasons for choosing to focus on the Marketing Initiative. The first is that a disproportionately high number of recipients (31.3 per cent of approved applicants at end 1989) choose this over the other support initiatives (Segal, Quince, and Wicksteed 1989). The second is that ever since the Bolton Report (1971) it has been widely accepted in the UK that small firms are either poor at marketing or that they do not practise it at all (e.g. Lamont 1972; Litvak and Maule 1980) and that absence of marketing expertise is a major obstacle to small firm performance (see, for example, Barnes, Pym, and Noonan 1982; Gibb and Scott 1985; Kinsey 1987; Verhage and Waarts 1988).

A third reason for choosing to look at the Marketing Initiative is supplied by the DTI's own analysis of the effectiveness of the Enterprise Initiative, undertaken by Segal, Quince, and Wicksteed (1989, 1991a, 1991b). This evaluation involved face-to-face, structured interviews with participating firms. Two panels of 420 firms were selected, 70 firms in each of the six initiatives (see Table 13.1). The first panel was interviewed first in late 1988/early 1989, then again approximately one year later (Segal *et al.* 1989 and 1991a). The second panel was interviewed in late 1989/early 1990 (Segal *et al.* 1991b), results of the second-stage interview had yet to appear at the time of writing.

Table 13.1 Enterprise Initiative evaluation schedule

Panel no.	1	2
First interview	Late 88/early 89	Late 89/early 90
Second interview	Late 89/early 90	Late 90/early 91*

Note: *Results yet to appear

The analysis of the data provides an evaluation of the scheme based on the following six broad criteria:

Client satisfaction: a measure of value for money.

Client implementation of recommendations: actual or anticipated.

Financial costs and benefits: in terms of implementation costs and actual or anticipated financial benefits directly resulting from implementation.

Estimated net employment gain: measured against the subsidy cost.

Additionality: a measure of whether participating firms would have made use of consultants in the absence of subsidy.

Future use of consultants: propensity to use outside consultants again, based on firms' experience of the Enterprise Initiative.

Collectively the three stages of the report exceed 350 pages. Below are summarized the findings that bear directly on the Marketing Initiative.

Underperformance: first panel

Client satisfaction

Firms were asked to rate the value for money of the consultancy in terms of (a) their own proportion of costs and (b) the total costs.[1] The mean scores were those shown in Table 13.2.

Table 13.2 First panel: satisfaction scores

	Overall	Marketing initiative
Proportion of costs	4.1	3.7
Total costs	3.3	3.0

Sources: Segal *et al.* 1989: (Table 6.8)

Unfortunately, the report does not provide statistical analysis of these data, nor the raw data from which this analysis can be derived. Nevertheless, Segal, Quince, and Wicksteed present this as evidence of the Marketing Initiative performing less satisfactorily than other Initiatives. Moreover, they note that marketing consultants also scored consistently below their counterparts on the other Initiatives in terms of the working relationship with the client company, identification of problems, relevance of recommendations, and the length of time taken to complete the work.

Implementation

Segal, Quince, and Wicksteed (1989: 54) found that 20 per cent of firms participating in the Marketing Initiative felt that the advice they received was not tailored to their particular needs, and observe that this figure was the highest for any Initiative (comparable data for all other five schemes are not provided). On a five-point scale rating of relevance of recommendations, the mean for Marketing was the lowest of the six, at 3.6. Again, these conclusions would appear to be based upon observation, rather than analysis. Nevertheless, the pattern which is emerging is consistently in the one direction.

Interestingly, these data were presented as evidence of a disinclination on the part of those participating in the Marketing Initiative to use consultants in the future, although the statistical analysis does not support this dichotomy.[2] However, the above data were gathered at a first interview conducted within twelve months of each firm's participation in the project. Further data gathered at a second interview, approximately twelve months later, suggest a clear hardening of this view with 49 per cent of respondents from the Marketing Initiative firms, compared with 26 per cent of respondents overall, stating that they had not accepted all of the recommendations and would not be implementing those which were not accepted (Segal *et al.* 1991a: 33, Table 8).[3] Expectations of financial benefits resulting from the consultancy were also reduced.

Overall, therefore, the results from the first panel show the Marketing Initiative under-performing when compared with the overall ratings of the six schemes.

Table 13.3 First panel: relevance scores

High	Overall	Marketing initiative
4.4	4.1	3.6

Attitudes towards future use of consultants

Attitudes towards future use of consultants are displayed in Table 13.4.

Table 13.4 Attitudes towards future use of consultants

	Overall	Marketing initiative
Percentage *more* likely to use consultants in future.	50	44
Percentage *less* likely to use consultants in future.	10	17
Percentage neutral	40	39
Number of respondents	415	68

Note: chi-squared = 2.69, df = 2, 5% SL = 5.99
Source: Segal *et al.* 1989: 29 (Table 4.11)

Under-performance: second panel

The inclusion of a second panel of firms in the evaluation was intended to take account of both teething troubles and of any self-selecting bias in candidate firms in the early days of the Initiative. The results of the first interview, shown in Table 13.5, confirm the trends detected in the first panel, and specifically the under-performance of Marketing Initiative firms (Segal *et al.* 1991b).

Table 13.5 Score data for second panel

	Overall	*Marketing initiative*
Firms considering the consultancy poor or less than satisfactory[4] (p. 50, Table 5.15)	28%	43%
Firms not accepting all of the recommendations[5] (p. 52, Table 5.19)	23%	41%
Firms considering advice not tailored to their circumstances[6] (p. 46, Table 5.6)	16%	30%

Notes:
A full assessment of the findings will be possible only when the fourth report, on the second stage of the second panel interviews, is published in 1993. However, the preliminary findings of the second panel interviews strongly support the conclusions drawn from the first panel, allowing us to discuss with confidence the implications of the survey results to date.

EXPLANATIONS

It was outside the scope of the Segal, Quince and Wicksteed evaluation to speculate at length on the reasons for the relative under-performance of the Marketing Initiative respondents:

> In the course of a short interview it is difficult to fathom the underlying reason for dissatisfaction. There were examples evident within the sample of poor consultancy in a technical sense. Certainly as numerous, if not more so, were cases where the firm's expectations of consultants were too high. This is a particular problem in Initiatives like Marketing which, by their nature, are general rather than specific and which have multiple objectives. (Segal *et al.* 1991b, section 7.9, p. 69.)

Nevertheless, they concluded that there were five categories of reasons for dissatisfaction (Segal *et al.* 1991b, Table 5.6.), which emerged from discussion during the interviews:

1 Lacked understanding of business
2 Recommendations too vague or too general
3 Recommendations 'off the shelf'
4 Recommendations directed towards an inappropriate area
5 Recommendations too expensive, or too risky to implement

Marketing Initiative firms appear in all five categories, with 'Lacked understanding of business' as the dominant reason, followed by 'Directed to inappropriate area' and 'Recommendations too vague or general'. However, the precise significance of these results is hard to determine, since it is unclear whether the categories were prompted or unprompted and whether multiple citations were included. Nevertheless, in the view of these authors, there are four possible explanations:

1. An 'experience curve' effect

There might be an 'experience curve' effect, related to the prior use of consultants. The data presented in Table 13.6 shows that those participating in the Marketing Initiative were significantly less likely to have used consultants previously than those in the sample overall.

Table 13.6 Prior experience of consultancy in general – no use of consultants before

	Overall	*Marketing initiative*
First panel[7]	47%	59%
Second panel[8]	56%	60%

Sources: First panel: Segal *et al.* 1989: 23, Table 4.1; Second panel: Segal *et al.* 1991b: 21, Table 3.1.

From these results, it is reasonable to expect higher dissatisfaction levels, assuming that firms get better results from outside advisers as their experience of using them increases. It has, however, already been noted that the nature of consultancy assignments varies considerably. Thus experience of managing one type of consultancy – say technical – might be of limited transfer value for managing another type, such as marketing. Therefore, we analysed the data further by looking solely at marketing firms' previous experience of *marketing* consultancy, compared with the other Initiatives' comparable prior experience (e.g. the experience of firms on the Quality Initiative of previous quality-focused consultancy). The data shows a significant difference between the percentage of Marketing Initiative firms which had previously used marketing consultants and the sample overall (Table 13.7). However, it should be noted that the level of experience of consultancy is generally very low, supporting the potential value of these Initiatives as training or developmental exercises. Nevertheless, whether or not prior experience contributes positively to a successful outcome in the consultancy process, that fact *of itself* does not further our understanding of the process.

Table 13.7 Prior experience of initiative-related consultancy – no use of consultants before

	Overall	*Marketing initiative*
No use of initiative-related consultants before		
First panel[9]	79%	84%
Second panel[10]	81%	84%
Sample size	418	70

Sources: First panel: Segal *et al.* 1989: 23, Table 4.1; Second panel: Segal *et al.* 1991b: 21, Table 3.1.

2. Poor or inappropriate consultants

It is possible that the consultants used on the Marketing Initiative might be less appropriate in some fashion than their counterparts on the other Initiatives. Indeed, Segal, Quince, and Wicksteed (1991b: 69) do report incidences of technically poor consultancy. However, their evaluation does not in itself provide grounds for believing that the quality of the Marketing Consultancy is inferior to the work undertaken on the other schemes. The Marketing Consultancy is administered for the DTI by the Chartered Institute of Marketing, the major vocational training and professional marketing institution in the UK. All consultants are screened by the Institute, and their work is subject to close scrutiny and quality control. The administration of the other five Initiatives is similarly contracted to appropriate professional bodies. Nevertheless, the Evaluation exercise does not provide a definitive answer one way or another, and so the question of the quality of the consultants, *in relation to this sector of the market*, remains open.

3. Unrealistic expectations

It is possible that owner–managers expect more from their consultants than can reasonably be delivered within the constraints and context of the particular exercise. Why, however, should this be particularly the case with the Marketing Initiative? Segal, Quince, and Wicksteed (1991a: 31) supply some observations on this subject:

- marketing is concerned with the development of a capability. Thus the gain to firms may take the form of improved long-term competitiveness, rather than a short-term pay-off.
- following from this, disappointment with the consultancy may reflect a misapprehension by the firm of the kind of benefit the consultancy was intended to deliver.

This view finds an echo in the study of Smallbone, North, and Leigh (1992: 7) previously discussed.

4. Poor strategy formulation and/or poor implementation

Focusing on the content of the consultancy report and its 'fitness for purpose', low satisfaction could be explained in terms either of the quality of the strategy or of its implementation. Unfortunately, the questions of strategy and implementation are largely unresolved by the Evaluation, which simply identifies whether implementation has taken place, and to what extent. The Evaluation also reports estimated costs of implementation, and anticipated (and, in some cases, actual) benefits. The obstacles to implementation, however, are not explored in detail.

A BLACK BOX?

The authors are of the view that a major obstacle to exploring further the possible causal factors identified above is posed by the nature of the data collection methodology. As is to be expected from a government-sponsored evaluation, the Segal, Quince, and Wicksteed studies were primarily concerned with quantifying costs and benefits. The resultant analytical structure could be modelled simplistically as in Figure 13.1.

The model looks to answer the question: is this a prudent or effective investment of time and resources in terms of the 'desirable deliverables' of SME competitiveness and increased employment? It assumes that the only factor affecting the outputs is the process which intervenes between input and output, the consultancy process. However, this process is not examined but, rather, treated as a 'black box'. Something is going on, but it is not clear exactly what that 'something' is. This is unfortunate, since one of the explicit aims of the Initiative is to change attitudes and improve both the marketing

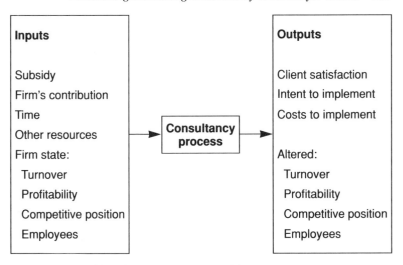

Inputs		Outputs
Subsidy		Client satisfaction
Firm's contribution		Intent to implement
Time	**Consultancy process**	Costs to implement
Other resources		
Firm state:		Altered:
Turnover		Turnover
Profitability		Profitability
Competitive position		Competitive position
Employees		Employees

Figure 13.1 The 'black box' consultancy model

orientation and the marketing activities of the owner–managers. As such, the consultancy is intended to be a *developmental process* and without an improved understanding of this process, it is hard to see how it is possible to develop generalizable inferences about the effectiveness of the consultancy or, indeed, to make suggestions as to how to improve the scheme.

MARKETING AND THE SMALL FIRM

Changing views on small firm marketing orientation

Recently, the prevailing view that small firms are generally poor at marketing or do not practise it at all (see e.g. Cohen and Lindbore 1972; Lamont 1972; Litvak and Maule 1980) has been challenged by a series of empirical studies (Hooley, West, and Lynch 1986; Dunn, Birley, and Norburn 1987; Peterson 1989; Antilla and Moller 1988; El-Rayyes and Birley 1992). These studies reveal the small firm both as recognizing the marketing concept and practising marketing, and provide evidence for small firm 'marketing orientation', defined as adopting the market concept (Konopa and Kalabro 1971; Kohli and Jaworski 1990).

There is, however, some divergence over what is to count as evidence of marketing orientation (Peterson 1989). One approach is to measure the owner/manager's tendency to agree or disagree with statements which embody the marketing concept (thus Barksdale and Darden 1971; Ford and Rowley 1979; Dunn, Birley, and Norburn 1987; Hooley, Lynch, and Shepherd 1988: cited in El-Rayyes and Birley 1992). The other is to regard attitudinal evidence as insufficient, but to look instead or in addition to 'signs that it [marketing orientation] has been translated into the structure and strategy of the firm (Hise 1965; McNamara 1972; Morris and Paul 1987; Miles and Arnold 1991; Meziou 1991)' (El-Rayyes and Birley 1992). El-Rayyes and Birley (1992: 3) analysed the research question: Do owner–managers understand concepts of market orientation, segmentation and targeting, customer closeness, and competition?

Respondents consisted of 128 small manufacturing firms in Bedfordshire, UK. Using previously validated research instruments, the authors conclude that their results 'tend to dispel the myth of a clear dichotomy with the bias towards a lack of marketing orientation' (1992: 13). Moreover, 'a large percentage of these owner–managers would appear to demonstrate a clear marketing orientation' (p. 13), with a substantial majority – typically between 70 per cent and 80 per cent – endorsing statements which embody various aspects of the marketing concept.

Of equal significance is the picture of *heterogeneity* which these results depict, of firms spread across a broad spectrum of 'more and less' marketing orientation. Through principal component and cluster analysis, the authors argue that the sample firms fall into four distinct categories which conform to or diverge from marketing orientation along different dimensions, such as segmentation and customer closeness (1992: 5–12).

If heterogeneity, not polarization, of small firm marketing orientation is indeed the norm rather than the exception, then many of the comments from both Segal, Quince, and Wicksteed (1991a, 1991b, 1992) and Smallbone, North, and Leigh (1992) begin to make sense: complaints of 'off the shelf' recommendations, failure to understand the business, advice which is not tailored to the needs of the specific firm – all perhaps signal consultancy approaches that attribute a simplistic, dichotomous stance of marketing/no marketing orientation to client owner–managers.

Developmental approach to small firm marketing

The heterogeneity issue is brought into sharper relief still when we come to the developmental literature concerning small firms and marketing. In this research stream, the other side of the marketing

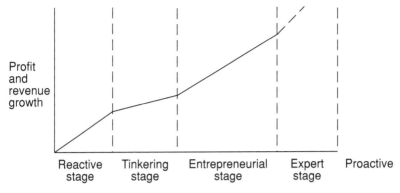

Figure 13.2 Stages of marketing development in small firms

orientation coin, management structure and practices, is subject to examination. Empirical studies suggest that, far from being a steady-state activity, marketing in small firms is typically a developmental activity that emulates the business life-cycle concept as presented by Carson (1985). See Figure 13.2.

Based on a longitudinal study of 80 small firms in Northern Ireland, this model identifies four developmental stages of marketing activity as new firms grow and prosper. *Stage 1*, the 'reactive stage', describes new firm entry into the market. In the majority of such cases, firms are started to meet an identified need – frequently in the form of an actual order – and the owner/manager is merely responding to a particular customer request. At this stage, Carson queries whether marketing in any real sense can be said to be taking place. In *Stage 2*, the 'tinkering stage', the firm has reached a point where re-ordering and word-of-mouth referral are no longer sufficient to sustain the business completely. This stage is characterized by spasmodic, unplanned, and isolated marketing activities, such as occasional advertising or an embryonic brochure. *Stage 3*, the 'entrepreneurial marketing' stage, is reached when the owner/manager explicitly recognizes the value of marketing in generating sales, and experiments with different activities. Characteristically instinctive and high risk, such marketing depends for its outcome on the innate aptitudes of the owner/manager. Carson defines *Stage 4*, 'expert' or 'proactive marketing', as 'methodical controlled marketing carried out by a marketing expert or specialist employed by the firm' (Carson 1990: 25), and sees this as a milestone which the small firm passes as it develops into a medium-sized business.

On the basis of this kind of model, we can reasonably predict heterogeneity of marketing orientation (defined in terms of management and structure) in any sizeable sample of small firms, as different firms pass through different stages in their development. Taken together with the empirical studies concerned with attitudinal marketing orientation, there are thus good *prima facie* grounds for thinking that two specific preconditions apply to successful small firms marketing consultancy:

1 the consultant needs to operate with a model that acknowledges the diversity of marketing practice and experience likely to be encountered in the small firm; and
2 the consultants' recommendations should be sensitive to the stage of marketing development at which the firm is operating.

These assertions are the subject of development in the final section of this paper, which discusses the generation and testing of specific research propositions.

THE STRATEGY/IMPLEMENTATION DIMENSION

In the discussion above concerning the interpretation of the Marketing Initiative Evaluation findings, it was argued that an important element in disentangling the possible contributory factors involved in firm satisfaction levels was the strategy/implementation dimension. Here we turn to the work of Bonoma (1984 and 1985). Bonoma's fieldwork studies of some 38 North American organizations are a landmark in scholarly understanding of implementation issues in marketing. The starting point was a sense of dissatisfaction with the knowledge base, the disquiet that strategy had preoccupied researchers at the expense of investigating implementation:

> Marketing science has made great strides toward strategic maturity in the last two decades. A substantial body of literature and corporate experience is available to help managers formulate marketing strategies. For example, pricing products on the basis of the value-added they provide to customers is an axiom of marketing strategy formulation. Yet when it comes to guiding the effective *implementation* of strategies, whether recommending a strategy as simple as 'price for value received' or as complex as managing a portfolio of markets and products, the academic literature is silent and the self-help books ring hollow. What rules are there for marketing practice that can help managers effectively translate strategies into market place results?
>
> (Bonoma 1985: 3).

Bonoma addressed the issue by observing both companies with an established reputation for effective implementation and companies that were suffering obstacles to achieving effectiveness. His findings confirm the initial hypothesis that marketing implementation impacts on marketing strategy at least as much as marketing strategy impacts on implementation: that is, whether the strategy is 'doable' is a critical dimension on which the quality of the strategy should be assessed. 'Doability' in turn hinges on the marketing culture and practice that prevail in the individual firm (Bonoma 1985: 7–8).

The strategy/implementation distinction developed by Bonoma is seen in the Marketing Initiative, where the consultant is tasked with producing a marketing plan that comprises both strategy and implementation. The consultant will be largely responsible for the formulation of the first; and the client firm will be largely – or wholly – responsible for the execution of the second. Success, measured in terms of client satisfaction, will depend on the quality of both. In simplified terms, there are four possible combinations (after Bonoma 1985, p. 12):

- Good strategy, poor implementation
- Poor strategy, good implementation
- Poor strategy, poor implementation
- Good strategy, good implementation

Since 'poor' implementation covers both unsatisfactory implementation and inability to implement, it would seem that the odds are stacked against a successful outcome.

Implementation, the focus of Bonoma's concerns, can be conceived both in terms of marketing practice and managerial skill. Out of the fieldwork, Bonoma devised a general-purpose analytic framework for the identification and mapping of marketing implementation problems (reproduced in the Appendix), which relates levels of marketing practice to desirable types of managerial skill. Bonoma also reached certain general conclusions about, first, the marketing strategy/marketing implementation relationship and, second, about practices associated with successful marketing implementation:

1 Strategies run into difficulty when they run directly counter to a business's engrained approach to marketing (Bonoma 1985: 29). Bonoma cites the example of an organization's attempt to get the sales force to market a new product on a 'price for value received' basis as against the old 'match the competition' basis (1985: 1–2). Clearly, such lack of fit does not necessarily mean the strategy cannot be implemented, but it does create an obstacle that must be surmounted.

2 Firms which implement their marketing successfully tend to be 'choosy' about which activities they support, give those activities substantial support, and focus on performing one or two major aspects of the marketing task extremely well, while aiming for adequacy in other areas (Bonoma 1985: 27, 43).

In virtually every case, the firms studied were not owner-managed but substantial organizations. Consequently the framework reproduced in the Appendix assumes a degree of sophistication and a resource base which are not found in a typical SME. Nevertheless, both Bonoma's approach and conclusions have appeal in shedding light on the problem under discussion.

THE WAY FORWARD

The foregoing review has identified a number of significant issues in furthering our understanding of small firms and marketing. The Enterprise Initiative firm base affords a particularly interesting opportunity of addressing these. In particular:

- the intervention of the consultancy process as demonstrated;
- the developmental expectations of the smaller firm;
- the nature of marketing developmental change in the smaller firm;
- the interrelationship of marketing planning, strategy, and implementation in the smaller firm.

The Evaluation exercise undertaken by Segal, Quince, and Wicksteed provides a richly researched context within which to conduct the research.

The marketing stage model of the smaller firm

If, as is argued above, marketing consultancy can be viewed as a developmental activity, then success, measurable in terms of enhancing the client firm's level of sophistication and capabilities, can be expected. It seems appropriate, therefore, to look to the empirically derived models which draw on the business life-cycle concept. It is proposed to use Carson's model (refer to Figure 13.2) as the basis for developing and testing propositions for the following reasons:

1 It is an empirically derived model, based on a small firm sample.
2 It has been developed from a substantial database of firms within the United Kingdom.

3 Carson's observations are supported by other examples in the literature (see, for example, Smith and Fleck 1987; Curran 1988).

The model and the review of the Initiative Evaluation led to the first research proposition, namely:

P1: That there is a significant link between a firm's satisfaction with the consultancy and an explicit shift in the firm's marketing practices and capabilities pre and post the consultancy.

This shift will be measured by categorizing the firm under one of the four stages (Figure 13.2 above) pre and post the consultancy.

To test the proposition that the small firm must pass through each stage sequentially as it raises the scope and capabilities of its marketing activities, we advance a related proposition:

P2: That the link identified in P1 only holds when the shift in the firm's marketing practices and capabilities pre and post the consultancy does not exceed a *one-stage* or *two-stage* increment (e.g. from Stage 1 to Stage 2, or from Stage 1 to Stage 3).

The reasoning behind this latter proposition is that a major cause of client dissatisfaction may well result from consultants' attempts to 'rush' the firm too quickly towards the 'expert' stage in their Marketing Plan, as a result of the dichotomous marketing/no marketing approach hypothesized earlier. Two-stage shifts are included on the basis that the firm may be expected to pass through a stage such as the tinkering or entrepreneurial stage *as it implements* the recommended strategy, given the time elapsed between the consultancy and the proposed research.

The strategy/implementation dimension

The next two research propositions use Bonoma's findings as the basis for exploring whether the strategy/implementation dimension plays a significant part in determining whether or not the outcome of the consultancy is satisfactory. (Our operating definition of marketing strategy is taken from Bonoma (1985: 7), which in turn derives from the work of Buzell *et al.*, Levitt, and Kotler: 'Marketing strategy is the analysis of alternative opportunities and risks to the firm, informed by environmental (e.g. competitive, social) and internal (e.g. production abilities) information, which leads management to choose a particular set of market, product and customer goals.') Proposition number three tests the notion that, to be 'implementable', strategy must fit – or not diverge too strongly – from prevailing practices and attitudes. It draws support from the fact that El-Rayyes and Birley (1992) were able to identify and name meaningful clusters of small firms in terms of their marketing orientation which, in turn, suggests that at the very least, embryonic marketing 'cultures' are in place.

P3:　The firm will be more likely to implement the marketing strategy if it perceives a close fit with current business practices and attitudes

The attitudes proposition draws from Bonoma's observation that firms which implement their marketing successfully tend to be 'choosy' about which activities they promote, to give those activities substantial support, and focus on performing one or two major aspects of the marketing task extremely well, whilst aiming for adequacy in other areas (Bonoma 1985: 27, 43). Adapting for small firms, we have:

P4　The firm will report higher satisfaction levels with implementation policies that focus on a limited range of marketing activities and which can be fully funded within the constrained resources available to the SME.

Research design

While the propositions owe their derivation to several streams of research literature, the authors are keenly aware that much of the supporting argument is based on inference and assumptions of parallel cases holding good. For this reason, a pilot case study has been developed to test the validity of these propositions.

CASE STUDY: STATELY HOME[11]

Background

Stately Home (SH) is a substantial country estate in the south of England. The house and gardens date from the fourteenth century and the property has been occupied by the same family for over four hundred years.

The house and gardens were first opened to the public in 1945 by the father of the present owner. Limited catering facilities were operated, which were subsequently expanded into a banqueting business, aimed at commercial and private customers. The period from 1945 until 1990 marks the first stage of business operations. Visitors to SH gradually increased, reaching a plateau of over 100,000 in the late 1970s, from which numbers slowly declined during the 1980s. Despite its historical and horticultural significance, however, SH received relatively few visitors in comparison with similar great houses in the vicinity during a time of rapid expansion in the 'heritage' industry. It is an inherently seasonal business, in which the cycle of activity begins in March and ends in October, with the exception of banqueting, which operates throughout the winter, although at reduced volume.

The present management describe the marketing practices in use at this time as 'virtually non-existent'. The prevailing belief was that visitors would be attracted to SH primarily through word of mouth, occasionally supplemented by the advertising of special events in the local press. The following anecdote characterizes the former attitude towards marketing. When the present Business Manager first arrived, he asked local storekeepers whether any of them would be prepared to keep stocks of SH literature. He was told that they had repeatedly requested such literature, in response to interest shown by visitors to the area. The Business Manager's predecessor declined to make any materials available, on the grounds that if potential visitors were given information about the House their curiosity would be satisfied and they would be unlikely to pay to visit.

Information presented here

The information presented here is extracted from interviews with senior management conducted in late January, shortly before the closing date for submission of this paper. Because of space limitations, the case deals chiefly with areas covering the four propositions previously identified.

The marketing consultancy

The marketing consultancy took place during January and February 1992, with implementation of the recommendations starting in February, while the report was in its closing stages.

The decision to undertake the consultancy exercise formed part of wider strategic changes in the organization. In 1990 the death of his father caused the present owner to inherit. This occasioned a complete review of the business and the institution of a new structure whereby SH – the house, gardens, and banqueting business – was formally separated from the agricultural activities of the Estate. The owner had had some previous involvement in the business.

Reporting to the owner is a Business Manager with responsibility for sales and marketing, and reporting to the Business Manager are managers with individual responsibility for finance and accounting, purchasing and personnel. The component parts of the business, such as banqueting, house, gardens, special events, and so forth, are also the specific responsibility of individuals and are costed as profit centres.

Situation just prior to the time of the consultancy

Financial: The business's turnover was approximately £250,000. It recorded a loss of £50,000, consistent with previous years.

Personnel: The business employed 13 full-time and 36 part-time staff.

Marketing channels: A small range of tour operators, unchanged for many years. Occasional small stand at a trade fair. Sporadic advertising in local press.

In-house expertise: Basically none.

Use of outside expertise: Basically none.

Experimentation with different marketing approaches: None.

Formal planning (marketing or otherwise): None.

Situation 12 months post-consultancy

Financial: The business turnover was approximately £420,000. It recorded a profit of £120,000, the first time in many years.

Personnel: The business now employs 15 full-time and 30 part-time staff.

Marketing channels: The business focuses heavily on press and public relations and maintains stands at all major trade fairs. It has built links with all major UK tour operators, and undertakes a small but growing overseas marketing activity.

In-house expertise: Steadily increasing, through exposure to professional marketing practice.

Use of outside expertise: The marketing consultancy which undertook the DTI sponsored exercise has been retained to assist in implementing the agreed plan.

Experimentation with different marketing approaches: A little, but only to refine the basic trade marketing approach.

Formal planning (marketing or otherwise): Quarterly.

Points emerging from discussion with management

Senior management was firmly of the opinion that the most significant variable in the business which had altered was marketing.

Improved operating efficiencies had made some impact on reducing costs, but the primary reason for the firm's turnaround was its changed approach to marketing.

Causes of success or failure inferred from our analysis of the Enterprise Initiative Evaluation

Our discussion explored the possible contributory factors already identified above, as follows:

'Experience curve' effect

The owner/manager had no prior experience of working with consultants, marketing or otherwise. However, the Business Manager, who has a background in small firm management, brought in to take charge of implementing the marketing consultancy's recommendations, *did* have previous (negative) experience of working with marketing consultants. His comments are reviewed in the next subsection.

Poor or inappropriate consultants

Senior management were emphatic that the consultants went to very considerable lengths to understand the nature of the business and to produce recommendations specific to the needs of a small firm with limited resources. The Business Manager had a generally poor opinion of marketing consultants. He made the following observations:

- Many consultancies lay claim to marketing expertise when in fact they only understand one aspect of marketing, such as advertising or press relations. This is the case with both small and large consultancies. There is, therefore, in his opinion, a tendency to conceive of the client's problem only in terms of the consultant's expertise (e.g. all 'marketing' problems can be solved by advertising); and a corresponding tendency to advise solutions which 'have worked for *x*' (i.e. off-the-shelf answers).
- The larger consultancies are unrealistic in their expectations of what smaller firms can (a) afford and (b) manage to implement.
- Both large and small consultancies are reluctant to advise on the daily management of marketing activities, such as maintaining customer databases, preferring to concentrate on the more glamorous activities (such as advertising campaigns and press launches) traditionally associated with marketing. The Business Manager believes that where small firms most need help is with the mundane activities.

Unrealistic expectations

At the outset of the consultancy, the firm agreed to a very focused brief with the consultants. The strategy was to concentrate on: turning the business around rapidly through building short-term sales; increasing visitor traffic; extending the visitor base to new geographic markets; and improving the firm's promotional activities. Both the consultants and the firm discarded other objectives as unrealistic within the scope of the exercise.

Management *did* acknowledge that some failure in marketing consultancy can be ascribed to unrealistic expectations on the part of client firms. The Business Manager believed (although he could not cite hard evidence) that many firms turned to marketing *in extremis*, when all else had failed. In these circumstances the situation had deteriorated to the point where marketing of itself could not reasonably be expected to save the firm from forced sale or insolvency.

Poor strategy formulation and/or poor implementation

The focus of the strategy altered during the consultancy process. Originally, the consultants' brief excluded pricing issues. In the course of the exercise, the consultants identified pricing as a key issue and, with the agreement of the client, conducted a price sensitivity analysis that resulted in a wholly new pricing structure, based on market segmentation. Management made the following points about the formulation of strategy and implementation:

- Strategy formulation was a joint process, shaped by the consultants' analysis but endorsed through discussion with management.
- Through endorsement, strategy was 'bought into' by the management team as it evolved.
- The key to making it happen was collaborative implementation, whereby the marketing plan was fine-tuned as it was progressively put into practice.
- Implementation was conceived at the outset as a staged process: the firm did not attempt everything on day 1.

The four propositions

Stately Home is the first of several cases which are being developed to assess the validity of the research methodology before passing to a larger sample size which, it is hoped, will yield statistically significant results. Accordingly the authors make no definitive claims for the findings arising from this single case: rather, they are presented to put the propositions in the context of the experiences of a representative small firm.

To recapitudate, the four propositions are:

P1: That there is a significant link between a firm's satisfaction with the consultancy and an explicit shift in the firm's marketing practices and capabilities pre and post the consultancy.

P2: That the link identified in P1 only holds when the shift in the firm's marketing practices and capabilities pre and post the consultancy does not exceed a one-stage or two-stage increment.

P3: The firm will be more likely to implement the marketing strategy if it perceives a close fit with current business practices and attitudes.

P4: The firm will report higher satisfaction levels with implementation policies that focus on a limited range of marketing activities and which can be fully funded within the constrained resources available to the SME.

Support for the propositions

P1: Management's depiction of marketing activities before the consultancy place the firm in Stage 2 of Carson's four-stage model, the 'tinkering' phase. Circumstances had forced the firm to make half-hearted, spasmodic attempts at marketing the business, but no systematic marketing effort had taken place. The evidence supplied by current management suggests that the business is now in, or entering, Stage 4, the 'expert' stage, as marketing has become the responsibility of a nominated senior manager, assisted by outside professionals.

The high satisfaction rating reported coupled with this clear shift in the firm's marketing capability would lend support to the proposition.

P2: That the transition is a two-stage shift tends to support the proposition; this is further underpinned by the Business Manager's comment that the firm's approach to marketing strategy implementation was quite intentionally incremental, to 'avoid biting off more than we could chew'.

P3: It is difficult to assess this proposition, because the marketing consultancy formed part of a wider strategic review that involved the recruitment of new management and the restructuring of the firm: the culture of the business was thus inevitably affected. However, the opinion of senior management was that the marketing strategy has been consistent with the underlying aim of the owner/manager, which is to maintain commercial viability without sacrificing the character and unique qualities of Stately Home, and allowing it to remain a family home as well a business.

P4:   This view is strongly supported by senior management, who have declared their objective to be that of becoming expert in trade marketing. This involves direct selling to tour operators, mainly by means of trade fairs, and maintaining a high profile in the relevant publications through an effective press relations campaign. The marketing budget reflects this commitment: as a percentage of turnover, this has been increased by a factor of three, to 15 per cent, following the consultancy.

APPENDIX 1

Table 13.8 Marketing practice: a taxonomy

Marketing implementation can be analysed at the level of	Effective implementation is achieved through INTERACTING	ALLOCATING	MONITORING	ORGANIZING
Actions	*How* are production and R&D colleagues encouraged to devote more time or effort to a single brand?	*How* is sales force territory allocation best done by a printing company?	*How* are salespeople best evaluated and compensated by a bulk chemicals firm?	*How* should the new product planning function of a market follower be organized in a high-loyalty business?
Programmes	*How* can sales and marketing effectively collaborate on a new national account programme?	*How* should prospects be selected for demonstration rides in a corporate jet?	*How* is a successful ad agency team best managed within a brand group for a new pipe introduction?	*How* should a sales force be reorganized to emphasize a marketing shift from 'dumb' to 'smart' terminals?
Systems	*How* should ownership of a competitive pricing intelligence system be parcelled between sales and marketing in an ethical drug company?	*How* should a regional bank set up centres, lock boxes, and computer service to maximise market share in a new cash management programme?	*How* does a mine machinery manufacturer monitor major trade promotion expenditure?	*How* should customer service engineers be redeployed to avoid hardware–software 'buck passing' in a computer graphics manufacturer?
Policies	*How* should a recall of a defective building component be managed by a major steel producer?	*How* should dollars and service resources be allocated to service key accounts by segment and country for a computer-aided design manufacturer?	*How* does a major securities firm regularly audit the marketing function?	*How* should the marketing team be reorganized by a company changing its 'theme'?

Source: Bonoma 1985: 37

NOTES

1 On a scale 1 [poor] to 5 [excellent], where 3 denotes indifference.
2 All subsequent statistical analysis of the data from this report has been conducted by the authors.
3 $z = 11.22$, $p(z>1.22) = 0.0000$
4 $z = 7.5$, $p(z<7.5) = 0.0000$
5 $z = -9.0$. $p(z<-9.0) = 0.0000$
6 $z = -8.75$, $p(z<-8.75) = 0.0000$
7 $z = -5.38$, $p(z<-5.38) = 0.0000$
8 $z = 1.98$, $p(z>1.98) = 0.023$
9 $z = -2.99$, $p(z<-2.99) = 0.0014$
10 $z = -1.86$, $p(z<-1.86) = 0.031$
11 The identity of the organization has been disguised.

REFERENCES

Antilla, M. and Moller, K. (1988) 'Marketing Capability in Small Manufacturing Firms', *5th Nordische Small Business Conference*, Norway.
Barksdale, H. and Darden, B. (1971) 'Marketers' Attitude Toward the Marketing Concept', *Journal of Marketing*, 35 (October): 29–36.
Barnes, J., Pym, G., and Noonan, A. (1982) 'Marketing Research: Some Basics for Small Businesses', *Journal of Small Business Management* (July).
Birch, D. (1980) *The Job Generation Process*, MIT Programme on Neighbourhood and Regional Change, Cambridge, MA.
Birley, S. (1986) 'The Role of New Firms: Births, Deaths and Job Generation', *Strategic Management Journal*, 7: 361–376.
Birley, S. and Westhead P. (1993) 'New Venture Environments: the Owner–Manager's View', in S. Birley and I. C. MacMillan (eds), *International Perspectives on Entrepreneurship Research 1992*, Amsterdam: North-Holland.
Bolton, Lord (1971) *Report of the Committee on Small Firms*, London: HMSO.
Bonoma, T. (1984) *Managing Marketing: Text, Cases and Readings*, New York: The Free Press.
Bonoma, T. (1985) *The Marketing Edge*, New York: The Free Press.
Carson, D. (1985) 'The Evolution of Marketing in Small Firms', *European Journal of Marketing*, 19 (5).
Carson, D. (1990) 'Some Exploratory Models for Assessing Small Firms' Marketing Performance', *European Journal of Marketing*, 24 (11).
Cohen, T. and Lindbore, R. (1972) 'How Management is Different for Small Companies', *American Management Association*.
Curran J. (1988) 'Training and Research Strategies for Small Firms', *Journal of General Management*, 13 (3).
Department of Employment (1991) The Government's Expenditure Plans, 1991, London: HMSO.
Department of Trade and Industry (1991) *The Government's Expenditure Plans, 1991*, London: HMSO.
Dunn, M., Birley, S., and Norburn, D. (1987) 'The Marketing Concept and the Smaller Firm', *Marketing Intelligence and Planning*, 4 (3).
El-Rayyes, B. and Birley, S. (1992) 'The Marketing Orientation of

Owner–managers', *Imperial College Management School Working Paper P9210/BP*, London.

Ford, D. and Rowley, T. (1979) 'Marketing and the Small Industrial Firm', *Management Decision*, 17 (2): 144–156.

Fothergill, S. and Gudgin, G. (1979) *The Job Generation Process in Great Britain*, Centre for Environmental Studies, Research Series, 32, London.

Gibb, A. and Scott, M. (1985) 'Strategic Awareness, Personal Commitment and the Success of Planning in Small Firms', *Journal of Management Studies*, 22 (6).

Hakim, C. (1989) 'Identifying Fast Growth Firms', *Employment Gazette*, 97: 29–41

Hise, R. (1965) 'Have Manufacturing Firms Adopted the Marketing Concept?', *Journal of Marketing*, 29 (July): 9–12.

Hooley, G., West, C., and Lynch, J. (1986) *Marketing in the UK: A Survey of Current Practice and Performance*, Institute of Marketing, Cookham, UK.

Hooley, G., Lynch, J., and Shepherd, J. (1988) *The Marketing Concept: Putting the Theory into Practice*, University of Bradford Management Centre, Bradford, UK.

Joyce, P. and Woods, A. (1992) 'Entrepreneurial Spirit in the United States – A Quantitative Study of the Period 1946–1986', *15th National Small Firms Policy and Research Conference*, Southampton, UK.

Kinsey, J. (1987) 'Marketing and the Small Manufacturing Firm in Scotland: Finding of a Pilot Survey', *Journal of Small Business Management*, 22 (6).

Kohli, A. and Jaworski, B.J. (1990) 'Marketing Orientation: The Construct, Research Propositions and Managerial Implications', *Journal of Marketing*, 54 (April 1–18).

Konopa, L. and Kalabro, P. (1971) 'Adoption of the Marketing Concept by Large Northeastern Ohio Manufacturers', *Akorn Business and Economic Review*, 2 (Spring): 9–13.

Lamont, L. (1972) 'Marketing Industrial Technology in the Small Business', *Journal of Marketing Management*, October: 387–396.

Litvak, J. and Maule, C. (1980) 'Entrepreneurial Success or Failure – Ten Years Later', *Business Quarterly*, 45 (4): 68–88.

Mason, C. and Harrison, R. (1990) 'The Regional Take-up of the Enterprise Initiative in Great Britain', *13th National Small Firms Policy and Research Conference*, Leeds, UK.

McNamara, C. (1972) 'The Present Status of the Marketing Concept', *Journal of Marketing*, 30 (October): 50–57.

Meziou, F. (1991) 'Areas of Strength in the Adoption of the Marketing Concept by Small Manufacturing Firms', *Journal of Small Business Management*, 29 (4): 72–78.

Miles, M. and Arnold, D. (1991) 'The Relationship Between Marketing Orientation and Entrepreneurial Orientation', *Entrepreneurship Theory and Practice*, Summer: 49–65.

Morris, M. and Paul, G. (1987) 'The Relationship Between Entrepreneurship and Marketing in Established Firms', *Journal of Business Venturing*, 2 (3).

North, D., Leigh, R., and Smallbone, D. (1992) *A Longitudinal Study of Adjustment Processes in Mature Small Firms in London During the 1980s*, Swindon: Economic and Social Research Council.

Owen, G. (1992) *Aid Regimes and Small Businesses in the UK, France and Belgium*, Swindon: Economic and Social Research Council.

Peterson, R. (1989) 'Small Business Adoption of the Marketing Concept vs Other Business Strategies', *Journal of Small Business Management*, 27 (1).

Schwartz, R., Southern, L., Teach, R., and Tarpley, F. (1992) 'Marketing to the Entrepreneur: the Public Service Providers', *Research at the Marketing/Entrepreneurship Interface*, G. Hills, and R. Laforge (eds).

Segal, Quince, and Wicksteed (1989) *Evaluation of the Consultancy Initiatives (First stage)*, London: HMSO.

Segal, Quince, and Wicksteed (1991a) *Evaluation of the Consultancy Initiatives (Second stage)*, London: HMSO.

Segal, Quince, and Wicksteed (1991b) *Evaluation of the Consultancy Initiatives (Third stage)*, London: HMSO.

Smallbone, D., North, D., and Leigh, R. (1992) 'Support for Mature SMEs: Developing a Policy Agenda', *15th National Small Firms Policy and Research Conference*, Southampton, UK.

Smith J. and Fleck, V. (1987) 'Business Strategies in Small High-Technology Companies', *Long Range Planning*, 20 (2): 63.

Storey, D.J. and Johnson, S. (1987) *Job Generation and Labour Market Change*, Basingstoke: MacMillan.

Storey, D.J., Keasey, K., Watson, R., and Wynarczyk, P. (1987) *The Performance of Small Firms*, London: Croom Helm.

Storey, D.J. (1992) 'Should We Abandon the Support to Start-up Business?', *15th National Small Firms Policy and Research Conference*, Southampton, UK.

Verhage, B.J. and Waarts, E. (1988) 'Marketing Planning for Improved Performance: A Comparative Analysis', *International Marketing Review*, 5 (2): 21.

14 A predictive model of litigation between channel members in a franchise channel of distribution

Stephen Spinelli, Jr and William D. Bygrave

INTRODUCTION

Nine characteristics of 75 US business format franchise systems were studied. These characteristics were compiled into data sets. The purpose of the study was to investigate the predictive value of these characteristics as independent variables, with system stores in litigation as the dependent variable. The cost of litigation was also studied with additional speculation regarding ancillary costs of conflict.

IS CONFLICT IN FRANCHISING INEVITABLE?

The objective of this paper is to outline the extent of franchising in the US economy, point out some theoretical structural flaws inherent in franchising, and comment on the predictive value of the operating parameters of franchise systems in forecasting conflict in the franchise relationship. Our research concentrated on business format franchising and dealt primarily in retail operations.

DEFINITION

540,000 franchised outlets had sales of over $750 billion in the USA, accounting for 35 per cent of all retail sales in 1991 (IFA 1991). The International Franchise Association believes that sales generated through franchising will rise to $1 trillion by the year 2000. Franchising has experienced real growth in every year since the US Commerce Department began keeping statistics in 1972. The British Franchise Association commissioned National Westminster Bank to conduct a survey of franchising in the United Kingdom in 1991. That survey revealed that 18,600 franchised outlets had sales of £4.8 billion, and were forecast to generate over £10 billion by 1996 (British Franchise Association 1992). The International Franchise Association estimates there are 62,000 franchised outlets outside the US and Britain (interview with IFA Director of Research, Terrien Barnes, January 1993). In 1992 alone 21,000 franchised outlets were added in the US (*Entrepreneur Magazine*, January 1993).

Franchising is an organizational form structured by a long-term contract (Miller and Grossman 1986). The owner, producer, or distributor (franchisor) of a service or trademarked product grants the exclusive rights to a distributor (franchisee) for the local distribution of the product or service. In return the franchisee pays an up-front fee and ongoing royalty and agrees to conform to quality standards (Justis and Judd 1986). This is consistent with Stern and El-Ansary's (1988) definition of a marketing channel of distribution as sets of interdependent organizations in the process of making a product or service available for use or consumption. Channel structure refers to the nature of the firm's involvement in the channel, the nature and extent of their interrelated roles, and the allocation of the channel's productive value (Stern and El-Ansary 1988).

A key aspect of franchising is the central role of the trademark (Caves and Murphy 1976). The franchisee cloaks himself in the identity of the trademark but operates as a separate legal entity, described as independently liable (Eaton and Joseph 1988). Therefore, franchising is the establishment of a relationship between independent firms who share an intangible asset, customer goodwill, embodied in the trademark. The intangible asset is enhanced or diminished by the delivery of the product or service to the customer. The value of the asset is derived by capitalizing the stream of earnings it will generate. The capitalization value is the basis for the franchise fee and royalty payment. The up-front fee, generally termed a franchise fee, is usually paid at the time the licence agreement is executed. A royalty is a scheduled payment on a monthly or weekly basis, calculated as a percentage of the total revenue generated by the franchisee firm. There is considerable variation in the magnitude of both types of fees (Sen 1991). These payments are an apportionment of the productive benefits derived from the shared intangible asset to the franchisor (Caves and Murphy 1976). The franchise firm enjoys the risk and return commensurate with outlet operation.

Two distinct types of franchising have developed and are described by Dicke (1991). Product franchising was created by the makers of complex durable goods who found existing wholesalers either unable or unwilling to market their products. These manufacturers built their own distribution systems. Company-owned outlets were found to be too costly and franchises were therefore established.

Business format franchising grew out of the concept of distribution channel development and control. It was formalized in the late 1950s by entrepreneurs who believed the outlet itself could be a product. Initially the motivation was to enhance efficiency through minimizing cost (franchised versus company-owned outlets) and later as a method of expanding revenue by prescribing detailed operational practices to protect and ultimately enhance the trademark. For franchising to survive it had to stand the test of creating bilateral gains for the channel members in this vertical integration (Williamson 1991). With the development of the modern economy and the evolution of contract law, the franchisor was able to extract economies of scale from channel development which gave the franchisees a competitive advantage over non-franchised business ownership. National and regional advertising and product purchasing are important examples of building the tradename and trademark value which may be sold to the franchisee firm on a limited, non-exclusive basis. The main difference between business format franchising and other market channels is that the downstream channel members play a significant part in the quality control of the final product or service (Sen 1991).

Business format franchising accompanies the trademark and distribution rights with information on the production processes and delivery system. Inherent in this is the assumption that the information exchange will ensure the maintenance of the trademark value (Caves and Murphy 1976). The value is then enhanced through the development and exploitation of economies of scale. Business format franchising usually includes a marketing plan, documented and enforced procedures, process assistance, and business development and innovation (Achrol and Etzel 1991). Business format franchising is an entire way of doing business and is a more complex relationship than product franchising because the method by which the asset is shared is stipulated in the license agreement (contract).

This complex channel system raises the question of coordination and control of the marketing functions (Simpson 1991). Each franchisee, as a downstream channel member, impacts the value of the intangible asset because the trademark becomes manifest in the delivery of the product or service to the customer. The performance of each outlet has direct pro rata impact on the total system revenue and the income stream to the franchisor. Indirect costs and benefits of individual performance are associated with agency concerns which ultimately affect trademark value. The relationship must necessarily be dynamic because no long-term contract can cover all the contingencies (Boyle

1991). Also, there is an interdependent effect of actions taken by parties either bilaterally or independently (Hart and Grossman 1986). There is continuing interaction between the franchisor and the franchisee involving general business discussion, feedback on marketing, and operations process adjustments. The level of interaction varies by franchise system but often exceeds the strictly interpreted contractual requirement (Dwyer, Schurr, and Oh 1987; Kaufman and Stern 1988; Mohr and Nevin 1990).

As noted, the franchise fee is paid and royalty stipulated in the licence agreement which is executed in advance of the actual franchisee firm's commencement of operation (Austin 1989). Two independent businesses, franchisor and franchisee, agree in advance on the probable outcome of a somewhat unknown series of events which will take place well into the future, leading to an apportionment of productive value. Because franchisors seldom negotiate their standard form of license agreement (Stansworth 1984), the apportionment of the productive value of the enterprise is used over a number of such relationships. That is, all the franchisee firms in a system typically pay the same franchise fee and royalty to the franchisor regardless of the particular input mix of the franchisee firm, like site location, local market potential, and entrepreneurial capacity of the franchisee.

Eighty-seven per cent of the outlets within the franchise system in the United States are operated by franchisee firms and thirteen per cent are operated by the franchisor (IFA 1991). Types of businesses generally included in business format franchising are restaurants, food and non-food retailing, personal and professional services (Justis and Judd 1986).

THE ROOTS OF CONFLICT: A THEORETICAL DISCUSSION

The franchisor establishes the business format for the purpose of enhancing the prospect of individual unit operating success. In order to provide the ongoing services required of the business format, including quality assurance monitoring, the franchisor must have much of the support overhead in place to service even a single franchisee. Therefore the franchisor has a high percentage of cost as necessarily fixed. As the system of franchisee firms and outlets grows, the franchisor's costs are spread over an ever-increasing base. The average cost to the franchisor per franchisee decreases as the number of outlets increase. On the revenue side the franchisor is motivated to maximize sales. The franchisor's ongoing income is derived from franchisee royalty payments, a percentage of *top line* sales paid to the franchisor.

System growth in number of outlets and individual outlet sales result in higher franchisor revenue applied against lower per-unit support costs. The franchisee firm, on the other hand, aspires to optimal unit sales, not necessarily maximum sales, in an effort to maximize profit. The franchisee's operating model has more variable expense than the franchisor. The implication is that there is divergent profit-maximizing behaviour which may be manifest in disagreements concerning pricing, promotion, and the development of additional outlets.

This conflict is exacerbated by the phenomenon of larger, more sophisticated franchisee firms supplanting the historical 'mom and pop' operator. With today's heightened level of competition in the marketplace, franchisees are necessarily more educated, possess capital, entrepreneurial drive, and organizational skills, and are capable of building fully-integrated companies. As a franchisee firm grows into multiple outlets and becomes increasingly self-reliant, the royalty paid for the business format becomes increasingly difficult to justify.

PROFIT-MAXIMIZING BEHAVIOUR

The franchisor and franchisee firms are established to divide tasks and in doing so reduce cost and/or enhance revenue (Williamson 1975; Caves and Murphy 1976). Traditional microeconomic theory serves as a framework to analyse this division of tasks and the profit-maximizing behaviour which results. We will endeavour to outline, in a basic form, the differences in optimal pricing between the franchisee and franchisor firms which may constitute a cause for structural conflict in the relationship.

Microeconomic theory assumes that both the franchisor and the franchisee firms are attempting to maximize profit (Coase 1936; Hayek 1945). Channel literature which has addressed the franchisee's hypothetical demand or average revenue (AR) function concludes that it is downward sloping and to the right (McGuire and Staelin 1983; Mittelstaedt and Stassen 1990). This reflects product and location differentiation that gives the franchisee the ability to vary price from their competitors in the marketplace. The coefficient of elasticity is different at every point along the AR line and decreases as price decreases. The only AR function which would not exhibit this property is one which has a constant elasticity to price over its entire range. The role of the franchisee in the franchise relationship is to deliver units of product or service to the consumer. Each unit of good or service carries a cost. To deliver the unit, some overhead is usually in place. Therefore, in the depiction of cost, the franchisee firm exhibits both fixed and variable expense. Thus there is a positive marginal cost to sales for the franchisee firm (Brickley, Dark, and Weisbach 1987).

Franchisor revenue is principally generated through franchise fees, royalties, and to a much lesser extent, the sale of goods and services. Initial fees are not directly related to output levels; they carry neither a marginal cost nor are a marginal revenue to the franchisor firm (Ozanne and Hunt 1971). Franchisors are loath to change the terms of their licence agreement among franchisees (Stansworth and Hough 1984). This is especially true in the setting of the royalty percentage. Hence the percentage of total revenue applied to royalties is generally fixed across the system. The sale of goods and services to the franchisee appears to be marginal both for cost and revenue. Some theoreticians would suggest that the basis on which the goods and services are sold to the franchisee dictates the effect on the franchisor firm's pricing behaviour. If the franchisor firm sells the goods at market price to the franchisee regardless of retail pricing considerations, then the effect of the sale is akin to the royalty on the franchisor firm's operating behaviour (Caves and Murphy 1976). This is exacerbated if the franchisor firm is simply negotiating national contracts and passing the deal on to the franchisee firms with a mark-up. If however, the franchisor firm participates in a promotional scheme by product or royalty discounts, then the franchisor and franchisee firm's cost curves are more closely aligned. Research has shown product sales from the franchisor firm to the franchisee firm to be inconsequential in magnitude to altering the basic cost or revenue functions of the franchisor firm. Therefore, the franchisor firm's average revenue curve will be substantively the sum of the franchisee's average revenue curves, already described as downward sloping and to the right. The elasticity of the AR curve will be the same at each price as that of the AR of the system's average franchisee.

Examining the franchisor's theoretical cost structure, the assumption is that the franchisor firm has only fixed cost. This is in line with the franchisor overhead placement requirement previously stated. This assumption could be relaxed to reflect a tiered placement of overhead. Tiered placement of overhead occurs as a result of staged growth. The first tier of overhead is put in place as required to meet contractual obligations for a prescribed number of outlets. Pressure, *vis-à-vis* task failure or relational issues mounts, and a second layer of overhead is placed to relieve the pressure and secure support obligations for a second group of outlets. Putting the tiered overhead effect aside for the moment, the franchisor has no cost directly attributable to the sale of each unit of good or service made by the franchisee. Therefore the franchisor firm has no marginal cost.

With the franchisee firm having a demand curve that is downward sloping to the right, a reduction in price yields an increase in the quantity of goods sold. A firm with no marginal cost maximizes profit with the price at which demand is exactly unit elastic, maximizing total revenue.

For the franchisee firm, each unit of good or service sold has an associated marginal cost. Increased sales increase marginal cost and, to a point, increase marginal revenue. With positive marginal cost, the franchisee's profit is maximized at a price elasticity of greater than 1.0. The franchisor's optimal price is set at an elasticity of exactly 1.0. This divergence in optimal pricing strategy means the franchisee firm's profit-maximizing price will be higher than the price which will maximize profit for the franchisor firm. Remember, the franchisor firm's revenue is principally generated from a fixed percentage of the franchisee firm's total revenue. Therefore the franchisor firm's pricing strategy is, *de facto*, the franchisee firm's pricing strategy.

Under the marginal cost scenario described above, total cost equals fixed cost for the franchisor. The total cost curve is parallel to the *x*-axis. The franchisee firm's total cost curve equals variable plus fixed costs. The franchisee firm's total cost curve is upward sloping and to the right. For both entities, profit equals total revenue less total cost. The profit-maximizing price for both entities is the point at which marginal revenue equals marginal cost. For the franchisor firm, $MC=0$. $MR=0$ where total revenue is maximized. When the lower price no longer generates an increase in volume sufficient to make up for the reduction in per-unit price, price will stabilize. With each unit increase in quantity of sales, a marginal cost is incurred by the franchisee. With the same pricing equation $MC=MR$, the franchisee will be motivated to lower price until MR equals MC. Franchisee $MC>0$ while franchisor firm $MC=0$ and therefore, franchisee profit-maximizing price > the franchisor firm's profit-maximizing price. See Figures 14.1 and 14.2.

Some qualifications need to be added to the framework. To the extent that sales increases in one outlet are the result of the cannibalization of sales from another outlet in the same franchise system, the revenue-maximizing effect to the franchisor firm is reduced (Rubin 1976). Also, the comparison being made is between the franchisor firm and the 'average' franchisee firm. Clearly, many franchisee firms will fall outside the average and have greater or lesser price behaviour divergence.

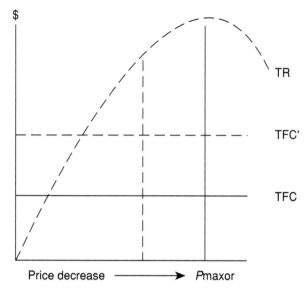

Figure 14.1 Franchisor profit-maximizing behaviour

Note: Absolute level of franchisor TFC does not affect pricing strategy, i.e. TFC to TFC'

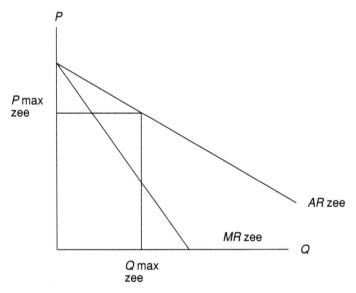

Figure 14.2 Demand function of a prototype zee

Economic theory points to the role of pricing within and between firms. Hayek (1945) proposes that the price system is an extraordinarily efficient mechanism for communicating information and inducing change. He asserts that adaptation is the central objective of economic organizations and focuses on the marketplace, with pricing as the key element. In the ideal marketplace, supply and demand are brought into equilibrium through the actions of autonomous participants, the consumer and the producer. Both parties respond to price changes so as to maximize their individual utility and profit (Williamson 1991). The profit-maximizing assumption is sometimes criticized as not being robust. Critics point to maximizing the long-term value of the company, or maximizing cash flow as better gauges of motivation (Mansfield 1990). Even given that criticism, a franchised retail operation is well suited to a traditional economic framework for analysis. Franchising centres on the sharing of the trademark. The value of the trademark is calculated as the future stream of earnings it will generate, over the term of the licence agreement (LaFontaine 1988). In retailing, cash flow is closely associated with profit. Therefore the profit-maximizing assumption can be altered to value or cash-flow maximizing, and not substantively change the analysis.

Because of the proliferation of franchising as explained in the introduction, it appears evident that if the problems of divergent pricing exist, they are outweighed by the advantages of the relationship. But do the differences in profit-maximizing behaviour sub-optimize the productive benefits of the relationship (increased bureaucracy, litigation, hard bargaining, opportunity cost), and are there ameliorating actions that could reduce the structural problems? We focus on pricing behaviour and subsequent litigation. However, there are a number of studies which analyse the costs of conflict in franchising (e.g. Austin and Winfrey 1988). None, however, specifically address the issue of litigation as a consequence of conflict.

THE RESEARCH QUESTIONS

Our research asks these questions:

1 Does conflict between the franchisor firm and the franchisee firm manifest itself in litigation?
2 Does this litigation correlate to franchisor or franchisee behaviour related to size of the system, rate of growth of the system, the size of the franchisee firm in terms of outlets, franchise stores acquired by the franchisor, financing provided by the franchisor, number of

franchised stores, number of franchisor-firm-operated stores, number of franchisee firm stores terminated, number of franchisee firm stores acquired by the franchisor firm, and total number of years in business for the franchisor?

DATA COLLECTION

The United States Federal trade Commission lists 4,031 franchisor firms. We drew a random sample of 75 companies from a pool reduced by the following criteria:

1   Business format franchising was the principal organizational form used by the firm, reducing the eligible companies to 2,851.
2   The company should have franchised for four or more years. This was an arbitrary number used to eliminate start-ups and franchise 'experimenters'. A number of companies were in business for more than four years but had only recently begun franchising. Another 900 companies were removed from the pool.
3   The company had to have or offer multiple unit franchise ownership. This brought the final number of eligible companies to 1,031.

Seven of the nine variables gathered for this study were based on personal experience and the intuitive belief about their impact on litigation. Following interviews with the International Franchise Association and three franchise litigation attorneys, two variables, franchisor-operated outlets and number of franchisees acquired by the franchisor, were added. Data was collected primarily from the United States Federal Trade Commission (FTC) mandated disclosure of information concerning the sale of franchises. The American Association of Securities Administrators has developed a disclosure format called the Uniform Franchise Offering Circular (UFOC) which fulfils the requirements of the federal law (see Addendum A, for example, UFOC Table of Contents). Additionally, fourteen states have disclosure requirements which are typically more stringent than the FTC. All UFOCs are on file in Washington DC at the Federal Trade Commission. State disclosure documents are typically found at the State Attorney General's office. Confusing or conflicting data was verified by direct contact with the franchisor or franchisee firm.

ANALYSIS OF THE DATA

Analysis of the data was performed to determine if the strength of the association between selected measures of franchisee and franchisor characteristics and litigation volume was sufficient to support our hypothesis.

Correlation analysis

Correlation analysis of the raw data resulted in the matrix reproduced in Table 14.1.

Data transformation

Where logarithmic transformation of the raw data resulted in an improved fit, transformed values were used for further analysis.

Regression analysis

Stepwise multiple regression of the potential variables revealed the logarithm of system size (LGOUTS) to be the strongest predictor of litigation volume, resulting in an R square value of 0.73. This also makes intuitive sense. As the system matures there is greater contact between the franchisee and franchisor and more opportunity for disagreement. However, the strength of this relationship may obscure the possible influence of other variables being considered. To test this, the system size variable was removed from the analysis.

Once system size is removed, the logarithm of system growth rate (LGGRTH) enters the equation as the strongest single predictor, yielding an R square value of 0.65.

This suggests that as the system grows, the higher the probability for inefficiency and diversion of resources from support of existing operational outlets to the development of new stores. The rate at which the franchisor firm attempts to spread its costs increases conflict.

Two more variables entered stepwise into the equation, increasing the R square value to 0.82 and 0.87, respectively. These variables are: (1) the logarithm of the variable AVFR (LGAVFR) and (2) the logarithm of the variable YRSN (LGYRSN).

The final equation is:

LGLITG = -.65327 + .78337(LGGRTH) + .708787LGAVFR) + .534580(LGYRSN)

| T | −5.506 | 12.128 | 7.942 | 4.861 |
| SIG. T | .0000 | .0000 | .0000 | .0000 |

(Adjusted R square = .86667: F = 141.83534 Signif F = .0000)

Table 14.1 Pearson correlation matrix

	LITG	OUTS	ZEES	OWND	YRSN	ACQD	TRMD	GRTH	AVFR
LITG	1.0000	.8511**	.7744**	.7099**	.4412**	.8390**	.8174**	.6689**	.5716**
OUTS		1.0000	.9587**	.6533**	.4995**	.7374**	.6100**	.8164**	.4910**
ZEES			1.0000	.4142**	.5125**	.5452**	.5407**	.7406**	.4158**
OWND				1.0000	.2450	.9484**	.5388**	.6295**	.4561**
YRSN					1.0000**	.3352*	.4232**	.2554	.2175
ACQD						1.0000	.6028**	.6299**	.4544**
TRMD							1.0000	.4609**	.5520**
GRTH								1.0000	.3551**
AVFR									1.0000

Notes: Key to variable names:
1. LITG = no. of franchise stores litigating with the franchisor
2. OUTS = no. of outlets in the system
3. ZEES = no. of franchised (versus company-operated) stores
4. OWND = no. of franchisor-operated stores
5. YRSN = no. of years in business
6. ACQD = no. of franchisee stores acquired by the franchisor
7. TRMD = no. of franchises terminated
8. GRTH = rate of growth
9. AVFR = average number of stores owned by franchisee firms
Rate of growth is calculated by dividing OUTS by YRSN
N of cases: 75; 1-tailed signif: * – .01; ** – .001

Discussion of the results

Regression analysis of our random sample has produced an equation with predictive value which includes three easily measured variables. The results appear to justify our belief that a rapidly growing franchise system with larger franchisees has a higher propensity to litigate. It should be noted that 91 per cent of the sample were presently in franchisee/franchisor litigation. Of the 9 per cent not in litigation, only one franchisor firm had more than 14 franchised outlets.

In an effort to begin quantifying the practical implications of litigation we interviewed three major US law firms and one British solicitor. The four attorneys do a majority of their work in franchising and all were litigators. Their clients include General Motors, Burger King UK franchisee firms, Pizza Hut, Midas Muffler, Taco Belle, and Jiffy Lube.

Although no two lawsuits are identical, the four attorneys easily agreed to a summary of the legal process common to franchise litigation in the US and the associated 3,340 billable hours. Rate per hour varied from $175 to $290. Therefore the range of cost for a fully executed lawsuit is $1,051,175 to $1,742,900. The 'average' lawsuit, as described by the attorneys, is settled at 50 per cent of the full process, or $500,000–$840,000 per litigant.

All four attorneys speculated that legal fees fell below the cost of executive time and opportunity cost.

Further development of this franchise litigation model can aid the planning process for both the franchisor firm and the franchisee firm. If rapid expansion is a key element of the decision to franchise, then the costs of litigation should be understood and made part of the planning process. A sophisticated use of such a model might help avert litigation through use of a planned exit agreement. The franchisee would be recruited and a growth schedule agreed upon. A put/call option on the franchisee firm is timed appropriately for a franchisee exit at a time which would maximize growth in outlets and minimize litigation and the associated costs of conflict. Eliminating these costs could result in better financial returns for both parties.

SUMMARY

The universe of US franchisor firms was narrowed to include companies four years old or older, offering business format franchises with multiple-store-ownership potential for franchisee firms. A random sample of seventy-five currently operating companies was examined.

The data set consisted of: (1) years in operation, (2) total system outlets, (3) company-operated outlets, (4) franchised outlets, (5) franchised outlets acquired by the franchisor, (6) average size (in terms of number of outlets) of the franchisee firm, (7) rate of system growth, (8) number of licence agreements terminated by the franchisor, (9) the number of stores currently in litigation.

The regression model with the greatest ability to predict litigation included rate of growth, average size of the franchisee firm, and years in business. The R square of the model is .86667. Ninety-one per cent of all the franchisor firms in the sample were currently in litigation. The cost of litigation was estimated at between \$500,000 and \$840,000 with speculation that the real cost, including management time and other opportunity costs, was far greater.

REFERENCES

Achrol, Ravi S. and Michael J. Etzel (1991) *Enhancing the Effectiveness of the Franchise Systems: Franchisee Goals and Franchisor Services*, The George Washington Univ. and the Univ. of Notre Dame.

Alpar, P. and D.M. Spitzar (1989) 'Response Behavior of Entrepreneurs in a Mail Study', *Entrepreneurship Theory and Practice*, 14 (2): 31–44.

Arrow, Kenneth J. (1985) 'The Economics of Agency', in *Principals and Agents: The Structure of Business*, J. Pratt and R. Zeckhauser (eds), Boston: Harvard Business School Press, 37–51.

Austin, Anne L. (1989) *American Export Intermediaries: Organizational Characteristics and Interfirm Relationships as Determinants of Performance*.

Austin, Anne L. and Frank L. Winfrey (1988) *Reciprocal Agency in Franchise Channels of Distribution*, Univ. of Wisconsin.

Axelrod, Robert M. (1984) *The Evolution of Cooperation*, New York: Basic Books.

Balakrishnan, Srinvasan and Issac Fox (1993) 'Asset Specificity, Firm Heterogeneity and Capital Structure', *Strategic Management Journal*, 14: 3–16.

Barnard, Chester I. (1938) *The Functions of the Executive*, Cambridge, MA: Harvard University Press.

Barnes, Terrien, Director of Research, International Franchise Association, Washington, D.C.

Bergen, Mark, Shantanu Dutta, and Orville C. Walker (1992) 'Agency Relationships in Marketing: A Review of the Implications and Applications of Agency and Related Theories', *Journal of Marketing*, 56 (July): 1–24.

Boulding, E. (1964) *Power and Conflict in Organizations*, New York, N.Y.

Boyle, Brett and Robert F. Dwyer (1991) *Measuring Interfirm Influence in Franchise Channels of Distribution*, Cincinnati: Univ. of Cincinnati Press.

Brickley, James A., Frederick H. Dark, and Michael S. Weisbach (1987) 'An Agency Perspective on Franchising', *Financial Management*, 20 (1): 27–35.

British Franchise Association (1992) *1991 NatWest/BFA Franchise Survey*, London: Howarth Publication.

Carney, M. and E. Gedajilovic (1991) 'Vertical Integration of the Franchise Systems: Agency Theory and Resource Explanations', *Strategic Management Journal*,12: 572–586.

Caves, Richard E. and William F. Murphy (1976) 'Franchising: Firms, Markets, and Intangible Assets', *Southern Economics Journal*, 42: 572–586.

Coase, Ronald H. (1937) 'The Nature of the Firm', *Economica*, 4 (386).

Dant R. and Schul (1992) 'Contract Resolution Processes in Contractual Channels of Distribution', *Journal of Marketing*, 56 (Jan): 38–54.

Dant, Rajiv P., Lawrence H. Wortzel, and Mohan Subramanian (1992) *Exploring the Relationship Between Autonomy and Dependence in Franchise Channels of Distribution*, Boston: Boston Univ. Press.

Dicke, Thomas Scott (1991)*Franchising in The American Economy, 1840–1980*, Ph.D. dissertation, Ohio State Univ.

Dillman, D.A. (1978) *Mail and Telephone Surveys*, New York: John Wiley.

Dwyer, F. Robert, Paul Schurr, and Sejo Oh (1987) 'Developing Buyer–Seller Relationships', *Journal of Marketing*, 51 (April): 11–27.

Eaton, Michael M. and Robert T. Joseph (1988) *Antitrust Issues In Franchising*, presented at the American Bar Associations's Fundamentals of Franchising Program.

Entrepreneur Magazine (1992) *13th Annual Franchise 500*, Jan.: 129–219.

Fama, E.F. and M.C. Jensen (1983a) 'Separation of Ownership and Control', *Journal of Law and Economics*, 26 (June): 301–325.

Fama, E.F. and M.C. Jensen (1983b) Agency Problems and Residual Claims', *Journal of Law and Economics*, 26 (June): 327–350.

Federal Trade Commission, US Government, Code of Federal Regulations, Title 16, Chapter 1, Subchapter D, Part 436 (16CRF436), effective 21 October, 1979.

Frazier, Gary L. and Raymond C. Rody, 'The Use of Influence Strategies in Interfirm Relationships in Industrial Product Channels', *Journal of Marketing*, Jan., 52–70.

Gross, Edward (1969) 'The Definition of Organizational Goals', *British Journal of Sociology*, 20: 277–294.

International Franchise Association and Horwath International (1991) *Franchising in the Economy 1990*, Evans City PA: IFA Publications.

Jakki, Mohr and John R. Nevin (1990) 'Communications Strategies in Marketing Channels: A Theoretical Perspective', *Journal of Marketing*, 54 (4): 36–51.

Jensen, Michael C. and William H. Meckling (1976) 'Theory of the Firm: Management Behavior, Agency Costs and Ownership Structure', *Journal of Financial Economics*, 3 (Oct.): 395–360.

Jick, D.J. (1979) 'Mixing Qualitative and Quantitative Methods: Triangulation in Action', in *Qualitative Methodology*, J. Van Maanen (ed.) Beverley Hills: Sage Publications.

Jobber, D. (1990) 'Choosing a Survey Method in Management Research', in *A Handbook for Management Research*, M.C. Smith and T. Danty (eds), London: Croom Helm, Ltd.

John, George (1991) 'An Empirical Investigation of Some Antecedents of Opportunism in a Marketing Channel.'

Justis, Robert A. and Richard Judd (1986) *Franchising*, Cincinnati OH: Southwest Publishing Co.

Kanuk, L. and C. Berenson (1975) 'Mail Surveys and Response Rates: A Literature Review', *Journal of Marketing Research*, 12 (Nov.): 440–453.

Kaufmann, Patrick J. and Louis W. Stern (1988) 'Relational Exchange Norms, Perceptions of Unfairness and Retained Hostility in Commercial Litigation', *Journal of Conflict Resolution*, September.

Klein, B. and K. Leffer (1983) 'The Role of Price Guaranteeing Quality', *Journal of Political Economy*, November: 659–686.

LaFontaine, Francine (1988) 'Agency Theory and Franchising: Some Empirical Results', *Rand Journal of Economics*, 23 (2): 263–283.

Lal, Rajiv (1990) 'Improving Channel Coordination Through Franchising', *Marketing Science*, 4 (Fall): 299–318.

Lockhart, C. (1978) 'Conflict Actions and Outcomes: Long-term Impacts', *Journal of Conflict Resolution*, 22 (4): 565–598.

Lusch, R.F. (1976) 'Sources of Power: Their Impact on Intrachannel Conflict', *Journal of Marketing Research*, 13 (Nov.): 382–390.

Macneil, I.R. (1974) 'The Many Futures of Contract', *Southern California Law Review*, 47: 691–816.

Macneil, I.R. (1978) 'Contracts: Adjustments of Long-Term Economic Relations Under Classical, Neo-Classical, and Relational Contract Law', *Northwestern Law Review*, pp: 854–905.

Macneil, I.R. (1980) 'Economic Analysis of Contractual Relations: Its Shortfalls and the Need for a "Rich Classificatory Apparatus"', *Northwestern University Law Review*, Feb.: 1018–1063.

Macneil, I.R. (1985) 'Relational Contracts: What We Do and Do Not Know', *Wisconsin Law Review*, 3: 483–525.

Martin, J. (1988) 'Franchising and Risk Management', *American Economic Review*, 78 (5): 954–967.

McGuire, Timothy W. and Richard Staelin (1983) 'An Industry Equilibrium Analysis and Downstream Vertical Integration', *Marketing Science*, 2 (Spring): 161–191.

Michael, Steven C. (1993) 'Why Franchising Works: An Analysis of Property Rights and Organizational Form Shares', presented at the 1993 Babson Conference on Entrepreneurial Research.

Miller, Arthur R. and Thomas L. Grossman (1986) *Business Law*, Glenview: Scott Foresman.

Mittelstaedt, Robert A. and Robert E. Stassen (1990) *Economic Sources of Conflict in Franchising Organizations*, Univ. of Nebraska and Univ. of Arizona.

Mundstock, George (1991) 'Franchises, Intangible Capital and Assets', *National Tax Journal*, 43 (3): 299–305.

Oppenheim, A.N. (1968) *Questionnaire Design and Attitude Measurement*, London: Heinemann.

Ozanne, Urban B. and Shelby D. Hunt (1971) *The Economics Effects of Franchising*, testimony to the Select Committee on Small Business, US Senate, 92 Congress, 1st Session.

Parsons, Talcott (1959) 'General Theory in Sociology', in *Sociology Today*, Robert K. Merton, Leonard Broom, and Leonard S. Cottrell, Jr. (eds), New York, NY: Basic Books.

Peterson, Alden and Rajiv P. Dant (1990) 'Perceived Advantages of the Franchise Option from the Franchisee Perspective: Empirical Insights From a Service Franchise', *Journal of Small Business Management*, 28 (3): 46–61.

Ping, Robert A. (1990) *Responses to Dissatisfaction in Buyer–Seller Relationships: Exit, Voice, Aggression, Loyalty, and Neglect*, Ph.D. dissertation, University of Cincinnati.

Pondy, Louis R. (1967) 'Organizational Conflict: Concepts and Models', *Administrative Science Quarterly*, 12 (Sept.): 296–320.

Raven, B.H. and A.W. Kruglanski (1970) 'Conflict and Power', in *The Structure of Conflict*, P. Swingle (ed.), New York: Academic Press, 69–109.

Robinson, R.B. and J.A. Pearce (1986) 'Product Life Cycle Considerations and the Nature of Stategic Activities in Entrepreneurial Firms', *Journal of Business Venture*, 1: 207–224.

Romano, Joseph and Andrew F. Seigel (1986) 'Counter-examples in Probability and Statistics'.

Rosenberg, Larry and Louis Stern (1971) 'Conflict Measurement in the Distribution Channel', *Journal of Marketing Research*, 8 (Nov.): 437–442.

Rubin, P.H. (1976) 'The Theory of the Firm and the Structure of the Franchise Contract', *Journal of Law and Economics*, 21: 223–234.

Scott, D. (1972) 'Evidence of the Importance of Financial Structure', *Financial Management*, 2: 45–50.

Seashore, Stanley E. (1983) 'A Framework for an Integrated Model of Organizational Effectiveness', in *Organizational Effectiveness: A Comparison of Multiple Models*, Kim S. Cameron and David A. Whetten (eds), New York: Academic Press.

Sen, Kabir Chandra (1991) *The Use of Initial Fees and Royalties in Business Format Franchising*, Ph.D. thesis, Washington University.

Shapiro, C. (1983) 'Premiums for High Quality Returns to Reputation', *Quarterly Journal of Economics*, November: 659–686.

Simon, H. (1979) 'From Substantive to Procedural Rationality', in *Philosophy and Economic Theory*, F. Hahn and M. Hollis (eds), Oxford: Oxford University Press.

Simpson, James Talmadge (1991) *An Empirical Investigation of the Impact of Governance of Marketing Channels of Distribution*, Ph.D. thesis, University of Michigan.

Stern. L.W. and A. El-Ansary (1988) *Marketing Channels*, Englewood Cliffs, NJ: Prentice Hall.

Stern, Peter and John Stanworth (1988) 'The Development of Franchising in Britain', *National Westminster Bank Quarterly Review (UK)*, May:38–48.

Stiglitz, J. (1972) 'Some Aspects of the Pure Theory of Corporate Finance: Bankruptcy and Takeover', *Bell Journal of Economics*, 3: 458–482.

Sudman, S. (1976) *Applied Sampling*, London: Academic Press.

Swinth, Robert L. (1974) *Organizational Systems for Management: Designing, Planning and Implementing*, Columbus, OH.

Williamson, O.E. (1975) *Markets and Hierarchies, Analysis and Antitrust Implications*, New York: Free Press.

Williamson, O.E.(1985) *The Economic Institutions of Capitalism*, New York, NY: Free Press.

Williamson, O.E. (1991) 'Comparative Economic Organization: The Analysis of Discreet Structural Alternatives', *Administrative Science Quarterly*, 36: 269–296.

Yin, Robert K. (1989) *Case Study Research, Design and Method*, Beverley Hills: Sage Publications (rev. edn).

Index